**PRENTICE-HALL SERIES IN MATHEMATICAL ECONOMICS**
Donald V. T. Bear, *Series Editor*

*Dennis J. Aigner*
　　　BASIC ECONOMETRICS

*David A. Bowers and Robert N. Baird*
　　　ELEMENTARY MATHEMATICAL MACROECONOMICS

*Michael D. Intriligator*
　　　MATHEMATICAL OPTIMIZATION AND ECONOMIC THEORY

*Ronald C. Read*
　　　A MATHEMATICAL BACKGROUND FOR ECONOMISTS

*Menahem E. Yaari*
　　　LINEAR ALGEBRA FOR SOCIAL SCIENCES

Elementary
Mathematical
Macroeconomics

*DAVID A. BOWERS* / *ROBERT N. BAIRD*

Case Western Reserve University

# Elementary Mathematical Macroeconomics

PRENTICE-HALL, INC., ENGLEWOOD CLIFFS, N.J.

*ELEMENTARY MATHEMATICAL MACROECONOMICS*
by David A. Bowers and Robert N. Baird

© 1971 BY PRENTICE-HALL, INC., ENGLEWOOD CLIFFS, NEW JERSEY

Printed in the United States of America

13-258327-5
Library of Congress Catalog Card Number 71-139473

Current printing (last digit)
10  9  8  7  6  5  4  3  2  1

PRENTICE-HALL INTERNATIONAL, INC., LONDON
PRENTICE-HALL OF AUSTRALIA PTY. LTD., SYDNEY
PRENTICE-HALL OF CANADA, LTD., TORONTO
PRENTICE-HALL OF INDIA PRIVATE LIMITED, NEW DELHI
PRENTICE-HALL OF JAPAN, INC., TOKYO

1589886

To Jean and Dee

# Series Foreword

The Prentice-Hall Series in Mathematical Economics is intended as a vehicle for making mathematical reasoning and quantitative methods available to the main corpus of the undergraduate and graduate economics curricula.

The Series has been undertaken in the belief that the teaching of economics will, in the future, increasingly reflect the discipline's growing reliance upon mathematical and statistical techniques during the past 20 to 35 years and that mathematical economics and econometrics ought not to be "special fields" for undergraduates and graduate students, but that every aspect of economics education can benefit from the application of these techniques.

Accordingly, the Series will contain texts that cover the traditional substantive areas of the curriculum—for example, macroeconomics, microeconomics, public finance, and international trade—thereby offering the instructor the opportunity to expose his students to contemporary methods of analysis as they apply to the subject matter of his course. The composition of the early volumes in the Series will be weighted in favor of texts that offer the student various degrees of mathematical background, with the volumes of more substantive emphasis following shortly thereafter.

As the Series grows, it will contribute to the comprehensibility and quality of economics education at both the undergraduate and graduate levels.

DONALD V. T. BEAR, *Series Editor*

# Preface

This book was originally designed for the advanced undergraduate course in macroeconomics, but we have found that it also serves quite well in the first graduate course in macroeconomic theory. Ideally, incoming graduate students should already have studied the material contained in this book, but in practice this is often not the case. Our experience has been that there are often gaps in their understanding of intermediate macroeconomic theory, especially among students who majored in other fields. We have had a considerable degree of success in filling these gaps using copies of an early draft of our manuscript.

Although the text is couched in mathematical terminology, the level of the mathematics is not very high. A knowledge of the partial derivative and the total differential is all that is required. Our own classroom experience indicates that the novice in mathematics who understands basic macroeconomic theory will most likely find that working through this book will help him develop proficiency in differential calculus. Correspondingly, the student with some mathematical background who has not previously studied economics will find that the mathematical format of the book is quite helpful in accelerating the pace at which he is able to learn macroeconomic theory.

Chapters 1 through 7 of this book merely restate the orthodox theory of aggregate demand in elementary mathematical terms. In these chapters, the well-prepared economics major will find little that is new to him. However, in Chapters 9 and 10 we present the theory of aggregate supply and its relationship to aggregate demand in a fashion that is substantially different from that of most contemporary textbooks. Well-prepared first-year graduate students might want to begin with Chapter 9 (slightly more than halfway through the book), referring to the previous chapters as the need arises.

For others making the allocation decision necessitated by too much material for the time available, Chapters 8 and 12 may be omitted without detracting from the understanding of the other chapters.

We are deliberately brief on contemporary policy debates. However, the material describing the determination of the equilibrium level of output, employment, and prices is more extensive than in other books, since we feel that a student must have a good grasp of the comparative statics of these matters before disputes concerning the dynamic matters of real-world policy can be intelligently considered. It has been our experience that material on disputes regarding economic policy is best covered by using one of the many excellent *Readings* books that have recently been published,* and new

* For example, Norman F. Keiser, ed., *Readings in Macroeconomics* (Englewood Cliffs, N.J.: Prentice-Hall, Inc., 1970); also, John Lindauer, ed., *Macroeconomic Readings* (New York: The Free Press, 1968).

collections will undoubtedly appear as the issues change over time. Also, such a readings book allows the instructor, at his discretion, to have the student review the original literature on many of the macroeconomic concepts presented here.

Of course, we owe a great debt of gratitude to many individuals who helped prepare this manuscript. Professor Donald V. T. Bear, editor of this series, gave us many helpful comments on the entire manuscript. Our colleagues, Professors Weldon Welfling, Gerhard Rosegger, and John Landon helped us resolve our own disagreements in several of the chapters. Mrs. Claire Gregory helped with the artwork and penned the equations, while Mrs. Joy Davis, Mrs. Dorothy Plezia, and Mrs. Betty Bates typed the original manuscript. Most recently, Mrs. Rita DeVries, our production editor at Prentice-Hall, has made the mechanics of actually getting the book into print look easy—and we know it was not.

We are also indebted to the students, graduate and undergraduate, at Case Western Reserve University whose response has guided the content and organization of this book and to the authors of earlier macroeconomic texts whose problems we can now more readily appreciate.

DAVID A. BOWERS / ROBERT N. BAIRD

# Contents

Elementary
Mathematical
Macroeconomics

# 1 | Some Fundamental Concepts

## I  MICROECONOMICS AND MACROECONOMICS

The traditional approach to the study of economic theory is to break the analysis into two separate investigations, each focusing on distinctly different types of behavior. On the one hand, microeconomics involves the study of the many separate units comprising the total economy, with emphasis placed on the individual consumer, the individual firm, and the individual market. On the other hand, macroeconomics is concerned with the aggregated variables such as output of the entire economy, the level of national employment, and the market rate of interest.

Because of the obvious relevance of differential calculus to the problems of profit maximization for the individual firm, the study of microeconomics has become more and more oriented toward mathematical exposition in recent years. This trend has meant not just increased sophistication in the economic models studied but also increased real understanding of economic implications that could not be adequately developed by purely verbal or graphic techniques. Despite the fact that the maximization problem is less ubiquitous in macroeconomics than in microeconomics, the former has also witnessed the same tendency toward mathematical elaboration. The concern of this book is to present in elementary mathematical form the basic theorems that comprise what is accepted today as orthodox macroeconomic theory. The advanced student will quickly see that there is no attempt to present material that has not yet found its way into traditional macroeconomic analysis. Rather, the focus of this book is on the systematic presentation of accepted concepts and not on the development of new ones. Moreover, with the exception of the aggregate production function and a few minor equations, the basic relationships discussed in the book are assumed to be linear. This allows the student with a limited mathematics background to see the relationships among the relevant variables without having to resort to complicated multi-graph diagrams from which it is impossible to compare elasticities directly. Accordingly, a knowledge of the derivative and the differential is all that is required for most of this book. In the first few chapters of the book, algebraic manipulations are generally presented in great detail. We believe that students with "rusty" or even weak mathematical backgrounds will acquire increased facility in the language of mathematics in these early chapters. Therefore, progressively more of the intermediate steps in long derivations are omitted in the later chapters, although the level of mathematical sophistication is not increased.

## II MACROECONOMIC VARIABLES

### I. Employment and Unemployment

To any economist concerned with the social performance of the economy, the level of employment is a key indicator. Employment is defined as the number of persons in the labor force currently holding a job. The labor force is defined as the number of persons actively seeking work at the prevailing wage rate. The level of unemployment is the difference between the labor force and the level of employment.

Since 1946, the United States has sought "full employment" as a national economic goal. Quotation marks are used here since no exact definition of full employment has been unanimously accepted. Because there are always some individuals in the labor force unable to find a job, it has been argued that economists cannot define zero percent unemployed as a reasonable economic target. For example, seasonal workers such as fruit pickers may be temporarily unemployed *as fruit pickers* although other jobs may be available. Other persons may be out of work because they are in a transition period between jobs. Finally, others may be actively seeking work but because of health conditions or other handicaps there may be no reasonable chance of their finding it. Economists traditionally exclude these and other similarly situated groups that account for some small percent of the labor force in defining "full employment." Accordingly, when about 4 percent of the labor force is unemployed, economists argue that full employment has been attained.[1]

### 2. The National Income Accounts

In addition to the level of employment, economists are also very much interested in the level of production or total output of the economy. Other things equal, an increase in the level of production is associated with increased national economic well-being. Several different variables are of importance as components of total output. The following explanations are not intended as complete descriptions of the national income accounts, but they are presented here in brief form as a review. Students seeking a more refined explanation should consult one of the references cited at the end of this chapter.

---

[1] The selection of 4 percent is somewhat arbitrary. Some economists argue that the figure should be lower; others, higher.

### Gross National Product

The level of GNP is defined to be the market value of all final goods and services produced in the United States during a given time period. Obviously, a more meaningful measure would be the actual number of physical goods produced, but the units are not commensurable. *Final* output indicates that the production of goods to be used as raw materials for further preparation during the same period is not to be counted. That is, steel produced for the manufacture of automobiles will be counted as part of the automobile—counting it when sold to the auto manufacturer would overstate the real value of production.

### Net National Product

Much of the total production defined under gross national product is not a net addition to the true wealth of the economy since it merely replaces equipment that wore out during the current period. Thus, the amount of depreciation must be subtracted from GNP to yield net national product.

### National Income

The level of net national product still overstates the true value of all final goods and services produced because the prices of these goods may reflect the various types of sales taxes. Accordingly, indirect business taxes must be subtracted from net national product to yield national income.[2]

### Personal Income

The level of national income is a measure of the nation's well-being resulting from production, but it does not equal the total income of all persons. Personal income can be determined by making relevant deductions from and additions to national income. The necessary deductions are retained corporate profits and social security taxes, neither of which are immediately available to individuals; while the proper additions are government transfer payments (such as unemployment compensation), which add to the incomes of individuals.

### Disposable Income

Total personal income does not measure that amount of money over which individuals can exercise complete discretion concerning its disposition since income taxes are mandatory in our economy. The subtraction of income taxes from personal income yields disposable income.

---

[2] Two other minor items differentiating NNP and NI are the statistical discrepancy and subsidies. Thus, NI = NNP − (indirect business taxes + statistical discrepancy) + subsidies.

### CONSUMPTION AND SAVING

The total amount of disposable income can be used according to what-ever preference systems are held by individuals receiving the income. That portion of income that individuals use for the purchase of final goods and services is defined as consumption, while the remainder is saving.

## 3. The Circular Flow

The definitions provided in the previous section are the components of gross national product. One very important concept should be noted, however, as it will be mentioned many times in subsequent chapters. This is simply that the national income accounts relate to *flow* variables, not *stock* variables. A stock variable is something that has a given numerical value at some point in time, say the number of gallons of water in a pond at some specific instant. A flow variable, on the other hand, is measured by a number of units that accumulate over time, say the number of gallons that have flowed into the pond in a month. Accordingly, the level of expenditures that has taken place over a given period of time is a flow, while the accumulated wealth of an individual or of society is a stock.

The breakdown of the national income accounts in the previous section has given a decomposition of gross national product, but there is an alter-native way of looking at GNP. The national income breakdown above looks at the income side of GNP. Alternatively, we can look at GNP from the expenditures side. Thus, consumption, the last component examined in the previous section, becomes the first component from the expenditures view-point, as consumers use their disposable incomes to purchase final goods and services. The other components are as follows.

### INVESTMENT

The business community finds that it must continually replace buildings and machinery that depreciate physically and grow obsolete as technology progresses or it must add to existing capital to accommodate growth. More-over, some goods are produced so that stockpiles may be accumulated. The sum of the capital account expenditures that businesses make for these items is defined as the level of private investment. Funds for these purchases are available from several sources, including retained corporate profits and consumer savings. The channeling of consumer saving to the corporate sector may take place directly through the purchase of *new* stocks and bonds or indirectly through deposits in commercial banks that are then lent to businesses. Note, however, that investment refers to expenditures for physical goods and not to the purchase of a financial asset.

It is important to note here the role played by inventory accumulation.

Goods produced but not sold nonetheless represent a portion of the value of final output and therefore should be defined as part of GNP. The traditional approach is to define inventory accumulation as part of business investment. It is possible that increased inventories are part of a planned buildup program of the business concerned or merely the result of overly optimistic production scheduling on the part of a manager who overestimated the demand for his product. This is an irrelevant distinction at this time.[3] In either case, increased inventories are part of business investment.

### GOVERNMENT EXPENDITURES

Just as the government withdraws taxes from the income stream, so government purchases increase the size of the expenditures stream. Although theoretically such purchases could be divided into consumption and investment expenditures, it has been found most useful analytically to treat them as a special category.

### IMPORTS AND EXPORTS

The final variables to receive our attention in this section are those derived from the international trade sector of the economy. The demand by foreigners for domestic goods also represents the sale of final goods and services and, therefore, should be added in as part of the expenditures side of GNP. Correspondingly, it should also be pointed out that individuals could also have used disposable incomes to purchase foreign goods as well as domestic ones. Thus, imports should be added to the uses of income breakdown of GNP.

All the variables above can be portrayed by the diagram in Figure 1–1, called the circular flow of income. Arrows indicate only the direction of the flows and not necessarily causal relationships. Notice that the streams have neither a definite beginning nor a definite end, as income is a continuous flow.

### 4.  Tabular Presentation, an Input-Output Table

In addition to the circular flow, the national income variables can also be read from the tabular presentation given in Table 1–1. This table arrays the economic structure of the nation into a given number of producing sectors, such as agricultural production, nonferrous mineral mining, coal mining, and fabricated metal products. Each of these sectors sells its output to other producing sectors and to the final sectors of consumers, investors,

---

[3] This distinction takes on crucial importance, however, in a later chapter.

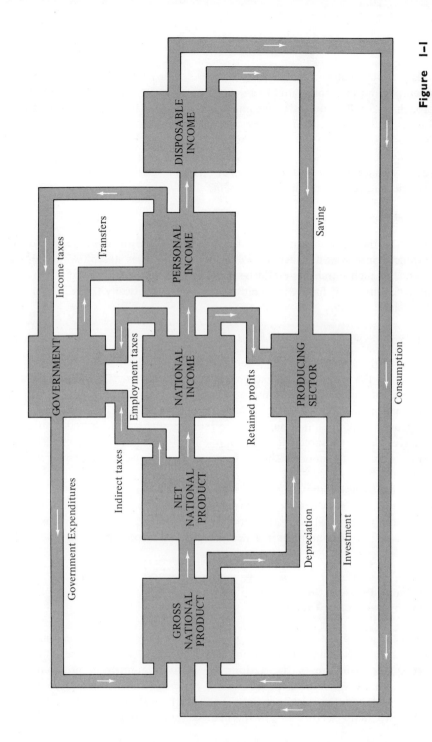

**Figure 1-1**

The Circular Flow of Income

## Table I-I

### National Income Components
#### (Millions of Dollars)

| | Purchases By | | | | | | | Final Demand | | | | | | Row Total |
|---|---|---|---|---|---|---|---|---|---|---|---|---|---|---|
| | 1 | 2 | 3 | 4 | 5 | 6 | 7 | C | I | G | Ex | Im | Total Final Demand | |
| Sales By 1 | 21,278 | 844 | 208 | 5,372 | 90 | 366 | 2,939 | 94,860 | 2,203 | 1,696 | 2,827 | −1,945 | 100,090 | 133,495 |
| 2 | 765 | 34,708 | 3,084 | 1,745 | 552 | 8,919 | 6,291 | 24,668 | 26,111 | 19,482 | 7,390 | −2,193 | 75,548 | 131,700 |
| 3 | 3,545 | 19,814 | 24,711 | 2,151 | 925 | 3,113 | 435 | 981 | 13,051 | 1,338 | 1,935 | −2,861 | 14,444 | 69,154 |
| 4 | 44,270 | 7,402 | 2,732 | 65,665 | 1,360 | 21,406 | 1,997 | 15,606 | 14,145 | 3,474 | 5,466 | −5,192 | 33,501 | 178,321 |
| 5 | 1,490 | 1,072 | 2,311 | 5,163 | 22,719 | 9,408 | 37 | 20,795 | 1,193 | 2,676 | 1,419 | −2,557 | 23,527 | 66,504 |
| 6 | 16,049 | 11,821 | 6,916 | 22,274 | 11,465 | 95,012 | 6,211 | 221,009 | 22,141 | 13,825 | 6,038 | −946 | 263,715 | 433,782 |
| 7 | 847 | 1,716 | 1,360 | 1,731 | 426 | 5,575 | 22 | 18 | −930 | 7,785 | 275 | −622 | 6,526 | 18,470 |
| Imports | 2,009 | 158 | 18 | 897 | — | 1,348 | — | 5,207 | 42 | 3,695 | 263 | −13,639 | −4,433 | |
| Value Added | 44,085 | 54,025 | 27,826 | 73,308 | 28,980 | 283,967 | 547 | 6,218 | 24,537 | 51,608 | 5,798 | −896 | 87,265 | 600,000 |
| Column Total | 133,495 | 131,700 | 69,154 | 178,321 | 66,504 | 433,782 | 18,470 | 389,358 | 102,584 | 105,604 | 31,410 | −28,955 | 600,000 | 1,035,974 |

SOURCE: Wassily Leontief, "The Structure of the American Economy," *Scientific American*, April 1965. Components may not add to totals because of rounding and the omission of very small magnitudes in aggregation.

government, and foreigners. The sales of these sectors are presented in the rows going across Table 1–1. Since each sale by one party is a purchase by a second party, Table 1–1 can also be viewed as the purchases by one sector from all other sectors, and these are in fact the interpretations to be given the entries in any single column. For example, the third entry in column 2 indicates that sector 2 purchased $19,814 million of intermediate goods from sector 3 during the time period in question. The row labeled "Value Added" is merely the difference between the total value of *all* output for each sector minus the current account costs of materials and supplies used in production. (That is, it is the column total minus the sum of the first eight entries in that column.) Hence, it is the value added to those materials and supplies by processing them. Value added is therefore roughly equivalent to the sum of all income payments for the factors of production, plus taxes and other payments to the various levels of government.

Using the previous paragraph as a guide, we can construct the variables entering into the national income accounts. Gross national product is merely the sum of consumption, investment, government, and net trade balance, or $600,000 million. Since the expenditures approach and the income approach must yield the same GNP figure, the sum of all value-added components will also equal GNP. Notice that because of the numerous sales of intermediate goods and services among processing sectors the value of total output is much larger than the value of GNP.[4]

### 5.  Monetary Variables

With the exception of the level of employment, every variable mentioned thus far has been expressed as a dollar value. Accordingly, money must play an important role in macroeconomic theory. The exact status of money in the economic system will not be discussed until Chapter 6, but some preliminary remarks are in order here.

The *stock* of money, once fixed, must be used to finance all the transactions referred to in Table 1–1. However, this is not to say that the money supply must be equal to the total volume of these transactions. It is obvious that a money supply of just a few dollar bills could finance any level of transactions as long as those bills could change hands with sufficient speed. Therefore, for any time period, there is a simple relationship relating the value of transactions, the stock of money, and its speed of turnover, called velocity. Stated simply, the transactions velocity of money, $V_T$, is equal to the value of all transactions, $T$, divided by the money stock, $M$:

[4] Although the example given is for a hypothetical GNP of $600,000 million, the entries are based on actual data for 1958. The sectors given roughly correspond to (1) final nonmetal, (2) final metal, (3) basic metal, (4) basic nonmetal, (5) energy, (6) services, and (7) other or "special." See Wassily Leontief, "The Structure of the American Economy," *Scientific American*, April, 1965.

$$V_T = \frac{T}{M} \quad \text{or} \quad T = MV_T \qquad (1\text{-}1)$$

Since economists are generally more concerned with the level of GNP than the value of all transactions, the concept of "income velocity" is also used quite often. Letting $Y$ represent GNP,

$$V_Y = \frac{Y}{M} \quad \text{or} \quad Y = MV_Y \qquad (1\text{-}2)$$

For the tabular presentation given in Table 1–1, a money stock of $150 billion would have yielded an income velocity of 4.0 (600 ÷ 150 = 4). In other words, the average dollar "turned over" four times in the purchase of all final goods and services during the specified time period.

## 6. Simplified Macroeconomic Models

The purpose of macroeconomic theory is to explain how equilibrium values of the variables above are determined. Rather than deal with the complete framework as presented thus far, however, most economists make some simplifying assumptions about the model in order to reduce the complexity and give additional clarification to the behavior of the more important variables. For example, social security taxes behave in a very predictable manner, but including them in a macroeconomic model adds very little in the way of overall explanation because their relative importance is not so great as other variables. Moreover, since the inclusion of social security taxes merely increases the number of interrelationships among the variables and complicates the entire analysis, most economists prefer to exclude them from the basic models altogether. Or, if they are to be included, the assumption is often made that they are no different than other taxes, so they are aggregated into a general category called "taxes." Other similar assumptions are made by the economist in an attempt to develop an accurate theory based upon as few fundamental relationships as possible. Three of the very basic models often cited follow.

### THE NO-GOVERNMENT NO-FOREIGN TRADE MODEL

In making their simplifying assumptions, many economists put forth a macroeconomic model based upon the absence of government expenditures, taxes, and foreign trade. Thus, the only relevant sectors are the business community (or producing sector) and consumers (or household sector). Under the added assumption that the consumers are responsible for all saving and that corporations retain no profits, the expenditures value for GNP is necessarily equal to the sum of consumption expenditures and investment expenditures. In the income approach, it is equal to consumption plus saving. Algebraically, letting $Y$, $C$, $I$, and $S$ stand for GNP, consumption expenditures, investment expenditures, and saving, respectively,

$$Y = C + I \tag{1-3}$$

and

$$Y = C + S \tag{1-4}$$

Therefore,

$$I = S \tag{1-5}$$

Equation (1-5) indicates that, in such a simplified system, investment (by definition) is equal to saving. This merely states that the incomes generated in the production of all final goods and services can be used only for purchasing those same goods or for saving. If consumers decide to purchase less than the total value of consumer goods produced, they increase their saving, and unsold consumer goods appear in the national income accounts as increased inventory investment by businessmen. If consumers purchase more than the total value of consumer goods produced, saving is decreased and the national income accounts record negative inventory investment. The analysis of the consequences of these situations will be discussed in greater detail in Chapters 3 through 5.

### GOVERNMENT INCLUDED

Once government is added to the model, the system becomes only slightly more complicated. The expenditures value of GNP is then equal to the sum of consumption, investment, *and* government expenditures; while the income approach is equal to consumption, saving, and taxes. Letting $G$ equal government expenditures and $T$ equal taxes,

$$Y = C + I + G \tag{1-6}$$

$$Y = C + S + T \tag{1-7}$$

Therefore,

$$S + T = I + G \tag{1-8}$$

Again, Eqs. (1-6) through (1-8) are really identities rather than true equations and merely express the fact that total contributions to income must be equal to total uses of income.

### FOREIGN TRADE INCLUDED

When the model above is expanded to include foreign trade, the purchase of imports serves as another use for the disposition of income, while foreign demands for domestic products contribute to the generation of income. Accordingly, letting $I_M$ equal imports and $X$ equal exports,

$$Y = C + I + G + X \tag{1-9}$$

$$Y = C + S + T + I_M \tag{1-10}$$

Therefore

$$S + T + I_M = I + G + X \tag{1-11}$$

If the analyst is interested only in the balance of trade rather than its individual components, Eq. (1-11) can be modified slightly. Define $N_X$ as net exports, so

$$N_X = X - I_M \tag{1-12}$$

and

$$I + G + N_X = S + T \tag{1-13}$$

A more complete analysis of the foreign trade model will be presented in Chapter 12.

## 7. "Real" Output and the Price Level

In many problems, economists seek to abstract from changes in the price level and to measure only changes in the level of "real" output or income. The common approach to measuring the real value of output, designated as $Q$, is to deflate the value of gross national product by some meaningful price index, $P$.

Thus:

$$Q = \frac{Y}{P} \tag{1-14}$$

Therefore,

$$Y = PQ \tag{1-15}$$

Note that Eq. (1-15) is just another way of expressing the basic definition of GNP as the dollar value of all final goods and services produced. The right-hand side of the equation is simply the total quantity of final output multiplied by the average price.

There are a host of methodological and practical problems in the construction of the price index and the measure of real output, but these problems are somewhat outside the scope of this book.

## 8. Summary of Basic Identities

The seven previous sections have presented several different definitions of GNP. Equating them all,

$$Y = C + I + G = C + S + T = PQ = MV_Y \tag{1-16}$$

By inspection, it is obvious that anytime there is a change in aggregate income and output in the economy, there must also be a corresponding change or group of changes in each segment of Eq. (1-16) that is set off by an equality sign. Suppose, for example, that GNP increases. Then it is necessarily true that

1. At least one or all among consumption, investment, or government expenditures must have increased.
2. At least one or all of consumption, saving, or taxes must have increased.
3. The price level or real output, or both, increased.
4. The money supply or the velocity of money, or both, increased.

An appreciation of the definitional relationships will forewarn the student to look for the results of a change in gross national product upon changes in the type of output $(C, I, G)$, upon changes in the allocation of income $(C, S, T)$, upon changes in real income $(Q, P)$, and upon changes in monetary variables $(M, V_Y)$.

## III IDENTITIES AND BEHAVIORAL RELATIONSHIPS

The relationships above are the somewhat arbitrary definitions that compose the language of macroeconomics. While these definitions imply various interrelationships that often prove useful in further analysis, however, it must be pointed out that these definitions per se can provide no behavioral relationships nor predictions. The fact that disposable income is equal to the sum of consumption and saving is in form similar to the fact that the total population of the United States is equal to the number of males plus the number of females. Each provides a statement of fact that can never be shown to be false; they are both tautologies.

In contrast to the definitional identities used in macroeconomics, there also exist some widely accepted behavioral relationships that have predictive ability. For example, it is generally accepted that if disposable income rises from one period to the next, personal consumption expenditures will also increase, but not by an equal dollar amount. From the definition of disposable personal income it follows, tautologically, that either savings or consumption *must* go up with a rise in income, but the contention that such an increase will be divided between the two in some particular fashion—say 90 percent to consumption and 10 percent to savings—is a postulated behavioral relationship which gives rise to a specific prediction for a particular time period and is subject to empirical verification or refutation.

While reading the following chapters, the student should be sure to keep in mind the difference between identities and behavioral relationships. Moreover, as a practical matter, he should thoroughly understand the standard definitions presented in Eqs. (1-1) through (1-15), as they will be relied upon constantly throughout the remainder of the text.

## IV  STATICS, COMPARATIVE STATICS, AND DYNAMICS

In this section, we seek to give workable definitions of the three common types of economic analysis: statics, comparative statics, and dynamics. Briefly stated, static analysis is the calculation of the equilibrium level of some economic variable (or variables) that results from a stated set of conditions. Comparative statics is the analysis of the change in the equilibrium value as a result of a change in the set of conditions determining that value. Dynamic analysis examines the path over time followed by the variable in adjusting from one equilibrium point to another. These three types of analysis can be illustrated by a simple model of supply and demand.

### 1.  Statics

Assume a simple supply-demand model in which the quantity supplied of some commodity at a given time is an increasing function of its current price and the quantity demanded is a decreasing function of current price. Equations to represent these two relationships might be

$$Q_s = aP \tag{1-17}$$

$$Q_d = b - cP \tag{1-18}$$

If we assume that prices will adjust to clear the market, then $Q_s$ must be set equal to $Q_d$. Simultaneous solution of Eqs. (1-17) and (1-18) yields the equilibrium price and the equilibrium quantity. These equilibrium values are

$$P_e = \frac{b}{a + c}$$

$$Q_e = \frac{ab}{a + c}$$

These values are said to represent a static equilibrium since they hold only for that one point in time for which Eqs. (1-17) and (1-18) are the correct supply and demand equations. Unfortunately, this is not very useful since economists are more interested in the consequences of change than in stationary values. Thus, the analysis must be expanded.

## 2.  Comparative Statics

We may push beyond the limitations of static analysis by inquiring into the consequences of a change in the value of one of the supply or demand parameters. For example, let the single parameter $a$ in the supply equation be increased by an amount $\Delta$, so that the quantity supplied will now be greater at all prices than it was in the former model. The supply and demand equations are

$$Q_s = (a + \Delta)P \tag{1-19}$$

$$Q_d = b - cP \tag{1-18}$$

The equilibrium price and quantity are now equal to

$$P_e = \frac{b}{a + \Delta + c} < \frac{b}{a + c}$$

$$Q_e = \frac{(a + \Delta)b}{a + \Delta + c} > \frac{ab}{a + c}$$

By comparing the new equilibrium values to the old, we see that the new price is lower than the old and that the new quantity is greater than the old. Thus, the comparison of different static equilibrium values, or comparative statics, tells us that increases in supply are accompanied by decreased equilibrium prices and increased equilibrium quantities.

A much simpler way of conducting the comparative static analysis would have been merely to calculate the sign of the partial derivatives of the static equilibrium values of price and quantity with respect to the supply parameter $a$. A positive sign for the derivative would indicate that the variable under inspection varies directly with $a$, while a negative sign would indicate an inverse relationship. Thus:

$$\frac{\partial P_e}{\partial a} = -\frac{b}{(a + c)^2} < 0 \tag{1-20}$$

$$\frac{\partial Q_e}{\partial a} = \frac{bc}{(a + c)^2} > 0 \tag{1-21}$$

The previous two equations confirm the results of the more tedious method pursued above.

## 3. Dynamics

Although comparative statics provides much more illumination than simple static analysis, it still does not indicate the intermediate steps involved in the movement from one equilibrium to another. As a matter of fact, it does not even tell us *if* it is possible to make the move. Dynamic analysis must be relied upon for this information.

The model used above may be made dynamic by assuming that supply does not react instantly to the current price but instead is an increasing function of the price in the previous period, as is common for many agricultural products. Thus, the "lagged" supply schedule might be

$$Q_{s,t} = aP_{t-1} \tag{1-22}$$

The subscript $t - 1$ indicates that we are talking about a time that is one period prior to the present. The demand schedule is

$$Q_{d,t} = b - cP_t \tag{1-23}$$

The market clearing equation is

$$Q_{s,t} = Q_{d,t} \tag{1-24}$$

The three previous equations can be solved to give us solutions for the values of price and quantity at any time $t$:

$$P_{e,t} = \frac{b}{c} - \frac{a}{c} P_{e,t-1} \tag{1-25}$$

$$Q_{e,t} = aP_{e,t-1} \tag{1-26}$$

Dynamic equilibrium requires that the price and quantity remain constant from one period to the next or that

$$P_{e,t} = P_{e,t-1} = P_{e,t-2} = P_e \tag{1-27}$$

$$Q_{e,t} = Q_{e,t-1} = Q_{e,t-2} = Q_e$$

Substitution of Eq. (1-27) into Eqs. (1-25) and (1-26) yields the dynamic equilibrium values

$$P_e = \frac{b}{a+c} \tag{1-28}$$

$$Q_e = \frac{ab}{a+c} \tag{1-29}$$

Note that the equilibrium values of price and quantity still have not changed from what the values were in the static model. However, we now have the advantage of being able to examine the process of change by examining Eqs. (1-25) and (1-26). For example, Eq. (1-25) is what is known as a "first-order difference equation," since the value of a variable in one period depends on the value of the same variable in the immediately preceding period. If we had known some original or base period value of price, say $P_0$, we could have developed a general solution of the difference equation in terms of $P_0$ by simple trial and error. The resulting solution is

$$P_{e,t} = \frac{b}{a+c} + \left(-\frac{a}{c}\right)^t \left(P_0 - \frac{b}{a+c}\right) \tag{1-30}$$

We can see now what was meant by the earlier statement that comparative statics cannot even tell us whether it is possible to reach a new equilibrium. For example, the value for price in Eq. (1-30) will converge to the equilibrium value of $b/(a+c)$ only if $(-a/c)$ is a fraction, and it will converge without fluctuations only if $(-a/c)$ is a positive fraction. When such convergence exists, the equilibrium is said to be *stable*. If the absolute value of $(-a/c)$ is greater than unity, the price will diverge from the equilibrium value by ever increasing amounts either cyclically or monotonically, and the equilibrium value is said to be an *unstable* equilibrium.

## V NOTATION

    The authors realize that it is very difficult for students to read different economics books when symbolic notation is not consistent among them. Moreover, the authors hesitate to impose yet another new notation upon the student. However, this particular book deals with so many relationships that neither the Roman nor Greek alphabets, singly or collectively, can be used to symbolize all the relevant variables and parameters without extensive repetition. Since we believe that it is better to learn a new system than to create the confusion necessitated by repetition of the same symbol for different variables, we have created a notation for this book that is different from most others. Although it is more complicated than many systems because of the use of subscripts, it is consistent throughout the book and, once learned, it is quite easy to remember.

All variables used in this book are symbolized by a capital letter, usually the first letter in the name of the variable. Thus, consumption is $C$, the money supply is $M$, and the wage rate is $W$. An important exception is the rate of interest, which is noted by the lowercase letter $r$, to prevent confusion with investment and to conform to a tradition of long-standing in the economics profession.

Parameters in the behavioral equations are lowercase letters and are subscripted. The lowercase letter used is the same as the letter used for the dependent variable in the equation. The subscript for the parameter is the same letter as the variable of which it is the coefficient. Thus, the traditional consumption function is written as

$$C = c_0 + c_y Y$$

In this equation, $C$ stands for consumption, $c_0$ is the intercept value of consumption (intercepts are always subscripted with 0), $Y$ is national income (another tradition), and $c_y$ is the coefficient of income. For this last symbol, note the correspondence of the lowercase letter $c$ to the dependent variable $C$ and the correspondence of the subscript $y$ to the independent variable $Y$.

One final point should be noted at this time. For the sake of simplicity, all parameters and variables in this book have positive values. If a relationship between two variables is negative, it will generally be indicated by the presence of a minus sign before one of those variables in the relevant equations.

**1.**   In Part IV, Section I of this chapter, the equilibrium values of price and quantity were given as

$$P_e = \frac{b}{a+c} \qquad Q_e = \frac{ab}{a+c}$$

Calculate the partial derivatives of these equilibrium values with respect to $b$ and to $c$ in order to determine the direction of the effect of a change in these parameters on the equilibrium values.

**2.**   Suppose that $Y_t = a + bY_{t-1}$ represents some meaningful economic relationship.

    **a.**   If the initial value of $Y$ is $Y_0$, solve for $Y_1$, $Y_2$, and $Y_3$ in terms of $Y_0$.

    **b.**   Using your solution for $Y_3$ as a guide, construct a general solution for $Y_t$ in terms of $Y_0$.

    **c.**   How does $Y_t$ behave over time if:
        $b$ is a positive fraction?
        $b$ is a negative fraction?
        $b$ is positive and greater than unity?

    **d.**   What is the limiting value of $Y_t$ as $t$ approaches infinity if $b$ is a fraction?

## RECOMMENDED REFERENCES

Ackley, Gardner, *Macroeconomic Theory*. New York: The Macmillan Company, 1962, Chapters I through IV.

Dernburg, Thomas F. and Duncan M. McDougall, *Macroeconomics*. New York: McGraw-Hill Book Co., 1968, Chapters 2 through 4.

National Bureau of Economic Research, *A Critique of the United States Income and Product Accounts*, Studies in Income and Wealth, Vol. 22. Princeton, N.J.: Princeton University Press, 1958.

For more information on difference equations, see

Allen, R. G. D., *Mathematical Economics*. New York: St. Martin's Press, 1956, Chapter 6.

Baumol, William J., *Economic Dynamics*. New York: The Macmillan Company, 1951, Chapter 9.

# 2 Consumption

The previous chapter has indicated that the largest single component of gross national product, $Y$, is personal consumption expenditures, $C$. Accordingly, any variable which has a significant effect upon consumption will also exert a strong influence upon GNP. It is the purpose of this chapter to examine those variables that are believed to be the determinants of consumption expenditures and to discuss how different functional relationships among them are usually specified. For those variables that are thought to be highly correlated with consumption, this examination will include an analysis of the entire form of the function. If the relationship is thought to be of only minor importance, the analysis will assess only the sign of the derivative.

## I THE CONSUMPTION FUNCTION

### I. National Income as an Explanatory Variable

As stated in Chapter 1,

$$Y = C + I + G$$

National income or gross national product ($Y$) is defined as the sum of consumption ($C$), investment ($I$), and government spending ($G$). (1-6)

This is not really an equation, however, but rather it is an identity or definition that must hold true for all values of C, I, and G. Thus, Eq. (1-6) in no way states that national income is *caused* by the three variables on the right-hand side. On the other hand, this does not rule out the possibility that one or more of the variables on the right-hand side might be determined by the single term on the left-hand side. As a matter of fact, this is exactly the behavioral relationship to be specified for the so-called "consumption function."

Keynes postulated in 1936 that the greatest single determinant of personal consumption expenditures was the level of national income and, although he himself made no empirical study to attempt verification of the statement, virtually every statistical investigation of the two variables has shown strong positive correlation. Accordingly, the first step in analyzing consumption is to specify that it is a function of income, or

$$C = f(Y)$$

The consumption function is some postulated relationship between consumption expenditures and income.

(2-1)

The relationship defined by Eq. (2-1) is called the *consumption function*.

Before beginning a formal analysis of the exact shape of the consumption function, it will be essential to consider a few definitions. For the moment, assume that taxes are equal to zero.

$$APC = \frac{C}{Y} = \frac{f(Y)}{Y}$$

The average propensity to consume ($APC$) is defined as the ratio of total consumption expenditures to the level of national income.

(2-2)

$$MPC = \frac{dC}{dY} = f'(Y)$$

The marginal propensity to consume ($MPC$) is defined to be the rate of change of consumption with respect to income.

(2-3)

Moreover, since $Y = C + S$, then $S = Y - C$, and the average propensity to save ($APS$) and the marginal propensity to save may be defined analogously to Eqs. (2-2) and (2-3).

$$APS = \frac{S}{Y} = \frac{Y - C}{Y}$$
$$= 1 - APC$$

The average propensity to save is the ratio of total savings to total income.

$$MPS = \frac{dS}{dY} = \frac{d(Y - C)}{dY}$$
$$= 1 - \frac{dC}{dY} = 1 - MPC$$

The marginal propensity to save is rate of change in savings associated with a change in income.

## 2. A Proportional Relationship

With the definitions above in mind, one can intuitively feel his way toward what the form of the consumption function might be. As income rises, one might logically expect that consumption also would rise, but not by so great an amount. Algebraically, this merely means that $0 < dC/dY < 1$. More simply, the marginal propensity to consume is a positive fraction.

Concerning the average propensity to consume, intuition is not so useful. On the one hand, it is possible that consumers on the aggregate might decide to spend a constant proportion $k$ of income, no matter how high or low the level of income. In that case,

$$APC = \frac{C}{Y} = k$$

The average propensity to consume is a constant, $k$.

$$MPC = \frac{dC}{dY} = k$$

The marginal propensity to consume is also the constant, $k$.

$$\frac{dC}{dY} = \frac{C}{Y}$$

The marginal propensity to consume equals the average propensity to consume.

This merely states that if the $APC$ is constant, then the $APC$ and $MPC$ must be equal. The only type of function which conforms to this criterion is one of simple proportionality, such as Eq. (2-4).

$$C = c_y Y$$

Consumption is a constant proportion, $c_y$, of income.

(2-4)

Then

$$APC = \frac{C}{Y} = c_y$$

and

$$MPC = \frac{dC}{dY} = c_y$$

Moreover, since such a function implies that consumption is always a constant fraction of income, it also indicates that the sum of investment and government spending must also be a constant share, no matter what the level of income.

**Illustration:**

| | |
|---|---|
| Let | $C = 0.8Y$ |
| Then | $APC = 0.8$ |
| and | $MPC = 0.8$ |
| If | $Y = 400$ |
| then | $C = 320 \qquad S = 80$ |
| Since | $Y = C + I + G$ |
| then | $I + G = 80$ |
| or 20% of total income. If | $Y = 500$ |
| then | $C = 400 \quad S = 100 \quad I + G = 100$ |
| or 20% of total income. | |

## 3. A Nonproportional Relationship

A second tenable assumption concerning the $APC$ is that, as income rises, individuals in the aggregate choose to devote a smaller fraction to consumption while allocating the remainder to increased savings. This assumption has great intuitive appeal, especially since it is often noticed that individuals with extremely low levels of income spend a high percentage of their income, while very wealthy individuals spend a relatively small fraction of current income for purposes of personal consumption. Although there are many different equations that could describe such a relationship, the simplest is a linear equation such as Eq. (2-5).

$$C = c_0 + c_y Y \qquad (2\text{-}5)$$

Then

$$APC = \frac{c_0}{Y} + c_y \qquad (2\text{-}6)$$

and

$$\frac{d(APC)}{dY} = -\frac{c_0}{Y^2} < 0 \qquad \text{The average propensity to consume varies inversely with the level of income.}$$

and

$$MPC = \frac{dC}{dY} = c_y \qquad (2\text{-}7)$$

These relationships indicate that a nonproportional linear consumption function generates a constant marginal propensity to consume and a declining average propensity to consume as income increases. The implication here is that although changes in consumption are always a constant fraction of the changes in income, the consumption share of GNP is perpetually declining as long as income is increasing. Thus, economic growth in such a model must be accompanied by an ever increasing share of national income being devoted to the sum of private and public investment.

**Illustration:**

Let
$$C = 100 + 0.8Y$$

Then
$$APC = \frac{100}{Y} + 0.8$$

and
$$MPC = 0.8$$

If
$$Y = 600$$

then
$$C = 580 \qquad S = 20$$
$$MPC = 0.8 \qquad APC = 0.97$$

Then
$$I + G = 20$$

or 3% of total income. If $Y = 700$

then
$$C = 660 \qquad S = 40$$
$$MPC = 0.8 \qquad APC = 0.94$$

Then $I + G = 40$

or 6% of total income. If $Y = 800$

then $C = 740$ $S = 60$

$MPC = 0.8$ $APC = 0.92$

Then $I + G = 60$

or 8% of total income.

One of many possible nonlinear consumption functions that generate declining $APC$'s is given by the quadratic equation, Eq. (2-8).

$$C = c_0 + c_y Y - c_{yy} Y^2 \qquad (2\text{-}8)$$

Restrictions placed on Eq. (2-8) are that $c_y$ is a positive fraction and that $c_{yy}$ is positive but less than $c_y$. In that case,

$$APC = \frac{c_0}{Y} + c_y - c_{yy} Y$$

$$\frac{d(APC)}{dY} = -\frac{c_0}{Y^2} - c_{yy} < 0$$

$$MPC = \frac{dC}{dY} = c_y - 2c_{yy} Y$$

$$\frac{d(MPC)}{dY} = -2c_{yy} < 0$$

With such a consumption function, *both* the $APC$ and $MPC$ decline at higher levels of income.

**Illustration:**

Let $C = 100 + 0.8Y - 0.0001Y^2$

Then $APC = \dfrac{100}{Y} + 0.8 - 0.0001Y$

and $MPC = 0.8 - 0.0002Y$

If $Y = 500$

then $C = 475$ $S = 25$

$MPC = 0.70$ $APC = 0.95$

Then $I + G = 25$

or 5% of total income. If $Y = 600$

then                              $C = 544$      $S = 56$

                                  $MPC = 0.68$   $APC = 0.91$

then                              $I + G = 56$

or 9% of total income. If    $Y = 700$

then                                  $C = 611$      $S = 89$

                                  $MPC = 0.66$    $APC = 0.87$

then                              $I + G = 89$

or 13% of total income.


Although many economists have expressed the belief that Eq. (2-8) is indeed the form of the relationship that actually exists between consumption and income, in practice economists have generally preferred to work with one of the two linear forms. The reasons for this are that linear relationships are easy to estimate statistically and that for small variations in independent variables, linear equations give reasonably good estimates of nonlinear functions. Accordingly, the remainder of this book will rely heavily upon linear equations for illustrative purposes.


## 4. Proportionality versus Nonproportionality

It would seem that the question of whether the consumption function is basically proportional or nonproportional could be resolved by a mere appeal to the facts. That is, by examining the past record relating consumption to income, one should be able to tell which of these relationships best fits the data in a statistical sense. Unfortunately, this is not the case. Using data for long periods of time, some economists have found that the "best" statistical fit is given by a proportional relationship, while others examining data for shorter periods have found that the relationship is basically nonproportional. The basic empirical defense of the proportional consumption function is based upon the separate works of Simon Kuznets and Raymond Goldsmith, who analyzed income and consumption expenditures in the United States between 1879 and 1954 and found that the average propensity to consume out of national income was very stable and about 0.87 in magnitude.[1] This

---

[1] See Simon Kuznets, *Uses of National Income in Peace and War*, Occasional Paper Number 6 (New York: National Bureau of Economic Research, 1942); and Raymond Goldsmith, *A Study of Savings in the United States* (Princeton, N.J.: Princeton University Press, 1955).

has been taken to be proof of a proportional relationship between consumption and income. On the other hand, studies made for cross sections of consumer groups for given years and other studies for short periods of time have indicated a nonproportional relationship. Because of the apparent inconsistencies involved in these studies, there have been several endeavors on the part of economists to attempt "reconciliation" of the two phenomena.

The first such attempt to explain the contradiction argued that the "true" consumption function was nonproportional but that its intercept tended to drift upward over time. The theory behind this argument suggests that increased urbanization, changing age distribution of the population, increases in accumulated wealth, and the rapid introduction of new products have all forced the consumption function upward over time.[2] However, this theory argues that the general shape of the consumption function has not changed as it has moved upward. Thus, the general equation for such a consumption function would be similar to Eq. (2-9),

$$C = c_0 + c_y Y + c_t t \qquad (2\text{-}9)$$

where $c_y$ and $c_t$ are both greater than zero and $t$ represents time. For a fixed time period, this is a linear consumption function with an intercept equal to $c_0 + c_t t$. The second phase of this argument suggests that the points observed for the "long-run" consumption functions actually lie on many different "short-run" functions but, by coincidence, the observed long-run values happened to lie along a straight line through the origin, as described by Eq. (2-10):

$$C = c_y^* Y \qquad (2\text{-}10)$$

where $c_y^*$ is greater than $c_y$.

**Illustration:**

Let the consumption function be

$$C_t = 100 + 0.5 Y + 20t$$

In that case, the consumption function can be graphed as a family of parallel lines, as given in Graph 2–1. Next, suppose that income in year zero is $250 and it increases by $50 every year ($Y = 250 + 50t$).

---

[2] This theory was first proposed by Arthur Smithies, "Forecasting Postwar Demand: I," *Econometrica*, June 1945, pp. 1–14.

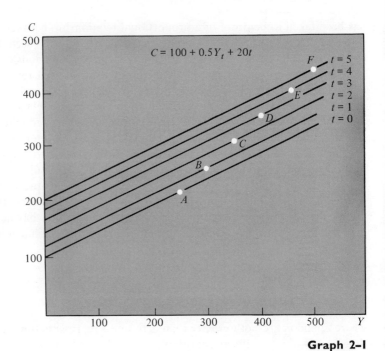

**Graph 2–I**

Upward-Shifting Consumption Function

Then

$$C_0 = 100 + 0.5(250) + 20(0) = 225$$

$$C_1 = 100 + 0.5(300) + 20(1) = 270$$

$$C_2 = 100 + 0.5(350) + 20(2) = 315$$

$$C_3 = 100 + 0.5(400) + 20(3) = 360$$

$$C_4 = 100 + 0.5(450) + 20(4) = 405$$

$$C_5 = 100 + 0.5(500) + 20(5) = 450$$

These values of consumption are labeled as points $A$ through $F$ on Graph 2–1. If one merely looks at the scatter diagram of these points, however, it appears that the relationship can be perfectly described by a proportional linear equation as shown in Graph 2–2. For the case at hand, the equation $C = 0.9Y$ generates the same values for consumption as the equation given above.

More recent studies have suggested that this appeal to coincidence is not a plausible one, since the factors cited above have not occurred rapidly

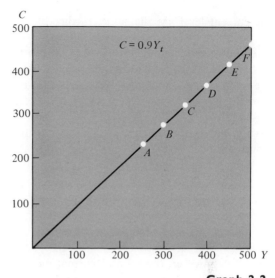

**Graph 2–2**

Long-Run Consumption Function

enough to shift the short-run function upward by the amounts that this theory requires. Secondly, if this explanation were true, Eqs. (2-9) and (2-10) could be solved simultaneously to find the relationship between income and time that brought this coincidence about. The solution is

$$Y = \frac{c_0}{c_y^* - c_y} + \frac{c_t t}{c_y^* - c_y}$$

Differentiating with respect to $t$,

$$\frac{dY}{dt} = \frac{c_t}{c_y^* - c_y} > 0 \tag{2-11}$$

Equation (2-11) implies that income must increase by a constant absolute amount in every time period in order to generate the "coincidence" required by this attempt at reconciliation. This is not the pattern of growth recorded for the period 1869–1938.

A second explanation of the apparent contradiction is a behavioral approach that asserts that individuals' tastes are conditioned by the highest level of income that they have enjoyed.[3] Moreover, when the highest level and

[3] See James Duesenberry, *Income, Saving, and the Theory of Consumer Behavior* (Cambridge, Mass.: Harvard University Press, 1949).

the current level are the same, further increases in income will be met by proportional increases in consumption. If income recedes from the peak level, however, the individual is reluctant to lower significantly the standard of living to which he had become accustomed, so decreases in consumption are not so large as the previously mentioned increases. Instead, the individual uses savings to cushion the decline in income. Similarly, as income is later pushed back toward the peak level, the $MPC$ remains at this lower value until savings have been replenished. This represents a "ratchet" type of consumption function. Letting $Y_p$ equal previous peak income,

$$APS = \frac{S}{Y} = s_1\left(\frac{Y}{Y_p}\right) + s_2$$

As long as income is rising from its previous peak, $Y = Y_p$, and the average propensity to save will be equal to the constant, $s_1 + s_2$. Should $Y$ be less than $Y_p$, however, the ratio of current income to peak income is a fraction, and the $APS$ declines ($APC$ increases) steadily as income falls. Correspondingly, as income rises back to the peak income, the $APS$ increases to the

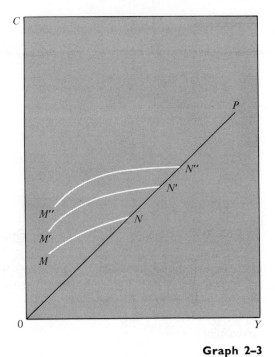

**Graph 2–3**

Ratchet Consumption Function

previous value of $s_1 + s_2$, after which it is again constant. For consumption,

$$APC = \frac{C}{Y} = \frac{Y - S}{Y} = 1 - \frac{S}{Y} = 1 - s_1\left(\frac{Y}{Y_p}\right) - s_2$$

or

$$C = (1 - s_2)Y - s_1\left(\frac{Y^2}{Y_p}\right) \quad \text{for} \quad Y < Y_p$$

$$C = (1 - s_1 - s_2)Y \quad \text{for} \quad Y = Y_p$$

and

$$MPC = (1 - s_2) - 2s_1\left(\frac{Y}{Y_p}\right) \quad \text{for} \quad Y < Y_p$$

$$MPC = 1 - s_1 - s_2 = 1 - APS \quad \text{for} \quad Y = Y_p$$

Graphically, this relationship appears in Graph 2–3. The ray $OP$ indicates the proportional consumption function for values of $Y = Y_p$. Once an individual's income is lowered, however, instead of falling back along $OP$, he drifts down one of the curves, $MN$, $M'N'$, etc. As income rises, he proceeds on the same path back to the intersection and then again up $OP$. An individual never moves down $OP$.

## 5. Disposable Income as an Explanatory Variable

Up to this point, consumption has been expressed as a function of national income. However, the explanation of the national income accounts in Chapter 1 showed that personal consumption and saving equal disposable income, not national income. Only if withdrawals from national income— taxes, retained earnings, etc.—are zero will national income and disposable income be equal. In order to make the present consumption hypothesis more realistic, this section will treat consumption as a function of disposable income that is equal to national income minus taxes. (Business withdrawals are considered to be zero for the present.) Consumption expressed as a function of disposable income is given by Eqs. (2-12) and (2-13).

$$C = f(Y_d) \tag{2-12}$$

$$C = f(Y - T) \tag{2-13}$$

where $Y_d$ designates disposable income and $T$ represents taxes. The $MPC$ is given by Eq. (2-14).

$$MPC = \frac{\partial C}{\partial Y} = f'(Y - T)\left(1 - \frac{dT}{dY}\right) \tag{2-14}$$

If taxes are invariant with respect to income, the second term on the right-hand side of Eq. (2-14) is unity. For the linear form,

$$C = c_0 + c_y(Y - T) = c_0 + c_y Y - c_y T \qquad (2\text{-}15)$$

The *MPC* for Eq. (2-15) is again $c_y$ if taxes are fixed.

In the more likely case, taxes are a function of income, and the tax equation may be written as Eq. (2-16).

$$T = g(Y) \qquad (2\text{-}16)$$

Substituting Eq. (2-16) into (2-13) yields consumption solely as a function of national income:

$$C = f[Y - g(Y)] = m(Y)$$

Differentiation with respect to $Y$ yields the *MPC*.

$$\frac{dC}{dY} = f'[Y - g(Y)][1 - g'(Y)] = m'(Y)$$

Again, in the linear case,

$$C = c_0 + c_y(Y - T) \qquad (2\text{-}15)$$

$$T = t_y Y - t_0 \qquad (2\text{-}17)$$

$$C = c_0 + c_y Y - c_y t_y Y + c_y t_0$$

$$\frac{dC}{dY} = c_y(1 - t_y) \qquad (2\text{-}18)$$

In Eq. (2-17), $t_y$ is a positive fraction equal to the marginal rate of taxation. In Eq. (2-18), $c_y(1 - t_y)$ will be a positive fraction that may be called the effective marginal propensity to consume out of national income. The importance of this composite parameter will be apparent in the following chapter.

## II OTHER DETERMINANTS OF CONSUMPTION

To this point, consumption has been treated as though it were a function of only an income variable. This is simply because income has been shown to be the single most important determinant of consumption. Completeness demands at least a cursory look at other variables, however, so the consumption function might be expanded to Eq. (2-19).

$$C = f(Y, r, A_F, A_R, P) \qquad (2\text{-}19)$$

where $r$ is the rate of interest; $A_F$, holdings of financial assets; $A_R$, holdings of real assets; and $P$, the price level.

## I. The Rate of Interest

Early economists believed that the rate of interest was the key variable in determining the shares of income that would be devoted to consumption and saving. As the rate of interest increased, saving would be more profitable, and individuals would be willing to cut back on consumption in order to save more. Mathematically, this requires the first derivative of consumption with respect to the rate of interest to be less than zero.

$$\frac{\partial C}{\partial r} < 0 \qquad (2\text{-}20)$$

More recent thought has raised some doubt about this type of relationship. Consider, for example, an individual who is planning to build an estate of given size. As the interest rate rises, he will find that he can accumulate this estate by saving less than he would have needed at the previously lower rate. Accordingly, he may decrease his rate of saving, in which case (2-20) would be positive. Even more important, many economists feel that any effect that the rate of interest exerts upon consumption is primarily traceable to the indirect relationship brought about by the influence of the interest rate upon the level of income, a topic reserved for Chapter 7. Because of these complicating factors, it is almost impossible to state confidently whether changes in the rate of interest are positively or negatively correlated with the level of consumption.

## 2. Financial Assets

Another variable that is often put forth as a possible determinant of consumption expenditures is the stock of financial assets in the economy. The theory implies that individuals with large holdings of financial assets spend more on consumption than individuals of the same level of income with lesser financial holdings. Mathematically, this theory can be formulated by the following dynamic equation:

$$C_t = c_0 + c_y Y_t + c_F A_{F,t-1} \qquad (2\text{-}21)$$

where $c_F > 0$. The subscript $t$ above indicates the time period. The financial assets variable is lagged by one period, since it would not be economically meaningful to include wealth at the end of the current period as a determinant of current consumption. The reason for this is that the addition to wealth in the current period equals the amount not consumed. Therefore, if current wealth is known, current consumption has already been determined.

The theory as presented above has a considerable intuitive appeal, especially since wealth accumulated during World War II is credited with stimulating much of the postwar buying surge. Moreover, econometric studies of the consumption function have revealed a positive coefficient for the wealth variable. However, certain qualifications should be introduced. First, in the United States, holdings of financial assets are concentrated in the hands of the higher-income groups who constitute a minority of all consumers. Therefore, the impact of the wealth variable is not large, absolutely speaking, and the coefficient $c_F$ in Eq. (2-21) is small in value for the household sector as a whole. Secondly, it is possible that the accumulation of financial assets only increases the desire for further acquisition of financial assets for some individuals. In that case it is possible for the coefficient of the wealth variable for those groups to be negative. Finally, the relationship between consumption and financial assets should take into consideration the effects of changes in the general price level. For financial holdings of fixed dollar value, a change in the general price level represents a change in the purchasing power of those assets. A decrease in general prices increases the real value of fixed dollar assets and may lead to an upward shift in the consumption function, while of course the reverse would hold for price increases. This phenomenon, called the "Pigou effect," has been widely discussed in the economic literature. Inclusion of the general price level into Eq. (2-21) yields

$$C_t = c_0 + c_y Y_t + c_F \left( \frac{A_F}{P} \right)_{t-1} \qquad (2\text{-}22)$$

where $P$ represents the general price level, and thus $A_F/P$ is the *real* value of financial assets. More will be said about the impact of prices in the next section.

### 3. Real Assets

Another possible determinant of consumption is the level of durable goods and other nonfinancial assets held by consumers. Again, however, the argument is not clear-cut concerning the direction of its effect. On the one hand, it is argued that an increase in holdings of durable goods represents a partial satisfaction of wants that will be reflected in decreased future consumption. The other side of the argument suggests that the purchase of durable goods generally leads to additional consumption expenditures for their maintenance and utilization. As with the previous variables, the net effect here is difficult to assess. In fact, the greatest influence of this variable is to be found not on the level of consumption but on its regularity over time. Durable goods are recorded as consumption at the time they are purchased, and the bunching of such purchases within short time spans may seriously alter the size of the short-run *MPC*. Moreover, even over periods as long as a year, a similar effect can be demonstrated, since economies with large inventories of consumer durables may postpone replacement demand for extended periods. Thus, while the net effect of consumer inventories of durable goods upon the level of consumption is at best uncertain, its effect upon cyclical behavior is a demonstrated fact.

### 4.  The Price Level

The influence of the price level upon the real value of financial assets has already been discussed above. However, many economists argue that an additional reason for including the average price level as a determinant of consumption is that the important variable in this analysis is not the dollar expenditures on consumption but the volume of output of the physical goods and services being produced. Accordingly, the dollar purchases should be deflated by a price index in order to indicate the "real" level of consumption. Alternatively, letting $Q_c$ represent the purchase of real consumer goods and $P$ the average price,

$$PQ_c = C$$

or

$$Q_c = \frac{C}{P} \tag{2-23}$$

Therefore, instead of writing current consumption expenditures as a function of current income, this theory suggests that real consumption is a function of real national income, or

$$\frac{C}{P} = f\left(\frac{Y}{P}\right) \tag{2-24}$$

While this theory does have considerable intuitive appeal, certain qualifications should again be pointed out. First of all, if one is interested in studying a cross-sectional consumption function (among different income groups at the same point in time), the distinction between the two types of functions is unnecessary. At a given point in time, the price level would be equal for all income groups, so an empirically fitted equation would yield the same parameter estimates for both equations. If one is instead interested in analyzing time-series behavior (for the same income group over different time periods), the two approaches may or may not yield different conclusions, but it is still difficult to decide on a priori grounds which technique is to be preferred.

A fundamental problem in selecting what type of time-series consumption function is applicable involves the decision as to how people react when confronted by changing prices and incomes. If in fact people do see through the money veil, then the best technique clearly is the "real" consumption function. However, people may be subject to a money "illusion" that disguises the real effects. Thus, in a period of proportionately rising prices and incomes, some groups may see only the rising incomes and thus increase the quantity of goods that they purchase, even though real income is the same. This would in fact be the pattern of behavior for an individual following a savings plan that calls for him to set aside a fixed dollar amount every time period. Correspondingly, another group may see only the price increases and therefore cut back on the quantity of consumer goods that they purchase. Thus, we cannot tell a priori exactly how people do behave.

The problem cited in the previous paragraph matters very little if the "true" consumption function is a proportional one. That is, suppose individuals react in such a way as to keep "real" consumption a constant fraction of "real" income. In that case, the "true" consumption function would be

$$\frac{C}{P} = c_y\left(\frac{Y}{P}\right) \tag{2-25}$$

However, multiplying through by $P$,

$$C = c_y Y \tag{2-4}$$

The same result would have held if the "true" behavior of consumers was to keep dollar expenditures on consumption a constant proportion of current income. Thus, if the relationship is proportional, statistical estimation techniques will yield the same estimate of $c_y$ no matter which type of function is assumed.

If the "true" consumption function is not proportional, then the two approaches will lead to different results. Suppose the following equation is the "true" function:

$$\frac{C}{P} = c_0 + c_y\left(\frac{Y}{P}\right) \tag{2-26}$$

Multiplying through by $P$ yields

$$C = c_0 P + c_y Y \tag{2-27}$$

If one mistakenly assumed that the form of the equation was a simple linear function of current income alone, the attempt to estimate the parameters of the equation would lead to misleading results. Equation (2-27) states that, in a period of rising prices and money incomes, each would have a positive effect on consumption. If one ignored the contribution of prices, however, he would attribute the rising consumption to income alone and therefore overestimate the magnitude of the $MPC, c_y$. Correspondingly, the reader may demonstrate for himself that if the "true" function were a nonhomogeneous linear function relating consumption in money terms to money income, the attempt to measure real consumption as a function of real income would tend to underestimate the value of the $MPC$.

The previous paragraphs indicate that the relationship of the price level to consumption expenditures is not a simple one. The exact technique to be employed depends on the researcher's assumption about the behavior of consumers as well as the objectives of his study. In this book, we shall continue to employ a function relating current consumption to current income. The reason for this is not that we assume the consumer to be subject to the money illusion but that this is an expedient technique for developing a model that ultimately will explain the determination of real output and the price level, with a minimum amount of complexity. The results can be generalized at that time to incorporate both types of consumption function.[4]

## 5. The "Permanent Income" Hypothesis[5]

A recent contribution to the theory of the consumption function suggests that the determinants of consumption expenditures cannot be isolated by examining the values of current economic variables and that one must examine the expected values of these variables in the future. This theory argues that when individuals set current consumption patterns, they are taking into account not only the value of their current incomes but also the values of the income receipts that they expect to have over a fairly long-run planning horizon. Consumption expenditures, according to the theory, need not be restricted to current income as long as the individual can borrow against future incomes. Thus, the constraint on current consumption expenditures is the present value of the expected future income stream, which, for a two-period planning horizon, is equal to

$$PV = R_1 + \frac{R_2}{1 + r} \tag{2-28}$$

[4] The general question of "real" versus current money behavioral relationships and the related question of "money illusion" is discussed in greater detail in the appendix to Chapter 10.

[5] See Milton Friedman, *A Theory of the Consumption Function* (Princeton, N.J.: Princeton University Press, 1957).

where

$$PV = \text{present value}$$

$$R_1 \text{ and } R_2 = \text{expected receipts}$$

$$r = \text{the rate of interest}$$

If the entire present value is spent for consumption expenditures in period 1, then all income receipts in period 2 would have to be used to retire the indebtedness incurred in period 1, so period 2 consumption would be zero. Obviously, then, the entire present value would not normally be used to finance current consumption. The question is then raised as to what the upper limit on consumption might be. A suggested answer here is that an individual might spend up to that amount that would leave his wealth constant over time. Wealth in this context is merely the total worth of the individual and would be equal to the present value of his future earnings, given by Eq. (2-28). The amount that could be spent without impairing this wealth would be the interest earnings on the wealth, or $rW$, which is defined as the individual's "permanent income." If current receipts are greater than permanent income, then the difference will be saved to maintain wealth and to finance future consumption. If current receipts are less than permanent income, then the difference is the amount that will be borrowed in order to finance current consumption.[6]

If permanent income is used entirely for consumption purposes, then the marginal propensity to consume out of wealth will be equal to the interest rate since

$$C = Y_p = rW \tag{2-29}$$

and

$$\frac{\partial C}{\partial W} = r \tag{2-30}$$

Since interest rates are normally below 0.10, the marginal propensity to consume out of wealth will be much smaller than the marginal propensity to consume out of income discussed earlier in this chapter.

By breaking income into permanent and transitory components, this theory also seeks to explain the apparent paradox between short-run and long-run consumption functions discussed earlier. Imagine that in some time period an individual receives an income payment that had not been antici-pated and that is not expected to be repeated in future years. This transitory payment will boost current income and wealth by the amount of the payment, but since the marginal propensity to consume out of wealth is quite small,

---

[6] For discrete time periods, consider that income is received at the beginning of the period and that expenditures are made at the end of the period.

most of the payment will be used for saving rather than consumption. Accordingly, short-run changes in income will lead to less than proportionate changes in consumption. If some unexpected income is received in one year and is expected to be repeated in future years, however, then current wealth is increased by the present value of all such future payments. This can be seen quickly by letting $U$ represent the unexpected payment. Then current wealth is

$$W = R_1 + U + \frac{R_2 + U}{1 + r} \tag{2-31}$$

$$W = R_1 + \frac{R_2}{1 + r} + \frac{U(2 + r)}{1 + r} \tag{2-32}$$

Since $(2 + r)/(1 + r)$ is greater than unity, wealth rises by more than the increase in income. With consumption a constant fraction of wealth, the increase in consumption will be much greater when the unexpected increase in income is incorporated in future expectations than when it is expected to be a one-shot phenomenon. Accordingly, the long-run function should be much steeper than the short-run function when consumption is plotted against current income.

## 6. Distribution of Income

A final consideration among the determinants of consumption should be the prevailing distribution of income in the economy. If the theory of a declining $MPC$ is true, higher-income groups will spend proportionately less of their income on consumption than do lower-income groups. Thus, any change in income that alters the income distribution will induce a different pattern of consumption than existed previously. This effect has been investigated statistically several times, however, and the net effect on consumption even for large-income redistribution measures has been shown to be quite small.

## III SUMMARY

The most important single variable helping to explain the variation in personal consumption expenditures is income, whether defined as gross national product or as disposable income. Important relationships between income and consumption are the average propensity to consume, defined to be the ratio of consumption to income, and the marginal propensity to consume, which is the derivative of consumption with respect to income.

Economists have developed several theories to try to explain apparent inconsistencies between long-run examinations of the consumption function that indicate a proportional relationship and short-run and cross-sectional studies that indicate a nonproportional function. Many of the attempts involve some ingenious insights, but no consensus has been generated as yet.

Other determinants of consumption besides income are thought to be the rate of interest, the stock of financial assets, the stock of real assets, the price level, and the distribution of income. The exact influence of the rate of interest is subject to some confusion because of the influence of the rate of interest upon the level of income. The stock of financial assets exerts a small but positive impact on consumption, although this is not consequential for a static model. Durable-goods holdings apparently influence the variability of the consumption expenditures more than the average level of consumption. Prices are important in measuring consumption if the researcher assumes that it is "real" consumption that responds to income changes. Finally, the distribution of income is theoretically significant in influencing the consumption function, but the observed magnitude of its impact has so far been small.

## EXERCISES

1. Given the following consumption function,

$$C = 10 + 0.6\,Y - 0.01\,Y^2$$

show how the APC and the MPC change as $Y$ changes.

2. Suppose that the true consumption function is

$$C = c_0 + c_y Y$$

where $C$ and $Y$ are, respectively, consumption expenditures and GNP measured in current dollars. Furthermore, suppose that an investigator attempted to estimate empirically a consumption function of the following form:

$$\frac{C}{P} = c_0 + c_y \left(\frac{Y}{P}\right)$$

where $C$ and $Y$ are as defined above and $P$ is a price index. If the latter function is estimated during a period of generally rising prices and income, would the value of the MPC in the second equation be less than, equal to, or greater than the MPC in the first equation?

## RECOMMENDED REFERENCES

Ackley, Gardner, *Macroeconomic Theory*. New York: The Macmillan Company, 1961, Chapters X and XI.

Ando, Albert, and Franco Modigliani, "The Life Cycle Hypothesis of Saving: Aggregate Implications and Tests," *American Economic Review*, March 1963, pp. 55–84.

Duesenberry, James S., *Income, Saving, and the Theory of Consumer Behavior*. Cambridge, Mass.: Harvard University Press, 1949.

Farrell, M. J., "The New Theories of the Consumption Function," *The Economic Journal*, December 1959, pp. 678–96.

Ferber, Robert, *A Study of Aggregate Consumption Functions*, Technical Paper No. 8. New York: National Bureau of Economic Research, 1953.

Friedman, Milton, *A Theory of the Consumption Function*. Princeton, N.J.: Princeton University Press, 1957.

Keynes, John Maynard, *The General Theory of Employment, Interest, and Money*. New York: Harcourt, Brace & World, Inc., 1936, Chapters 8 and 9.

Kuznets, Simon, *Uses of National Income in Peace and War*, Occasional Paper Number 6. New York: National Bureau of Economic Research, 1942.

Smithies, Arthur, "Forecasting Postwar Demand: I," *Econometrica*, June 1945 pp. 1–14.

Zellner, Arnold, "The Short-Run Consumption Function," *Econometrica*, October 1957, pp. 552–67.

# 3 Simple Equilibrium

# And The Multiplier

The previous chapter has examined the determinants of consumption expenditures and concluded that consumption may be best explained as a function of either total or disposable income. The purpose of this chapter is to incorporate the behavioral consumption function into the GNP identity in order to arrive at a simple equilibrium model, assuming that investment and government spending are given. Section I analyzes equilibrium with instantaneous adjustments among the variables, while Section II deals with various lagged relationships. In each section, behavior is analyzed for both the general form and the linear form of the consumption function.

## I INSTANTANEOUS ADJUSTMENT

### 1. The Simple Multiplier

The general form of the consumption function was given in the previous chapter as Eq. (2-1).

$$C = f(Y)$$ 
Consumption is a function of total income

(2-1)

Again, this is a *behavioral* equation that considers consumption as being dependent on, or caused by, the level of income. On the other hand, it will be remembered that the basic GNP equation, Eq. (1-6), is always true.

$$Y = C + I + G$$

Total income is the sum of consumption, investment, and government purchases of goods and services.

(1-6)

In order to construct a behavioral equation of GNP, Eq. (2-1) must be substituted into Eq. (1-6) to yield Eq. (3-1), for which we assume an explicit solution for $Y$ is obtainable.

$$Y = f(Y) + I + G \tag{3-1}$$

$$Y = g(I, G)$$

The level of income is a function of the exogeneous variables, $I$ and $G$.

(3-2)

Equation (3-2) states that if values for $I$ and $G$ are given, the value of $Y$ is uniquely determined. This value of $Y$ may be called the equilibrium level of income. Naturally, as $I$ or $G$ take on new values, $Y$ must change accordingly, so $\partial Y/\partial I$ and $\partial Y/\partial G$, called the investment and government-spending multipliers, are of considerable interest. These may be derived by differentiating Eq. (3-1) implicitly.

$$\frac{\partial Y}{\partial I} = f'(Y)\frac{\partial Y}{\partial I} + 1$$

$$\frac{\partial Y}{\partial I} = \frac{1}{1 - f'(Y)}$$

Similarly,

$$\frac{\partial Y}{\partial G} = \frac{1}{1 - f'(Y)} \qquad (3\text{-}3)$$

Assuming a linear function,

$$C = c_0 + c_y Y$$

Then

$$Y = c_0 + c_y Y + I + G$$

or

$$Y = \frac{1}{1 - c_y}(c_0 + I + G)$$

If consumption is a linear function of income, then income is a linear function of government and investment. Then

$$\frac{\partial Y}{\partial I} = \frac{\partial Y}{\partial G} = \frac{1}{1 - c_y} = m \qquad \text{The multiplier, } m, \text{ is the reciprocal of the marginal propensity to save.}$$

$$(3\text{-}4)$$

and the multiplier, $m$, is the same for both private investment and government spending. The multiplier itself is a function of $c_y$, the marginal propensity to consume. As the $MPC$ takes on larger values, the multiplier increases in value also, as shown by Eq. (3-5).

$$\frac{dm}{dc_y} = \frac{1}{(1 - c_y)^2} > 0 \qquad \text{The multiplier varies directly with the marginal propensity to consume.}$$

$$(3\text{-}5)$$

Expressing $Y$ as a differential,

$$dY = \frac{\partial Y}{\partial I}\,dI + \frac{\partial Y}{\partial G}\,dG \qquad (3\text{-}6)$$

Any change in $I$ or $G$ will lead to a change in $Y$ equal to the product of the change times the multiplier.

**Illustration:**

Let $\quad C = c_0 + c_y Y = 20 + 0.8\,Y \qquad I = 50 \qquad G = 50$
Then $\quad Y = 20 + 0.8\,Y + 50 + 50 \quad$ or $\quad Y = 600$
If $\quad dI = 10 \qquad dG = 0$

then from Eq. (3-6),

$$dY = \left(\frac{1}{1 - 0.8}\right) 10 = 50$$

The new level of income will be 650, or the change in income will be five times the change in investment. The new level of consumption will be

$$C = 20 + 0.8(650) = 540$$

so,

$$Y = 540 + 60 + 50 = 650$$

The same procedure may be used for a more complicated consumption function, such as the one in Eq. (3-7).

$$C = c_0 + c_y Y - c_{yy} Y^2 \qquad c_{yy} < c_y \tag{3-7}$$

In that case

$$Y = c_0 + c_y Y - c_{yy} Y^2 + I + G$$

Use of the quadratic formula yields[1]

$$Y = -\ \frac{-(1 - c_y) + [(1 - c_y)^2 + 4c_{yy}(c_0 + I + G)]^{1/2}}{2c_{yy}}$$

The multipliers are

$$\frac{\partial Y}{\partial I} = \frac{\partial Y}{\partial G} = \frac{1}{[(1 - c_y)^2 + 4c_{yy}(c_0 + I + G)]^{1/2}} > 0$$

## 2. Fixed Taxes and the Balanced Budget Theorem

Perhaps more interesting is the equilibrium model generated by the inclusion of taxes, so that consumption is a function of disposable income, as in Eq. (2-13).

$$C = f(Y - T) \tag{2-13}$$

---

[1] The negative solution is necessarily ignored since negative levels of income are meaningless.

Substituting Eq. (2-13) into (1-6) yields

$$Y = f(Y - T) + I + G = g(I, G, T) \qquad (3\text{-}8)$$

Let taxes be an exogenous variable $(dT/dY = 0)$ and differentiate Eq. (3-8) to find the government-spending multiplier and private investment multiplier.

$$\frac{\partial Y}{\partial I} = f'(Y - T)\frac{\partial Y}{\partial I} + 1$$

$$\frac{\partial Y}{\partial I} = \frac{1}{1 - f'(Y - T)} \qquad (3\text{-}9)$$

where $f'(Y - T)$ has been defined as the *effective MPC* in Chapter 2. Since income is now a function of fixed taxes, as well as of $I$ and $G$, Eq. (3-8) may also be used to derive $\partial Y/\partial T$, called the *tax multiplier*.

$$\frac{\partial Y}{\partial T} = -\frac{f'(Y - T)}{1 - f'(Y - T)} < 0 \qquad (3\text{-}10)$$

One very interesting feature of this model may be seen by examining the change in income that results from equal changes in government spending and taxes. In other words, what will be the total impact on income if new government spending is matched by new taxes, so that the budget remains marginally balanced? Examine the total differential of Eq. (3-8):

$$dY = \frac{\partial Y}{\partial I}\, dI + \frac{\partial Y}{\partial G}\, dG + \frac{\partial Y}{\partial T}\, dT \qquad (3\text{-}11)$$

Under the assumptions above, $dI = 0$, $dG = dT$; so

$$dY = \frac{\partial Y}{\partial G}\, dG + \frac{\partial Y}{\partial T}\, dG = \left(\frac{\partial Y}{\partial G} + \frac{\partial Y}{\partial T}\right) dG$$

But

$$\frac{\partial Y}{\partial G} + \frac{\partial Y}{\partial T} = \frac{1}{1 - f'(Y - T)} - \frac{f'(Y - T)}{1 - f'(Y - T)} = 1$$

and

$$dY = dG \qquad (3\text{-}12)$$

The conclusion here is that even if new taxes equal new spending, the net effect of such a budgetary operation will still exert an expansionary influence upon income since the change in income will be equal to the change in government spending. This statement has been named the *balanced budget theorem*. One explanation of this result may be found in the differences in the *MPC* of the private sector versus the public sector. If the budget is balanced marginally, then the effective marginal propensity to spend (with respect to tax revenues) of the government is unity. Accordingly, any transfer of funds from the private sector to the public sector raises the marginal propensity to spend for the economy as a whole and thus generates a higher level of national income.

For the linear case, the consumption function is provided by Eq. (2-15).

$$C = c_0 + c_y Y_d$$
$$C = c_0 + c_y(Y - T) \tag{2-15}$$

Substitution of Eq. (2-15) into (1-6) yields the income equation.

$$Y = \left(\frac{1}{1 - c_y}\right)(c_0 + I + G - c_y T) \tag{3-13}$$

The investment, government, and tax multipliers may be found by differentiating Eq. (3-13).

$$\frac{\partial Y}{\partial I} = \frac{\partial Y}{\partial G} = \frac{1}{1 - c_y}$$

$$\frac{\partial Y}{\partial T} = -\frac{c_y}{1 - c_y}$$

Note that

$$\frac{\partial Y}{\partial G} + \frac{\partial Y}{\partial T} = \frac{1}{1 - c_y} - \frac{c_y}{1 - c_y} = \frac{1 - c_y}{1 - c_y} = 1$$

**Illustration:**

Let $\quad C = c_0 + c_y(Y - T) = 20 + 0.8(Y - 30)$ $\quad\quad I = 50 \quad\quad G = 50$

Then $\quad Y = 20 + 0.8(Y - 30) + 50 + 50$

$\quad\quad\quad Y = 480$

and $\quad C = 20 + 0.8(480 - 30) = 380$

In the identity $\quad Y = 380 + 50 + 50 = 480$

which checks. Let government spending and taxes both increase by 10,

or $\quad dG = dT = 10$

Let $\quad dI = 0$

Then $dY = (5)(10) + (-4)(10) = 10$

Thus, $Y$ increases by 10 to 490. For the new value of $C$,

$$C = 20 + 0.8(490 - 40) = 380$$

In the identity     $Y = 380 + 50 + 60 = 490$

which checks. Since the change in income is exactly equal to the change in government spending, the original values of consumption and investment will be unaffected.

## 3. Variable Taxes and the Balanced Budget Theorem

The previous analysis may be extended one step further by making taxes a function of national income, as would be the case if income taxes were relied upon heavily for government revenues. The linear case for this model is discussed below.

Equation (2-17) presented the variable tax equation. Substituting this equation and Eq. (2-15) into the GNP identity yields the following solution for $Y$.

$$T = t_y Y - t_0 \tag{2-17}$$

$$C = c_0 + c_y(Y - T) \tag{2-15}$$

$$Y = \frac{c_0 + I + G + c_y t_0}{1 - c_y(1 - t_y)} \tag{3-14}$$

Solving for the investment and government multipliers,

$$\frac{\partial Y}{\partial I} = \frac{\partial Y}{\partial G} = \frac{1}{1 - c_y(1 - t_y)} \tag{3-15}$$

and $c_y(1 - t_y)$ may be called the effective $MPC$.

Equation (3-15) presents a multiplier that will always be smaller than the multiplier given in Eq. (3-4) as long as the marginal rate of taxation ($t_y$) is greater than zero. This means that if autonomous changes in investment (or government spending) occur, the induced changes in income will be smaller than under a system where taxes are constant ($t_y = 0$). In other words, rising taxes absorb some of the increase in income that would have otherwise been generated. Conversely, if income is declining, taxes decrease to cushion that decline. This principle has therefore been given the name of *built-in stability*, and the income tax has been designated as one of the *automatic stabilizers*.

Equations (2-17) and (3-14) can also be used to demonstrate the balanced budget theorem. Assume that government expenditures are to increase by an amount $dG$ and that the government wants to balance these expenditures by increased taxes of $dT$ to ensure that the budget remains balanced at the margin. Thus, the tax rate must be adjusted so that after the new equilibrium has been attained, $dG$ must equal $dT$. Algebraically, the analysis is as follows:

$$dY = \frac{dG}{1 - c_y(1 - t_y)} - \frac{c_y(c_0 + I + G + c_y t_0)}{[1 - c_y(1 - t_y)]^2} dT_y \qquad (3\text{-}16)$$

$$dT = t_y\, dY + dt_y Y = dG \qquad (3\text{-}17)$$

$$dt_y = \frac{dG - t_y\, dY}{Y} \qquad (3\text{-}18)$$

and

$$Y = \frac{c_0 + I + G + c_y t_0}{1 - c_y(1 - t_y)}$$

Substitution into Eq. (3-16) for $dt_y$ and $Y$ yields

$$dY = \frac{dG}{1 - c_y(1 - t_y)} - c_y \frac{(c_0 + I + G + c_y t_0)}{[1 - c_y(1 - t_y)]^2} (dG - t_y\, dY)$$

$$\times \left\{ \frac{[1 - c_y(1 - t_y)]}{c_0 + I + G + c_y t_0} \right\}$$

$$dY = \frac{dG - c_y\, dG + c_y t_y\, dY}{1 - c_y(1 - t_y)}$$

and

$$dY(1 - c_y) + c_y t_y\, dY = dG(1 - c_y) + c_y t_y\, dY \qquad dY = dG$$

Extension of the model has not affected the basic result. If the budget is to be balanced marginally, the increase in the equilibrium level of income will be equal to the change in government expenditures, and the overall effect will be expansionary. The balanced budget multiplier is still unity.

**Illustration:**

Let $C = 20 + 0.8(Y - T)$     $I = 50$     $G = 50$     $T = 0.25\,Y - 100$

So    $C = 20 + 0.8(Y - 0.25\,Y + 100) = 100 + 0.6\,Y$

and    $Y = 100 + 0.6\,Y + 50 + 50$

or     $Y = 500$

      $T = 0.25(500) - 100 = 25$

Next assume that government expenditures increase to 150 and that the tax *rate* is raised to 0.375, investment remaining constant.

Then    $C = 20 + 0.8(Y - 0.375Y + 100)$

and

$$Y = 100 + 0.5Y + 50 + 150 = 600 \qquad T = (0.375)(600) - 100 = 125$$

The increase in taxes is equal to the increase in expenditures, so the budget has remained balanced at the margin. Nonetheless, income has risen by the amount of the increase in government spending.

Notice that the figures used above cannot be fitted into Eq. (3-18). This is simply because Eq. (3-18) applies only to instantaneous rates of change, while the numerical example uses large, discrete changes. However, the principle remains valid.


## II  LAGGED ADJUSTMENT, A DYNAMIC MODEL

### I.  A Lagged Consumption Function

Some studies have suggested that a lag exists between the time that current income is received and the time that expenditures are made from that income. Proponents of this type of hypothesis suggest that individuals need time to become accustomed to new levels of income before new levels of consumption are generated, that time must pass before individuals accept new levels of income as permanent, or simply that institutional forces prevent the simultaneous spending of current income for current consumption.[2] Whatever the reason, the implication of the theory is that consumption is a function of income from the previous pay period rather than the current one. Algebraically,

$$C_t = c_0 + c_y Y_{t-1}$$

Consumption in the present time period depends on the level of income in the previous time period.

(3-19)

where the subscript $t$ refers to the time period. Since income in period $t - 1$ is the sum of consumption, investment, and government spending in that

---

[2] This is one empirical approach to the "permanent income hypothesis" mentioned earlier.

period, Eq. (3-19) can be rewritten as

$$C_t = c_0 + c_y(C_{t-1} + I_{t-1} + G_{t-1}) \tag{3-20}$$

or, more simply

$$C_t = A + c_y C_{t-1} \tag{3-21}$$

where

$$A = c_0 + c_y(I_{t-1} + G_{t-1})$$

assuming that $I$ and $G$ are constant. Equation (3-21) is a first-order nonhomogeneous difference equation, which may be solved for $C_t$ as an explicit function of the variable $t$. The solution is

$$C_t = A\left(\frac{1 - c_y^t}{1 - c_y}\right) + c_y^t C_0 \tag{3-22}$$

where $C_0$ is the original value of consumption in the initial period when $t = 0$. The economic meaning of the equation is that if some original equilibrium level of income is altered by an increase in, say, autonomous investment, then the level of consumption in the following period will change by an amount equal to the marginal propensity to consume (out of previous income) multiplied by the change in income in the preceding period. The change in consumption will generate a new value for current income, even if investment stabilizes at the new level or even falls back to the old one, so this in turn leads to an induced change in consumption for the next period. This geometric progression continues through an infinite number of terms or, more practically, until the increments approach zero. Since $c_y$ is always a positive fraction, $c_y^t$ approaches zero monotonically, and $1 - c_y^t$ approaches unity, so $C_t$ in Eq. (3-22) approaches $A/(1 - c_y)$ monotonically as $t$ becomes larger and larger. What happens to income during this process depends on whether the autonomous variable that kicked off the whole process continues at its new level or falls back to its old value. Let us consider both of these cases.

## 2. Continuous Injection

The general theory of income determination and the multiplier is not significantly affected when a lagged consumption function replaces the instantaneous relationship. The only real difference is that the investment or government multiplier for the lagged model states that the new equilibrium level of income will be a multiple of the change in $I$ or $G$ but that this multiplier holds only for the new equilibrium value at $t = \infty$ and not for any single disequilibrium value during the interim period. Consider the following linear model, which assumes that consumption is a function of total income. Let

$$C_t = c_0 + c_y Y_{t-1} \tag{3-19}$$

Then

$$Y_t = c_0 + c_y Y_{t-1} + I_t + G_t \tag{3-23}$$

The general solution of Eq. (3-23) is as follows:

$$Y_t = (c_0 + I_t + G_t)\left(\frac{1 - c_y^t}{1 - c_y}\right) + c_y^t Y_0 \tag{3-24}$$

where $Y_0$ is the initial value for income. Suppose that this system is originally in equilibrium. Then, let investment increase and remain at that higher level for all succeeding periods. In other words, this new level of investment is maintained for all succeeding periods. Equilibrium will be attained when there is no change in income from one period to the next. This requires that

$$Y_t - Y_{t-1} = 0 \tag{3-25}$$

or

$$Y_e = Y_t = Y_{t-1} \tag{3-26}$$

For Eq. (3-25) to hold, $c_y^t$ must converge to zero as $t$ increases. Since $c_y$ is the marginal propensity to consume and is less than unity, this condition is satisfied, and the equilibrium level of income may be written as

$$\lim_{t \to \infty} Y_t = Y_e = \frac{c_0 + I_t + G_t}{1 - c_y} \tag{3-27}$$

The investment and government expenditures multipliers may be found by taking the partial derivative of Eq. (3-27) with respect to either $I_t$ or $G_t$.

$$\frac{\partial Y_e}{\partial I_t} = \frac{\partial Y_e}{\partial G_t} = \frac{1}{1 - c_y} \tag{3-28}$$

This is again the familiar multiplier derived above. The change in the *equilibrium* value of $Y$ will be the product of the multiplier and the change in either $I$ or $G$.

Before offering an illustration, we should point out one other important characteristic of this system. If the consumer bases his purchasing decisions upon previous income, then there will very likely be a discrepancy between his planned saving and his realized saving. Moreover, the difference will exactly equal the difference in income from one period to the next. Define planned saving as the difference between previous income and current consumption:

$$S_p = Y_{t-1} - C_t \qquad (3\text{-}29)$$

Actual or realized saving will be the difference between current income and current consumption:

$$S_r = Y_t - C_t \qquad (3\text{-}30)$$

Therefore,

$$S_r - S_p = Y_t - Y_{t-1} \qquad (3\text{-}31)$$

Equilibrium in a dynamic system can be obtained only when income does not change from one period to the next or

$$Y_t = Y_{t-1} = Y_e \qquad (3\text{-}25)$$

Thus, Eqs. (3-25) and (3-31) together imply that, in equilibrium, planned saving must equal realized saving or

$$S_r = S_p \qquad (3\text{-}32)$$

Moreover, since realized saving will always be equal to the fixed value of investment, it will also be true that, in equilibrium, planned saving will be equal to investment. This statement is offered here merely as a mechanical proposition, supported in the following illustration. Theoretical support will be offered in Chapter 5.

**Illustration:**

For Table 3–1, let $\quad C_t = 100 + 0.6\,Y_{t-1}$

If $I = 100$, the original equilibrium is defined by the first row of the table. Next, let investment increase by 10 and remain at that higher level for each succeeding period. In period 1, even though income has increased by 10, consumption remains the same since it depends on the previous period's income. Moreover, even though planned saving is also unchanged, realized saving has increased by 10. Only in period 2 does consumption begin to "feel" the changing income, and the rising consumption then pushes income up even more. With rising income, planned saving also rises, eventually approaching equality with realized saving and investment. The equilibrium solution is found by substituting the consumption function into the GNP identity:

$$Y_t = (100 + 110)\left(\frac{1 - 0.6^t}{1 - 0.6}\right) + 0.6^t(500)$$

Since as $\qquad t \to \infty \qquad 0.6^t \to 0$

$$Y_e = \frac{210}{1 - 0.6} = (525)$$

Thus, the investment multiplier is 2.50. The last row of Table 3–1 demonstrates the new equilibrium position, with planned saving equal to investment.

**Table 3–I**

Equilibrium and a Lagged Consumption
Function (Continuous Injection)

| PERIOD | $Y$ | $C$ | $S_p$ | $S_r$ | $I$ | $G$ |
|--------|-----|-----|-------|-------|-----|-----|
| Equil. | 500 | 400 | 100 | 100 | 100 | 0 |
| 1 | 510 | 400 | 100 | 110 | 110 | 0 |
| 2 | 516 | 406 | 104 | 110 | 110 | 0 |
| 3 | 519.60 | 409.60 | 106.40 | 110 | 110 | 0 |
| 4 | 521.76 | 411.76 | 107.84 | 110 | 110 | 0 |
| 5 | 523.31 | 413.31 | 108.45 | 110 | 110 | 0 |
| . | | | | | | |
| . | | | | | | |
| . | | | | | | |
| $\to \infty$ | 525 | 415 | 110 | 110 | 110 | 0 |

## 3. Single Injection

In the previous section, it was assumed that the new level of income was generated by an increase in either investment or government spending and that this increase was maintained through all succeeding periods. If the increase in $I$ or $G$ had been a "one-shot" injection, income would rise initially, but then succeeding periods would witness erosion of this higher level until it ultimately fell back to the original equilibrium value. Again, equilibrium would be attained when planned saving and investment were equated.

**Illustration:**

Let $C_t = 100 + 0.6\,Y_{t-1}$ as before.

Equilibrium is demonstrated by the first row of Table 3–2. In period 1, investment rises by 10 to 110 but then falls back to 100 for all following periods. In period 2, however, consumption "feels" the increase in income from the previous period and rises by 60 % of that amount, thus cushioning the decline in current income brought about by the return of investment to its earlier level. In the ensuing periods, consumption and planned saving both decline until equilibrium is reached. Applying the formula for a geometric progression to calculate the total increments to income yields the following:

$$\sum_{t=1}^{\infty} (Y_t - Y_0) = 10 + 6 + 3.6 + 2.16 + \cdots$$

$$= 10 + 10(0.6) + 10(0.6)^2 + 10(0.6)^3 + \cdots$$

$$= \frac{10}{1 - 0.6} = 25$$

Thus, the sum of all the increases in income over the initial value equals the multiplier times the original temporary increase in investment.

**Table 3–2**

Equilibrium and a Lagged Consumption
Function
(Single Injection)

| PERIOD | $Y$ | $C$ | $S_p$ | $S_r$ | $I$ | $G$ |
|--------|-----|-----|-------|-------|-----|-----|
| Equil. | 500 | 400 | 100 | 100 | 100 | 0 |
| 1 | 510 | 400 | 100 | 110 | 110 | 0 |
| 2 | 506 | 406 | 104 | 100 | 100 | 0 |
| 3 | 503.60 | 403.60 | 102.40 | 100 | 100 | 0 |
| 4 | 502.16 | 402.16 | 101.44 | 100 | 100 | 0 |
| . | | | | | | |
| . | | | | | | |
| . | | | | | | |
| $\rightarrow \infty$ | 500 | 400 | 100 | 100 | 100 | 0 |
| Sum of Increments | 25 | 15 | 10 | 10 | 10 | 0 |

## III SUMMARY

Substitution of the consumption function into the GNP identity yields a very simple model of income determination. In this model, the values of consumption and income depend on the fixed values of private investment and government expenditures. Accordingly, consumption and income are said to be *endogenous* variables (determined by the system), while investment and government expenditures are called *exogenous* variables (fixed in value or independent of the system). In a more complete model containing taxes,

additional variables are introduced although the model remains concep-
tually unchanged. Partial derivatives of the equilibrium equation are the
so-called "multipliers," which represent the rate of change in income with
respect to the exogenous variables. Of special interest are the government
expenditures multiplier and the tax multiplier. The former of these will
always have the largest absolute value and it will be positive, whereas the
tax multiplier will be negative. The implication here, that equal increases in
government spending and taxes will nonetheless lead to an increase in income,
has been called the *balanced budget theorem*.

When a lagged consumption function replaces an instantaneous function, a dynamic model results in which the multipliers take on different interpretations. For a case where either government spending or investment
changes to some new and permanent level, the change in the equilibrium
level of income will be equal to the multiplier times the change in the exogenous variable. Where the change in that variable is only temporary, the
sum of all changes in income over the disequilibrium periods will be equal to
the multiplier times the temporary change in the exogenous variable.

## EXERCISES

1. Given the model

$$Y = C + I$$

$$C = c_0 + c_y Y$$

derive the formula for the investment multiplier and show how the multiplier
changes as the *MPC* changes.

2. Given the dynamic model

$$Y_t = C_t + I_t$$

$$C_t = c_y Y_{t-1}$$

derive the multiplier showing the effect of a change in

    **a.** $I_t$ on $Y_t$;

    **b.** $I_{t-1}$ on $Y_t$;

    **c.** $I_{t-2}$ on $Y_t$;

    **d.** Generalize your findings to show the effect of a change in $I_{t-n}$ on $Y_t$.

3. In addition to making expenditures on goods and services, the government also spends money merely by giving it to individuals for such things as
social security benefits and unemployment compensation. Such payments
are called government transfers $(F)$. Since many of these payments vary

inversely with income, assume that

$$F = f_0 - f_y Y$$

Furthermore, since transfer payments contribute to personal income,

$$Y_d = Y - T + F$$

a. Incorporate these two equations into the model presented on page 50 and find a new equation for the investment multiplier.

b. In your new solution, find $\partial Y/\partial t_0$ and $\partial Y/\partial f_0$. What is the implication of your answer?

## RECOMMENDED REFERENCES

Salant, William A., "Taxes, Income Determination, and the Balanced Budget Theorem," *Review of Economics and Statistics*, May 1957, pp. 152–61.

Samuelson, Paul A., "The Simple Mathematics of Income Determination," *Income, Employment, and Public Policy*. New York: W. W. Norton & Company, 1948.

# 4 The Investment Function

Investment, as defined in Chapter 1, includes business expenditures for plant, capital equipment, and inventories. Since there are very many well-developed theories to explain these components, the theory of investment is in this sense an advanced area of economic thought. On the other hand, investment theory must also be regarded as underdeveloped because these various explanations have not been unified into a single general explanation. To some extent, this is because of the heterogeneity of investment expenditures. That is, inventory investment probably responds to different economic factors than plant and equipment expenditures do. Furthermore, the exact link between the desired stock of capital and the rate at which that stock is attained by new investment has not been completely explained.

Investment expenditures have two distinct types of effects on the functioning of the economy. In the first place, an increase in the stock of capital augments the productive capacity of the economy. Investment is therefore a major factor in determining productive capability or potential aggregate output. The other, more immediate, effect of investment is the increase in aggregate demand that it generates. The present section is primarily concerned with the second of these two aspects. Accordingly, it will be helpful in this chapter to think of investment expenditures in terms of current dollar magnitudes rather than "real" or price-deflated values. Real changes in capacity will be considered in Chapter 11. In the present chapter, current investment expenditures may take on either positive or negative values, with inventory liquidation as the best example of the latter.

Section I defines the standard terms and discusses the orthodox theory of investment in a static equilibrium model, and Section II relates investment to the optimum capital stock. In Sections III and IV, dynamic models linking investment to past expenditures are developed.

## I THE MARGINAL EFFICIENCY OF CAPITAL AND THE RATE OF INTEREST

### 1. The Marginal Efficiency of Capital

Much contemporary investment theory utilizes the Keynesian concept of the "marginal efficiency of capital," $E$, which is defined implicitly as follows:[1]

$$P_s = \frac{N_1}{(1+E)} + \frac{N_2}{(1+E)^2} + \cdots + \frac{N_n}{(1+E)^n} = \sum_{i=1}^{n} \frac{N_i}{(1+E)^i} \qquad (4\text{-}1)$$

where

$P_s =$ supply price of capital or other investment goods
$N_i = $ *expected* net earnings in dollars in the $i$th period after the investment is made
$E =$ marginal efficiency of capital.

In other words, the marginal efficiency of capital (*MEC*) is the rate of discount required to equate the stream of expected incomes from the investment to the cost of the investment. The term "marginal" refers to the fact that this is an investment that has not yet been undertaken but is the highest-yielding investment available to the business community and would be the next (marginal) investment to be undertaken—if, in fact, any at all is undertaken.

Note that by the nature of the definition of the marginal efficiency of capital one cannot solve for a generalized algebraic statement of it in terms of supply price ($P_s$) and the expected earnings ($N_i's$). Its definition, Eq. (4-1), is an $n$th-degree equation and a general solution is impossible if $n$ is unspecified. For illustrative purposes, we can assume that the period of discount equals the life of the capital so that $n = 1$ and Eq. (4-1) becomes

$$P_s = \frac{N}{(1+E)} \qquad (4\text{-}2)$$

or, when solved for the *MEC*,

$$E = \frac{N}{P_s} - 1 \qquad (4\text{-}3)$$

Equation (4-3) indicates the marginal efficiency of capital to be the "yield" of a one-period investment or what others have called the "rate of return over cost." For example, if a \$100 machine is expected to produce a net cash return of \$110, then $E = 10\%$; i.e.,

$$E = \tfrac{110}{100} - 1 = 1.10 - 1.0 = 0.10$$

It is apparent from Eq. (4-1) and perhaps more so from Eq. (4-3) that if the marginal efficiency of capital, $E$, is considered the dependent variable, it

---

[1] J. M. Keynes, *The General Theory of Employment, Interest, and Money* (New York: Harcourt, Brace & World, Inc., 1936), pp. 135–41.

will vary directly with changes in expected net earnings (the $N_i$'s) and inversely with changes in the supply price ($P_s$). Partial derivatives of Eq. (4-3) demonstrate this clearly:

$$\frac{\partial E}{\partial N} = \frac{1}{P_s} > 0 \tag{4-4}$$

$$\frac{\partial E}{\partial P_s} = -\frac{N}{P_s^2} < 0 \tag{4-5}$$

It is generally held that changes in expected earnings or the supply price come about as a result of investment expenditures. The usual assumption is that as additional investment is undertaken, expected net earnings of further investment will fall and the supply price of capital will rise. Both of these assumptions make sense at the microeconomic level, but at the macroeconomic level the fall in expected net earnings is sometimes disputed. For example, an investment boom may be self-sustaining for some time by leading to *higher* expected net earnings. For the moment, however, we shall accept both of the assumptions stated previously. Therefore,

$$\frac{dN_i}{dI} < 0 \qquad \text{Expected earnings decline as investment increases.}$$

$$\frac{dP_s}{dI} > 0 \qquad \text{The cost (supply price) of capital equipment increases as investment increases.}$$

Accepting these assumptions causes the *MEC* to be a decreasing function of the rate of investment. This can be demonstrated by differentiating a generalized form of Eq. (4-1) and evaluating the sign of the derivative of $E$ with respect to $I$. Equation (4-1) states that the marginal efficiency of capital is a function of $P_s$ and the $N_i$'s; i.e.,

$$E = f(P_s, N_1, N_2, \ldots, N_n) \tag{4-6}$$

$$dE = \frac{\partial E}{\partial P_s} dP_s + \sum_{i=1}^{n} \frac{\partial E}{\partial N_i} dN_i$$

$$\frac{dE}{dI} = \frac{\partial E}{\partial P_s} \frac{dP_s}{dI} + \sum_{i=1}^{n} \frac{\partial E}{\partial N_i} \frac{dN_i}{dI} < 0 \tag{4-7}$$

The $n + 1$ terms on the right-hand side are all products of derivatives that differ in sign, as established (or assumed) above. Therefore, each individual term is negative and, of course, the total is negative. Thus, the *MEC* is a decreasing function of $I$.

Theoretically, then, there exists at any point in time some negative relationship between the rate of investment and the marginal efficiency of capital. This negative relationship is frequently referred to as the *MEC schedule*. Since it actually is a relationship between *investment* and expected yields rather than between total *capital* and yields, some authors refer to it as the "marginal efficiency of investment schedule."[2] Assume for illustrative purposes the following linear relationship:

$$I = i_0 - i_E E \qquad (4\text{-}8)$$

## 2. The Rate of Interest

Assuming that businessmen have the alternatives of either making investment expenditures directly on capital goods or earning the going rate of interest by the purchase of financial assets (or by repaying outstanding liabilities), the net rate of profit on an investment opportunity requiring the purchase of capital goods is the difference between the relevant rate of interest $(r)$ and the expected rate of return $(E)$. As long as $E$ is greater than $r$, the businessman with available funds believes that he would make larger profits by making investment expenditures than by purchasing a financial asset. As indicated by Eqs. (4-7) and (4-8) above, however, $E$ decreases as $I$ is increased. If the rate of interest is assumed constant (or exogenously determined), the quantity of investment undertaken per time period would, in equilibrium, be that amount that just forces $E$ down to $r$, at which point the expected net gain from a higher rate of investment is zero. Hence, in equilibrium,

$$E = r \qquad (4\text{-}9)$$

If one is concerned only with comparative statics and assumes that the equilibrium condition in Eq. (4-9) always holds, then investment becomes a function of only the rate of interest. The linear approximation of this relationship may be obtained by substituting Eq. (4-9) into (4-8) to yield

$$I = i_0 - i_r r \qquad (4\text{-}10)$$

This negative relationship between the rate of investment and the interest rate is also frequently referred to as the *MEC* schedule or, as mentioned above, the *MEI* schedule. This schedule will be of major importance in the complete economic model depicted in Chapters 5 through 10.

[2] See Eq. (4–10) for another relationship also referred to as the marginal efficiency of capital (or investment) schedule. Section II of this chapter also discusses these concepts.

## II  INVESTMENT AND THE OPTIMUM CAPITAL STOCK

The previous section explains investment expenditures by employing a static model in which the independent variable is the rate of interest. In that section, we also explained that some economists have named the investment-interest rate schedule the "marginal efficiency of investment," that some have called it the "marginal efficiency of capital," and that some have called it both. The purpose of this section is to try to shed a little more light on this point and to highlight some of the subtleties involved.

The basic problem here is that the traditional Keynesian analysis given in Section 4–I derives a relationship between the level of investment and the rate of interest, while some elements of modern capital theory imply a relationship between the level of the capital stock and the rate of interest. At first glance, these approaches appear to be inconsistent. If investment is a function of the current interest rate, then the capital stock (the sum of all past investment) must be a function of past interest rates. On the other hand, if the capital stock is a function of the current interest rate, then the level of investment must be a function of the change in the interest rate. These inconsistencies will be addressed below.

### I.  The Optimum Capital Stock

We can solve for the profit-maximizing or optimum capital stock and the resulting rate of investment by making two critical assumptions regarding the *average* rate of return on the capital stock: (1) The average rate of return, $\bar{E}$, on the capital stock, $K$, will vary inversely with the size of the capital stock; and (2) the passage of time will cause the average rate of return on a *fixed* capital stock to rise as a result of technological change, growth of the labor force, or other factors. This latter assumption is a necessary one for the equilibrium level of investment to be greater than zero. Otherwise, the optimum capital stock, once achieved, would require no further investment.

To illustrate these concepts as simply as possible, let us assume that the average rate of return on the existing stock of capital is viewed by investors as the ratio of the present value of the expected stream of future incomes to the capital stock. In that case,

$$\bar{E} = \frac{N}{K}$$

The average expected rate of return on the capital stock is the ratio of the present value of expected earnings, $N$, to the capital stock, $K$.

(4-11)

In order to state our assumptions that this rate of return will fall with increases in the capital stock and increase with the passage of time, we may use the following linear equation:

$$\bar{E} = e_t t - e_K K \tag{4-12}$$

Total profit to businessmen is equal to the total return on the capital stock minus the opportunity cost of investing the same amount of money at the going market rate of interest:

$$\pi = \bar{E}K - rK$$
$$= (\bar{E} - r)K \tag{4-13}$$

The optimum stock of capital, noted as $K^*$, will be equal to the actual stock of capital when profit has been maximized. To find this optimum capital stock, we need only maximize $\pi$ in Eq. (4-13). Substitution of Eq. (4-12) into (4-13) yields

$$\pi = (e_t t - r)K - e_K K^2$$

To find the maximum profit for any time period, we must take the partial derivative of the previous equation with respect to $K$ and then set the derivative equal to zero.

$$\frac{\partial \pi}{\partial K} = e_t t - r - 2e_K K = 0 \tag{4-14}$$

or

$$K^* = \frac{e_t}{2e_K} t - \frac{1}{2e_K} r \tag{4-15}$$

Thus, Eq. (4-15) shows that the optimum stock of capital varies directly with the passage of time and inversely to the rate of interest.

One other very interesting and important point should be noted at this time. Remember that the marginal rate of return on capital (or the marginal efficiency of capital) can be defined as the change in the present value of the stream of incomes as the size of the capital stock is increased by small increments. By combining Eqs. (4-11) and (4-12), we can obtain

$$N = e_t t K - e_K K^2 \tag{4-16}$$

and

$$\frac{\partial N}{\partial K} = e_t t - 2e_K K \tag{4-17}$$

Moreover, by solving Eq. (4-14) for the rate of interest instead of for the optimum capital stock,

$$r = e_t t - 2e_K K \tag{4-18}$$

Notice that the right-hand sides of Eqs. (4-18) and (4-17) are the same. At the profit-maximizing equilibrium, the market rate of interest and the marginal efficiency of capital will be equated. This is simply another way of deriving the relationship already stated in Section I of this chapter.

For students familar with the microeconomic theory of the firm, the foregoing can also be phrased in terms of such theory. Consider a profit-seeking business that hires capital and labor inputs that jointly produce the final output of the firm. At the profit-maximizing output, the ratio of the factor prices will be equal to the ratio of the marginal products. Thus, if the price of one of the factors decreased, the use of that factor would increase (and its marginal product would fall) and the use of the other factor would decrease (its marginal product would rise) until the ratio of the marginal products would again equal the new price ratio. In other words, the relatively less expensive factor is substituted for the relatively more expensive factor. This implies that a decrease in the interest rate (the price of capital to the firm) would increase the amount of capital being employed.

## 2. The Level of Investment

Equation (4-15) shows the optimum capital stock as a function of both time and the interest rate. If we assume temporarily that businesses *always* maintain the optimal amount of capital, then investment expenditures for any period will merely be the change in the optimal capital stock for that period. This level of investment may be determined by differentiating Eq. (4-15) with respect to $t$.

$$\frac{dK^*}{dt} = I = \frac{e_t}{2e_K} - \frac{dr}{dt} \frac{1}{2e_K} \tag{4-19}$$

In other words, the level of investment is a function of the change in the interest rate and not of its absolute level. In periods when the rate of interest remains constant ($dr = 0$), the level of investment will be fixed at $e_t/2e_K$.

Equation (4-19) is clearly inconsistent with Eq. (4-10); yet each is appealing on theoretical grounds. Fortunately, the inconsistency is not so irreconcilable that one of the theories must be completely discarded. The underlying assumption of Eq. (4-19) is that the optimal level of the capital stock is always maintained. However, this is not likely to be the case. Because of bottlenecks in production, tightness in labor markets, deficiencies of funds, and many other factors, a firm is not likely to make up a large deficiency in its capital stock in one year. Instead, it may try to eliminate the deficiency over a number of different periods.

One model that assumes lags in investment expenditures is the so-called "stock-adjustment model." This model is based upon the idea that a firm might eliminate a set fraction of its capital stock deficiency in any given time period. To illustrate, let us first rewrite Eq. (4-15) as a difference equation. For purposes of simplicity, let us also omit the time variable so that the optimal capital stock depends only on the rate of interest.

$$K_t^* = k_0 - \frac{1}{2e_K} r \qquad (4\text{-}20)$$

If the firm in question makes up only a fraction of its capital deficiency in any given period, then

$$I_t = \Delta K_t = K_t - K_{t-1}$$  The change in the capital stock is a fraction
$$= \alpha(K_t^* - K_{t-1})$$  $\alpha$ of the optimum stock minus the previous stock.

$$(4\text{-}21)$$

In this model, $\alpha$ is known as the "speed of adjustment." By substitution of Eq. (4-20) into (4-21),

$$I_t = \alpha k_0 - \frac{\alpha}{2e_K} r - \alpha K_{t-1}$$

$$= \alpha(k_0 - K_{t-1}) - \frac{\alpha}{2e_K} r$$

For any given time period, when the previous capital stock is fixed, the current level of investment is a function of only the current rate of interest, just as in Eq. (4-10). If the rate of interest is low, the optimal capital stock is high, and current investment is likely to be great. Correspondingly, if the rate of interest is high, the optimum capital stock is low, and current investment will probably be small. Therefore, the apparent inconsistency mentioned above can be resolved if changes in the capital stock for any given period are only a fraction of the surplus or deficiency in that stock.

Several reasons for failure to attain the optimum capital stock were briefly mentioned above. We might now pay more attention to this matter. Suppose that a sudden drop in the interest rate, say from 7 to 5%, increased the nation's optimal capital stock by $100 billion. Ideally, firms would then like to spend that amount for investment in the next year in order to get back at the optimal level. Even if there are adequate sources of financing for these investment projects, however, it may be unprofitable to make this large an investment expenditure immediately. The producers of capital goods may have a present capacity that is not large enough to accommodate such production efficiently. If businesses attempt to force production of $100 billion, material and labor bottlenecks will send the prices of investment goods up and the rate of return on investment down. Rather than accept a decrease in the rate of return, it will be more profitable to parcel out the investment expenditures over a number of years so that price increases may be held down.[3]

## III CONSUMPTION AND TOTAL EXPENDITURES AS DETERMINANTS OF INVESTMENT

Many forms of investment are sensitive to the level of sales being experienced by businessmen. This may be due to shifts in the *MEC* schedule if it is assumed that businessmen's expectations of future net earnings on present investment are heavily influenced by the present and immediately past levels of demand. Such voluntary increases in investment must not be confused, however, with the purely technical requirements of increased inventories and capital equipment brought about by increased sales when the economy is already at capacity. In other words, we are not talking about how much investment *must* be made in order to meet the increased sales, but rather how much investment *will* be made in response to these sales. The relationship is behavioral, not technical. The businessmen may overreact or underreact from what is required from the purely technical point of view. Whether the expected yields are realized or not is irrelevant for purposes of evaluating the effect of investment on aggregate demand in the short run.

### 1. Investment as a Function of Consumption

One fairly common assumption about investment expenditures is that investors desire to maintain some constant ratio of inventory or other capital stock $(K)$ to sales to consumers $(C)$. Hence,

$$\frac{K}{C} = k_c$$

Or, in a dynamic model,

$$K_t = k_c C_t \tag{4-22}$$

[3] Two interesting graphic treatments of this problem may be seen in John Lindauer, *Macroeconomics* (New York: John Wiley & Sons, Inc., 1968), and Edward Shapiro, *Macroeconomic Analysis*, 2nd ed. (Harcourt, Brace & World, Inc., 1970).

Taking first differences of Eq. (4-22) gives

$$\Delta K_t = I_t = k_c \, \Delta C_t = k_c(C_t - C_{t-1}) \qquad (4\text{-}23)$$

The change in capital stock is by definition the amount of investment. The far right-hand side of the equation uses the definition of the change in period $t$ as being the difference between the consumer sales in the present period $(C_t)$ and the sales in the previous period $(C_{t-1})$. Under these definitions, investment in any period will vary directly with consumption in that period and inversely with consumption in the previous period.

## 2. Investment as a Function of Total Income

The previous section related investment to final sales to consumers. Governments also purchase final goods, however, and what one businessman purchases as an investment is the sale of a final product by another businessman. As a result, it is frequently assumed that investment is not only a function of the level of consumption but of investment and government expenditures as well. That is, investment is a function of total income.

If one assumes as above that investors seek to keep a constant ratio of capital stock to total sales, the following relationship is obtained:

$$\frac{K_t}{Y_{t-1}} = k_y \quad \text{or} \quad K_t = k_y Y_{t-1} \qquad (4\text{-}24)$$

Taking first differences gives the following relationship between investment and income:

$$I_t = k_y(Y_{t-1} - Y_{t-2}) \qquad (4\text{-}25)$$

The reader should note the difference between the form of Eqs. (4-23) and (4-25):

$$I_t = k_c(C_t - C_{t-1}) \qquad (4\text{-}23)$$

$$I_t = k_y(Y_{t-1} - Y_{t-2}) \qquad (4\text{-}25)$$

Equation (4-23) assumes investment to be linearly dependent on the *current* period's increase in consumption $(C_t - C_{t-1})$, but in Eq. (4-25) investment is related to the *previous* period's increase in income $(Y_{t-1} - Y_{t-2})$. The reason for this asymmetry is as follows. Since $Y_t$ contains $I_t$ as a component [Eq. (1-3)], a model using a relationship between $Y_t$ and $I_t$ assumes instantaneous adjustments *within* a single time period and does not allow for an adequate time lag in making business decisions. For similar reasons, many writers prefer the lagged consumption function presented in Chapter 3 to the instantaneous functions of Chapter 2. It would have been methodologically "better" to have used $C_{t-1}$ and $C_{t-2}$ in Eq. (4-23); but many well-known writers have used the formulation as given, even though it implies that investment adjusts immediately to changes in consumption *within* a single period. This creates no great difficulty for most of these writers, however, because they assume that $C_t$, unlike $Y_t$, will be independent of $I_t$ for any single time period by adopting the lagged consumption function mentioned above. Thus,

$$I_t = k_c(C_t - C_{t-1})$$

$$C_t = c_y Y_{t-1}$$

By substitution,

$$I_t = k_c c_y(Y_{t-1} - Y_{t-2})$$

The last equation therefore successfully avoids the problem of intraperiod adjustments. More will be said about this in Section IV of this chapter.

## IV THE ACCELERATION PRINCIPLE

The acceleration principle refers to the relationship between final sales and investment, some possible forms of which were discussed in the previous section. However, the accelerator per se is basically a microeconomic concept with important macroeconomic implications. In microeconomics, it refers to the fact that under certain conditions small fluctuations in the level of sales at the retail level will give rise to much larger fluctuations in sales at the wholesale and manufacturing levels. In macroeconomics, it refers not only to this pyramiding of demand fluctuations back through the channels of distribution but also to any hypothesized relationship between the rate of investment and either the level of consumption or total income. We shall consider each of these concepts in turn.

### I. The Accelerator as a Microeconomic Concept[1]

In its simplest form, the accelerator rests upon the assumption that the firm or industry at each level of distribution seeks to maintain its capital stock at some constant ratio to sales, similar to Eqs. (4-23) and (4-25) above.

---

[1] For the original formulation of the accelerator concept, see J. M. Clark, "Business Acceleration and the Law of Demand: A Technical Factor in Economic Cycles," *The Journal of Political Economy*, Vol. XXV, No. 3 (March 1917).

If we consider two levels of distribution, the manufacturer and the retailer, and assume that each adjusts his capital stock in the present period in accordance with the sales experienced in the previous period, we obtain the following model:

$$K_{rt} = k_c C_{t-1} \tag{4-26}$$

$$K_{mt} = k_W \cdot W_{t-1} \tag{4-27}$$

where

$K_{rt} =$ capital stock and inventory of the retailer
$K_{mt} =$ capital stock and inventory of the manufacturer
$C_t =$ final sales to consumers by the retailer
$W_t =$ final sales to retailer by the manufacturer

By definition,

$$I_t = \Delta K_{rt} + \Delta K_{mt} \tag{4-28}$$

$$W_t = \Delta K_{rt} + C_t \tag{4-29}$$

Taking first differences of Eqs. (4-26) and (4-27) gives

$$\Delta K_{rt} = k_c \, \Delta C_{t-1} = k_c (C_{t-1} - C_{t-2}) \tag{4-30}$$

$$\Delta K_{mt} = k_W \, \Delta W_{t-1} = k_W (W_{t-1} - W_{t-2}) \tag{4-31}$$

Substituting the expression for $W_t$ given in Eq. (4-29) into (4-31),

$$\Delta K_{mt} = k_W [(\Delta K_{rt-1} + C_{t-1}) - (\Delta K_{rt-2} + C_{t-2})] \tag{4-32}$$

Substituting the expression for $\Delta K_{rt}$ given in Eq. (4-30) into (4-32) gives

$$\Delta K_{mt} = k_W [(k_c C_{t-2} - k_c C_{t-3} + C_{t-1}) - (k_c C_{t-3} - k_c C_{t-4} + C_{t-2})] \tag{4-33}$$

Equation (4-30) is an expression for the retailer's investment as a function of retail sales, and Eq. (4-33) is an expression for the manufacturer's investment as a function of retail sales. Substituting both of these equations into Eq. (4-28) gives total investment as a function of retail sales.

$$I_t = (k_c + k_W)C_{t-1} + (k_c k_W - k_c - k_W)C_{t-2} - 2k_c k_W C_{t-3} + k_c k_W C_{t-4} \tag{4-34}$$

It is important to note that the coefficients in Eq. (4-34) sum to zero regardless of the values for $k_c$ and $k_W$. As a result, if final sales hold constant for four periods, then $C_{t-1} = C_{t-2} = C_{t-3} = C_{t-4}$, and investment falls to zero.

The time path of investment resulting from a "one-shot" change in the level of final sales is simply a sequential listing of the coefficients of Eq. (4-34) multiplied by the change in final sales; i.e.,

| $t$ | $C_t$ | $I_t$ |
|---|---|---|
| 0 | $C_0$ | 0 |
| 1 | $C_0 + \Delta C$ | 0 |
| 2 | $C_0$ | $(k_c + k_W) \Delta C$ |
| 3 | $C_0$ | $(k_c k_W - k_c - k_W) \Delta C$ |
| 4 | $C_0$ | $(-2k_c k_W) \Delta C$ |
| 5 | $C_0$ | $(k_c k_W) \Delta C$ |
| 6 | $C_0$ | 0 |

**Illustration:**

Let $k_c = 2 \qquad k_W = 10$

Then $I_t = 12C_{t-1} + 8C_{t-2} - 40C_{t-3} + 20C_{t-4}$

Also, let sales rise from 10 in period 0 to 11 in period 1; then fall back to 10 for all ensuing periods. In that case, the time path is as follows:

| $t$ | $C_t$ | $I_t$ |
|---|---|---|
| 0 | 10 | 0 |
| 1 | 11 | 0 |
| 2 | 10 | 12 |
| 3 | 10 | 8 |
| 4 | 10 | $-40$ |
| 5 | 10 | 20 |
| 6 | 10 | 0 |

If the change in final sales is a permanent one, the time path of investment is simply the cumulative changes given in the "one-shot" case above; i.e.,

| $t$ | $C_t$ | $I_t$ |
|---|---|---|
| 0 | $C_0$ | 0 |
| 1 | $C_0 + \Delta C$ | 0 |
| 2 | $C_0 + \Delta C$ | $(k_c + k_W) \Delta C$ |
| 3 | $C_0 + \Delta C$ | $[(k_c + k_W) + (k_c k_W - k_c - k_W)] \Delta C$ |
| 4 | $C_0 + \Delta C$ | $[(k_c + k_W) + (k_c k_W - k_c - k_W) - 2k_c k_W] \Delta C$ |
| 5 | $C_0 + \Delta C$ | 0 |

In this case, investment returns to zero in the fifth period since the sum of all coefficients in Eq. (4-30) is zero.

**Illustration:**

Let $k_c = 2$     $k_W = 10$

Then $I_t = 12C_{t-1} + 8C_{t-2} - 40C_{t-3} + 20C_{t-4}$

Assume further that consumer purchases rise from 10 in period 0 to 11 in periods 1 through 5. The time path is as follows:

| $t$ | $C_t$ | $I_t$ |
|-----|-------|-------|
| 0 | 10 | 0 |
| 1 | 11 | 0 |
| 2 | 11 | 12 |
| 3 | 11 | 20 |
| 4 | 11 | $-20$ |
| 5 | 11 | 0 |

The magnitude of the fluctuations brought about by the accelerator depend on the magnitude of the capital-sales ratios, $k_c$ and $k_W$, but in no case can these fluctuations be explosive. In models employing only the accelerator, induced investment always settles down to zero after the requisite number of periods.

## 2. The Macroeconomic Accelerator

The accelerator in macroeconomic models can be any particular relationship of investment to changes in consumption or total income. Equations (4-23) and (4-25) are linear forms of such relationships.

$$I_t = k_c \, \Delta C_t = k_c(C_t - C_{t-1}) \tag{4-23}$$

$$I_t = k_y \, \Delta Y_{t-1} = k_y(Y_{t-1} - Y_{t-2}) \tag{4-25}$$

The accelerator in a simple macroeconomic model using Eq. (4-23) is as follows:

$$Y_t = C_t + I_t = C_t + k_c C_t - k_c C_{t-1} \tag{4-35}$$

or

$$Y_t = (1 + k_c)C_t - k_c C_{t-1}$$

It is obvious from Eq. (4-35) that if consumption has been constant for two periods ($C_t = C_{t-1}$), then the model is in equilibrium at $I_t = 0$ and $Y_t = C_t$. As a result, the analysis of the comparative statics of this model is of little interest. The dynamics of the model are also quite simple. A "one-shot" disturbance generates the following time path:

| $t$ | $C_t$ | $+$ | $I_t$ | $=$ | $Y_t$ |
|-----|-------|-----|-------|-----|-------|
| 0 | $C_0$ | | 0 | | $C_0$ |
| 1 | $C_0 + \Delta C$ | | $k_c \Delta C$ | | $C_0 + (1 + k_c) \Delta C$ |
| 2 | $C_0$ | | $- k_c \Delta C$ | | $C_0 - k_c \Delta C$ |
| 3 | $C_0$ | | 0 | | $C_0$ |

**Illustration:**

Let $\quad k_c = 2$

Then $\quad I_t = 2(C_t - C_{t-1})$

$\qquad Y_t = 3C_t - 2C_{t-1}$

Assume that consumption rises to 11 in period 1 only.

Then

| $t$ | $C_t$ | $+$ | $I_t$ | $=$ | $Y_t$ |
|-----|-------|-----|-------|-----|-------|
| 0 | 10 | | 0 | | 10 |
| 1 | 11 | | 2 | | 13 |
| 2 | 10 | | $-2$ | | 8 |
| 3 | 10 | | 0 | | 10 |

Using the relation between total income and investment, Eq. (4-25), as the accelerator gives the following macroeconomic model when consumption is exogenously determined:

$$I_t = k_y(Y_{t-1} - Y_{t-2}) \tag{4-25}$$

$$Y_t = C_t + I_t = C_t + k_y Y_{t-1} - k_y Y_{t-2} \tag{4-36}$$

The analysis of the comparative statics of this model is not particularly interesting either since, in equilibrium, $Y_t = C_t$ and $I_t = 0$, as before.

However, the dynamic analysis of the previous models is somewhat more complex. Equation (4-36) can be rewritten in the standard form for a second-order, nonhomogeneous, linear difference equation:

$$Y_t - k_y Y_{t-1} + k_y Y_{t-2} - C_t = 0 \tag{4-36}$$

The time path of $Y_t$ after an exogenous shock in the form of a change in $C_t$ is shown in Table 4–1. Numerical examples of each case are given in Table 4–2. In that table, the values existing at time period $t = 0$ are assumed to have existed for at least two periods before. Thus, each system begins in a state of equilibrium.

## Table 4–I

Dynamics of a Simple Accelerator Model
with Investment a Function of Total
Income and Consumption Exogenously
Determined*

$$\text{Eq. (4-25)} \quad I_t = k_y(Y_{t-1} - Y_{t-2})$$

$$\text{Eq. (4-36)} \quad Y_t - k_y Y_{t-1} + k_y Y_{t-2} - C_t = 0$$

| VALUE OF ACCELERATOR $(k_y)$ | TIME PATH OF TOTAL INCOME $(Y_t)$ |
|---|---|
| a. $1.0 > k_y > 0$ | Damped cycles converging on equilibrium |
| b. $k_y = 1.0$ | Unending cycles of constant magnitude |
| c. $4.0 > k_y > 1.0$ | Explosive cycles departing ever further from equilibrium |
| d. $k_y \geq 4.0$ | Monotonically departing ever further from equilibrium |

* For details of the characteristic equations involved in obtaining these results, see R. G. D. Allen, *Mathematical Economics* (New York: St. Martin's Press, 1956), pp. 187ff.

## Table 4–2

Investment as a Function of Total Income,
Consumption Exogenously Determined

$$\text{Eq. (4-25)} \quad I_t = k_y(Y_{t-1} - Y_{t-2})$$

$$\text{Eq. (4-36)} \quad Y_t = C_t + k_y Y_{t-1} - k_y Y_{t-2}$$

| | a. $k_y = 0.05$ | | | | b. $k_y = 1.0$ | | |
|---|---|---|---|---|---|---|---|
| $t$ | $C_t$ + | $I_t$ | = $Y_t$ | $t$ | $C_t$ + | $I_t$ | = $Y_t$ |
| 0 | 10 | 0 | 10 | 0 | 10 | 0 | 10 |
| 1 | 11 | 0 | 11 | 1 | 11 | 0 | 11 |
| 2 | 11 | 0.5 | 11.50 | 2 | 11 | 1 | 12 |
| . | . | . | . | | | | |
| 4 | 11 | −0.12 | 10.88 | 3 | 11 | 1 | 12 |
| . | . | . | . | | | | |
| 6 | 11 | −0.03 | 10.97 | 4 | 11 | 0 | 11 |
| . | . | . | . | | | | |
| 8 | 11 | 0.06 | 11.06 | 5 | 11 | −1 | 10 |
| . | . | . | . | | | | |
| | | | | 6 | 11 | −1 | 10 |
| . | . | . | . | | | | |
| ∞ | 11 | 0 | 11.00 | 7 | 11 | 0 | 11 |
| | | | | 8 | 11 | 1 | 12 |
| | | | | 9 | 11 | 1 | 12 |

**Table 4-2** (Continued)

| | c. $k_y = 2.0$ | | | | d. $k_y = 9$ | | |
|---|---|---|---|---|---|---|---|
| $t$ | $C_t$ | $+$  $I_t$ | $=$  $Y_t$ | $t$ | $C_t$ | $+$  $I_t$ | $=$  $Y_t$ |
| 0 | 10 | 0 | 10 | 0 | 10 | 0 | 10 |
| 1 | 11 | 0 | 11 | 1 | 11 | 0 | 11 |
| 2 | 11 | 2 | 13 | 2 | 11 | 4 | 15 |
| 3 | 11 | 4 | 15 | 3 | 11 | 16 | 27 |
| . | . | . | . | 4 | 11 | 48 | 59 |
| 7 | 11 | $-16$ | $-5$ | 5 | 11 | 128 | 139 |
| . | . | . | . | 6 | 11 | 320 | 331 |
| 11 | 11 | 64 | 75 | . | . | . | . |
| . | . | . | . | $\infty$ | 11 | $\infty$ | $\infty$ |
| 15 | 11 | $-256$ | $-245$ | | | | |
| . | . | . | . | | | | |
| $\infty$ | 11 | $\pm\infty$ | $\pm\infty$ | | | | |

## 3. A Digression on the Dynamics of Macroeconomic Models

Certain general characteristics of this type of dynamic model need to be mentioned. In general, such models have equilibrium values for $Y_t$ that will be repeated indefinitely if they are achieved and held for two periods. If the equilibrium value is the historical value for two previous periods, one can project the value of $Y_t$ at that value for as many periods into the future as the exogenous variables and structural parameters remain unchanged.[5]

If the model is assumed to be in disequilibrium, there are five general types of time paths relative to the equilibrium value that may result if no further changes in the structural parameters or exogenous variables occur. They are as follows:

a. *Income variable moves monotonically toward equilibrium.* In this case the dependent variable, $Y_t$, asymptotically approaches the new equilibrium position, $Y_{e2}$, from the initial equilibrium position, $Y_{e1}$, after an exogenous shock that changes the equilibrium from $Y_{e1}$ to $Y_{e2}$.

[5] This comes from the fact that the reduced form solution is a *second* order difference equation. If it were third order, the equilibrium would have to have held for three periods before one could be sure it would hold indefinitely.

b. *Income departs monotonically ever further from equilibrium.* In this case the dependent variable initially moves toward the new equilibrium position but just keeps right on going. The absolute rate of increase grows while the percentage rate of growth asymptotically approaches a constant rate; i.e., the percentage rate grows at a decreasing rate.

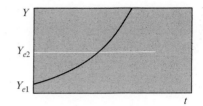

c. *Income fluctuates in cycles of ever-increasing magnitude departing ever further from equilibrium.* In this case income initially moves toward the new equilibrium, overshoots it, comes back toward it, and overshoots it in the opposite direction. This pattern repeats itself with peak–trough values being further from the new equilibrium value with each successive cycle. These are the so-called "explosive cycles."

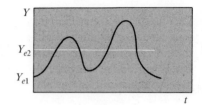

d. *Income fluctuates in cycles of constant magnitude.* In this case income first overshoots the new equilibrium, then returns and overshoots it in the opposite direction by an equal amount before reversing direction again. In this case the same pattern is repeated indefinitely with cycles of constant magnitude.

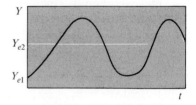

e. *Income fluctuates in cycles of diminishing magnitude.* As indicated by the subtitle, in this case each successive peak and trough of income is closer to the new equilibrium level. These peaks and troughs asymptotically approach the new equilibrium level. These are the so-called "damped" cycles.

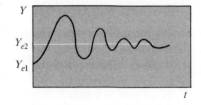

## 4. The Accelerator with the Multiplier

In the previous model, it was assumed that consumption was given (exogenous) and that the level of investment expenditure responded to these "autonomous" consumption expenditures. A very common extension of this model is to add a consumption function relating consumption in one time period to total income in the previous period, as discussed in Section II of Chapter 3. The discussion there treated investment and government expenditures as autonomous and noted that an increase in such expenditures raised the equilibrium level of income by some multiple of the increase in autonomous expenditures. If investment is made a function of the level of consumption, and consumption is assumed to be a function of total income, the resulting system is called a "multiplier-accelerator" model. For example,

$$Y_t = C_t + I_t + G_t \tag{1-4}$$

$$C_t = c_0 + c_y Y_{t-1} \tag{3-19}$$

$$I_t = k_c(C_t - C_{t-1}) \tag{4-23}$$

Solving the system for $Y_t$ gives

$$Y_t = (1 + k_c)c_y Y_{t-1} - k_c c_y Y_{t-2} + c_0 + G_t \tag{4-37}$$

In equilibrium, $Y_t = Y_{t-1} = Y_{t-2}$, and Eq. (4-37) reduces to

$$Y_t = \frac{c_0 + G_t}{1 - c_y} \tag{4-38}$$

This is the same equilibrium level of total income given in Section I of Chapter 3 except that $I_t = 0$ and thus does not appear in the numerator. Since induced investment is zero in equilibrium, the addition of the accelerator does not change the comparative statics of the multiplier model as discussed previously.

The dynamics of the model, first discussed in the literature by Paul Samuelson,[6] are perhaps more interesting. It should be noted that if such a model is in equilibrium for two time periods, it will remain there unless some variable or parameter is arbitrarily changed. The time path of total income when disequilibrium values result from a change (usually assumed to be in either $c_0$ or $G_t$) depends on the values of the parameters $k_c$ and $c_y$. Since $c_y$ is the marginal propensity to consume, its value will always lie between zero and plus one. The possible time paths of total income are presented as functions of $c_y$ and $k_c$ in Table 4–3, with numerical examples given in Table 4–4. In the numerical examples the system starts at a position of equilibrium with investment equal to zero. Government expenditures are initially assumed to be 5 and then rise to 6, creating a disequilibrium situation.

[6] "Interaction Between Multiplier Analysis and the Principle of Acceleration," *The Review of Economics and Statistics*, May 1939, pp. 75–78.

## Table 4–3

Dynamics of Multiplier-Accelerator Model

Eq. (3-19)  $C_t = c_0 + c_y Y_{t-1}$

Eq. (4-23)  $I_t = k_c(C_t - C_{t-1})$

Eq. (4-37)  $Y_t = (1 + k_c)c_y Y_{t-1} - k_c c_y Y_{t-2} + c_0 + G_t$

| Values of Marginal Propensity to Consume, $c_y$, and the Accelerator Coefficient, $k_c$ | Time Path of Total Income, $Y_t$ |
|---|---|
| a.  $c_y > \dfrac{4k_c}{(1 + k_c)^2}$ ; $k_c < 1.00$ | Moves monotonically toward equilibrium |
| b.  $c_y > \dfrac{4k_c}{(1 + k_c)^2}$ ; $k_c > 1.00$ | Monotonically departing ever further from equilibrium |
| c.  $\dfrac{1}{k_c} < c_y < \dfrac{4k_c}{(1 + k_c)^2}$ | Explosive cycles departing ever further from equilibrium |
| d.  $c_y = \dfrac{1}{k_c}$ | Unending cycles of constant magnitude |
| e.  $c_y < \dfrac{1}{k_c}$ | Damped cycles converging on equilibrium |

## Table 4–4

Time Paths of a Multiplier-Accelerator Model

Eq. (3-19)  $C_t = c_0 + c_y Y_{t-1}$

Eq. (4-23)  $I_t = k_c(C_t - C_{t-1})$

Eq. (4-37)  $Y_t = (1 + k_c)c_y Y_{t-1} - k_c c_y Y_{t-2} + c_0 + G_t$

a.  $c_y = 0.8; k_c = 0.25$

| $t$ | $G_t$ | $+$ | $C_t$ | $+$ | $I_t$ | $=$ | $Y_t$ |
|---|---|---|---|---|---|---|---|
| 0 | 5.00 | | 45.00 | | 0 | | 50.00 |
| 1 | 6.00 | | 45.00 | | 0 | | 51.00 |
| 2 | 6.00 | | 45.80 | | 0.20 | | 52.00 |
| 3 | 6.00 | | 46.60 | | 0.20 | | 52.80 |
| 4 | 6.00 | | 47.24 | | 0.16 | | 53.40 |
| 5 | 6.00 | | 47.72 | | 0.12 | | 53.84 |
| 6 | 6.00 | | 48.07 | | 0.09 | | 54.16 |
| 7 | 6.00 | | 48.33 | | 0.06 | | 54.39 |
| 8 | 6.00 | | 48.51 | | 0.05 | | 54.56 |
| 9 | 6.00 | | 48.65 | | 0.03 | | 54.68 |
| . | . | | . | | . | | . |
| . | . | | . | | . | | . |
| . | . | | . | | . | | . |
| ∞ | 6.00 | | 49.00 | | 0 | | 55.00 |

**Table 4-4** (Continued)

### b. $c_y = 0.8; k_c = 5.0$

| $t$ | $G_t$ | $+$ | $C_t$ | $+$ | $I_t$ | $=$ | $Y_t$ |
|---|---|---|---|---|---|---|---|
| 0 | 5.00 | | 45.00 | | 0 | | 50.00 |
| 1 | 6.00 | | 45.00 | | 0 | | 51.00 |
| 2 | 6.00 | | 45.80 | | 4.00 | | 55.80 |
| 3 | 6.00 | | 49.64 | | 19.20 | | 74.84 |
| 4 | 6.00 | | 64.87 | | 76.16 | | 147.03 |
| 5 | 6.00 | | 122.63 | | 288.77 | | 417.39 |
| 6 | 6.00 | | 338.91 | | 1,081.44 | | 1,426.36 |
| 7 | 6.00 | | 1,146.09 | | 4,035.86 | | 5,187.95 |
| 8 | 6.00 | | 4,155.36 | | 15,046.37 | | 19,207.73 |
| 9 | 6.00 | | 15,371.18 | | 56,079.10 | | 71,456.28 |
| 10 | 6.00 | | 57,170.03 | | 208,994.22 | | 266,170.25 |
| . | . | | . | | . | | . |
| . | . | | . | | . | | . |
| . | . | | . | | . | | . |
| $\infty$ | 6.00 | | $\infty$ | | $\infty$ | | $\infty$ |

### c. $c_y = 0.5; k_c = 5.0$

| $t$ | $G_t$ | $+$ | $C_t$ | $+$ | $I_t$ | $=$ | $Y_t$ |
|---|---|---|---|---|---|---|---|
| 0 | 5.00 | | 15.00 | | 0 | | 20.00 |
| 1 | 6.00 | | 15.00 | | 0 | | 21.00 |
| 2 | 6.00 | | 15.50 | | 2.50 | | 24.00 |
| 3 | 6.00 | | 17.00 | | 7.50 | | 30.50 |
| . | . | | . | | . | | . |
| . | . | | . | | . | | . |
| . | . | | . | | . | | . |
| 9 | 6.00 | | 90.94 | | 105.00 | | 201.94 |
| . | . | | . | | . | | . |
| . | . | | . | | . | | . |
| . | . | | . | | . | | . |
| 19 | 6.00 | | $-6,948.68$ | | $-9,004.66$ | | $-15,947.34$ |
| . | . | | . | | . | | . |
| . | . | | . | | . | | . |
| . | . | | . | | . | | . |
| 24 | 6.00 | | 641,728.35 | | 752,298.92 | | 394,033.28 |
| . | . | | . | | . | | . |
| . | . | | . | | . | | . |
| . | . | | . | | . | | . |
| $\infty$ | 6.00 | | $\pm\infty$ | | $\pm\infty$ | | $\pm\infty$ |

**Table 4–4** (Continued)

d. $c_y = 0.8$; $k_c = 1.25$

| $t$ | $G_t$ | $+$ | $C_t$ | $+$ | $I_t$ | $=$ | $Y_t$ |
|---|---|---|---|---|---|---|---|
| 0 | 5.00 | | 45.00 | | 0 | | 50.00 |
| 1 | 6.00 | | 45.00 | | 0 | | 51.00 |
| 2 | 6.00 | | 45.80 | | 1.00 | | 52.80 |
| 3 | 6.00 | | 47.24 | | 1.80 | | 55.04 |
| 4 | 6.00 | | 49.03 | | 2.24 | | 57.27 |
| 5 | 6.00 | | 50.82 | | 2.23 | | 59.05 |
| 6 | 6.00 | | 52.23 | | 1.77 | | 60.00 |
| . | . | | . | | . | | . |
| . | . | | . | | . | | . |
| 13 | 6.00 | | 45.77 | | $-1.77$ | | 50.00 |
| . | . | | . | | . | | . |
| . | . | | . | | . | | . |
| 20 | 6.00 | | 52.23 | | 1.77 | | 60 |
| . | . | | . | | . | | . |
| 27 | 6.00 | | 45.77 | | $-1.77$ | | 50 |
| . | . | | . | | . | | . |
| 34 | 6.00 | | 52.23 | | 1.77 | | 60 |
| . | . | | . | | . | | . |
| $\infty$ | 6.00 | | $\geq 45.77$ $\leq 52.23$ | | $\pm 1.77$ | | $\geq 50$ $\leq 60$ |

e. $c_y = 0.75$; $k_y = 1.25$

| $t$ | $G_t$ | $+$ | $C_t$ | $+$ | $I_t$ | $=$ | $Y_t$ |
|---|---|---|---|---|---|---|---|
| 0 | 5.00 | | 35.00 | | 0 | | 40.00 |
| 1 | 6.00 | | 35.00 | | 0 | | 41.00 |
| 2 | 6.00 | | 35.75 | | 0.94 | | 42.69 |
| 3 | 6.00 | | 37.02 | | 1.58 | | 44.60 |
| 4 | 6.00 | | 38.45 | | 1.79 | | 46.24 |
| 5 | 6.00 | | 34.68 | | 1.54 | | 47.22 |
| 6 | 6.00 | | 40.41 | | 0.42 | | 47.33 |
| 7 | 6.00 | | 40.50 | | 0.11 | | 46.61 |
| 8 | 6.00 | | 34.95 | | $-0.68$ | | 45.27 |
| 9 | 6.00 | | 38.95 | | $-1.25$ | | 43.71 |
| 10 | 6.00 | | 37.78 | | $-1.47$ | | 42.31 |
| 11 | 6.00 | | 36.73 | | $-1.31$ | | 41.42 |
| 12 | 6.00 | | 36.07 | | $-0.83$ | | 41.24 |
| . | . | | . | | . | | . |
| . | . | | . | | . | | . |
| 18 | 6.00 | | 39.54 | | 0.74 | | 46.28 |
| . | . | | . | | . | | . |
| . | . | | . | | . | | . |
| 24 | 6.00 | | 36.78 | | $-0.65$ | | 42.13 |
| . | . | | . | | . | | . |
| $\infty$ | 6.00 | | 38.0 | | 0 | | 44.00 |

The model presented above, which relates consumption to income and investment to consumption, is the most common form of treatment of multiplier-accelerator interaction. However, one variation of the accelerator relationship assumes investment to be a function of total income, as given previously by Eq. (4-25). This changes the dynamics of the model significantly, making it generally less stable. A model of this type is identical to the one just considered, with the exception that the investment equation, Eq. (4-25), replaces Eq. (4-23).

$$Y_t = C_t + I_t + G_t \qquad (1\text{-}4)$$

$$C_t = c_0 + c_y Y_{t-1} \qquad (3\text{-}19)$$

$$I_t = k_y(Y_{t-1} - Y_{t-2}) \qquad (4\text{-}25)$$

Solving the model for $Y_t$ gives

$$Y_t = (k_y + c_y)Y_{t-1} - k_y Y_{t-2} + c_0 + G_t \qquad (4\text{-}39)$$

In equilibrium, $Y_t = Y_{t-1} = Y_{t-2}$ and the solution reduces to

$$Y_t = \frac{c_0 + G_t}{1 - c_y} \qquad (4\text{-}38)$$

Again, this is similar to the case of the multiplier alone—the addition of the accelerator does not change the comparative statics significantly since $I_t = 0$

### Table 4–5

Dynamics of Multiplier-Accelerator Model

Eq. (3-19)   $C_t = c_0 + c_y Y_{t-1}$

Eq. (4-25)   $I_t = k_y(Y_{t-1} - Y_{t-2})$

Eq. (4-39)   $Y_t = (k_y + c_y)Y_{t-1} - k_y Y_{t-2} + c_0 + G_t$

| VALUES OF MARGINAL PROPENSITY TO CONSUME, $c_y$, AND THE ACCELERATOR COEFFICIENT, $k_y$ | TIME PATH OF TOTAL INCOME, $Y_t$ |
|---|---|
| a.   $k_y < 1.00; c_y \geq 2\sqrt{k_y} - k_y$ | Moves monotonically toward equilibrium |
| b.   $k_y > 1.00; c_y \geq 2\sqrt{k_y} - k_y$ | Monotonically departing ever further from equilibrium |
| c.   $k_y > 1.00; c_y < 2\sqrt{k_y} - k_y$ | Explosive cycles departing ever further from equilibrium |
| d.   $k_y = 1.00; c_y < 2\sqrt{k_y} - k_y$ | Unending cycles of constant magnitude |
| e.   $k_y < 1.00; c_y < 2\sqrt{k_y} - k_y$ | Damped cycles converging on equilibrium |

in equilibrium. However, changing investment from a function of consumption to a function of total income significantly changes the dynamic adjustments in this model. Assuming the marginal propensity to consume is between zero and plus one, it can be shown that the time paths for disequilibrium income follow the patterns given in Table 4–5. Table 4–6 gives a numerical illustration for each possibility.

## Table 4–6

Time Paths of Another Multiplier-
Accelerator Model

Eq. (3-19)  $C_t = c_0 + c_y Y_{t-1}$

Eq. (4-25)  $I_t = k_y(Y_{t-1} - Y_{t-2})$

Eq. (4-39)  $Y_t = (c_y + k_y)Y_{t-1} - k_y Y_{t-2} + c_0 + G_t$

a.  $c_y = 0.8;\ k_y = 0.25$

| $t$ | $G_t$ | + | $C_t$ | + | $I_t$ | = | $Y_t$ |
|---|---|---|---|---|---|---|---|
| 0 | 5.00 | | 45.00 | | 0 | | 50.00 |
| 1 | 6.00 | | 45.00 | | 0 | | 51.00 |
| 2 | 6.00 | | 45.80 | | 0.25 | | 52.05 |
| . | . | | . | | . | | . |
| 4 | 6.00 | | 47.32 | | 0.21 | | 53.54 |
| . | . | | . | | . | | . |
| 6 | 6.00 | | 48.19 | | 0.11 | | 54.30 |
| . | . | | . | | . | | . |
| 8 | 6.00 | | 48.62 | | 0.06 | | 54.67 |
| . | . | | . | | . | | . |
| . | . | | . | | . | | . |
| . | . | | . | | . | | . |
| ∞ | 6.00 | | 49.00 | | 0 | | 55.00 |

b.  $c_y = 0.5;\ k_y = 5.0$

| $t$ | $G_t$ | + | $C_t$ | + | $I_t$ | = | $Y_t$ |
|---|---|---|---|---|---|---|---|
| 0 | 5.00 | | 15.00 | | 0 | | 20.00 |
| 1 | 6.00 | | 15.00 | | 0 | | 21.00 |
| 2 | 6.00 | | 15.50 | | 5.00 | | 26.50 |
| 3 | 6.00 | | 18.25 | | 27.50 | | 51.75 |
| 4 | 6.00 | | 30.88 | | 126.25 | | 163.13 |
| 5 | 6.00 | | 86.56 | | 556.88 | | 649.44 |
| 6 | 6.00 | | 329.72 | | 2,431.56 | | 2,767.28 |
| 7 | 6.00 | | 1,388.64 | | 10,589.22 | | 11,983.86 |
| 8 | 6.00 | | 5,996.93 | | 46,082.89 | | 52,085.82 |
| 9 | 6.00 | | 26,047.91 | | 200,509.81 | | 226,563.72 |
| 10 | 6.00 | | 113,286.86 | | 872,389.47 | | 985,682.32 |
| . | . | | . | | . | | . |
| . | . | | . | | . | | . |
| . | . | | . | | . | | . |
| ∞ | 6.00 | | ∞ | | ∞ | | ∞ |

**Table 4–6**   (Continued)

c.   $c_y = 0.8; k_y = 1.25$

| $t$ | $G_t$ | $+$ | $C_t$ | $+$ | $I_t$ | $=$ | $Y_t$ |
|-----|-------|-----|-------|-----|-------|-----|-------|
| 0  | 5.00 |  | 45.00 |  | 0     |  | 50.00 |
| 1  | 6.00 |  | 45.00 |  | 0     |  | 51.00 |
| 2  | 6.00 |  | 45.80 |  | 1.25  |  | 53.05 |
| 3  | 6.00 |  | 47.44 |  | 2.56  |  | 59.49 |
| .  | .    |  | .     |  | .     |  | .     |
| .  | .    |  |       |  |       |  |       |
| .  | .    |  | .     |  | .     |  | .     |
| 7  | 6.00 |  | 57.56 |  | 3.42  |  | 66.98 |
| .  | .    |  | .     |  | .     |  | .     |
| .  | .    |  |       |  |       |  |       |
| .  | .    |  | .     |  | .     |  | .     |
| 15 | 6.00 |  | 27.69 |  | −6.77 |  | 26.92 |
| .  | .    |  | .     |  | .     |  | .     |
| .  | .    |  |       |  |       |  |       |
| 22 | 6.00 |  | 93.12 |  | 20.86 |  | 119.97 |
| .  | .    |  | .     |  | .     |  | .     |
| .  | .    |  | .     |  | .     |  | .     |
| .  | .    |  | .     |  | .     |  | .     |
| ∞  | 6.00 |  | $\pm\infty$ |  | $\pm\infty$ |  | $\pm\infty$ |

d.   $c_y = 0.8; k_y = 1.00$

| $t$ | $G_t$ | $+$ | $C_t$ | $+$ | $I_t$ | $=$ | $Y_t$ |
|-----|-------|-----|-------|-----|-------|-----|-------|
| 0  | 5.00 |  | 45.00 |  | 0     |  | 50.00 |
| 1  | 6.00 |  | 45.00 |  | 0     |  | 51.00 |
| 2  | 6.00 |  | 45.80 |  | 1.00  |  | 52.80 |
| 3  | 6.00 |  | 47.24 |  | 1.80  |  | 55.04 |
| 4  | 6.00 |  | 49.03 |  | 2.24  |  | 57.27 |
| 5  | 6.00 |  | 50.82 |  | 2.23  |  | 59.05 |
| 6  | 6.00 |  | 52.23 |  | 1.77  |  | 60.00 |
| .  | .    |  | .     |  | .     |  | .     |
| .  | .    |  | .     |  | .     |  | .     |
| .  | .    |  | .     |  | .     |  | .     |
| 13 | 6.00 |  | 45.77 |  | −1.77 |  | 50.00 |
| .  | .    |  | .     |  | .     |  | .     |
| .  | .    |  | .     |  | .     |  | .     |
| .  | .    |  | .     |  | .     |  | .     |
| 20 | 6.00 |  | 52.23 |  | 1.77  |  | 60.00 |
| .  | .    |  | .     |  | .     |  | .     |
| .  | .    |  | .     |  | .     |  | .     |
| 27 | 6.00 |  | 45.77 |  | −1.77 |  | 50.00 |
| .  | .    |  | .     |  | .     |  | .     |
| .  | .    |  | .     |  | .     |  | .     |
| 34 | 6.00 |  | 52.23 |  | 1.77  |  | 60.00 |
| .  | .    |  | .     |  | .     |  | .     |
| .  | .    |  | .     |  | .     |  | .     |
| ∞  | 6.00 |  | $\geq 45.77$ <br> $\leq 52.23$ |  | $\pm 1.77$ |  | $\geq 50.00$ <br> $\leq 60.00$ |

**Table 4-6** (Continued)

e. $c_y = 0.8$; $k_y = 0.75$

| t | $G_t$ | + | $C_t$ | + | $I_t$ | = | $Y_t$ |
|---|---|---|---|---|---|---|---|
| 0 | 5.00 | | 45.00 | | 0 | | 50.00 |
| 1 | 6.00 | | 45.00 | | 0 | | 51.00 |
| 2 | 6.00 | | 45.80 | | 0.75 | | 52.55 |
| 3 | 6.00 | | 47.04 | | 1.16 | | 54.20 |
| 4 | 6.00 | | 48.36 | | 1.24 | | 55.60 |
| 5 | 6.00 | | 49.48 | | 1.05 | | 56.53 |
| 6 | 6.00 | | 50.22 | | 0.70 | | 56.92 |
| . | . | | . | | . | | . |
| . | . | | . | | . | | . |
| . | . | | . | | . | | . |
| 13 | 6.00 | | 48.50 | | −0.23 | | 54.27 |
| . | . | | . | | . | | . |
| . | . | | . | | . | | . |
| . | . | | . | | . | | . |
| 20 | 6.00 | | 49.20 | | 0.08 | | 55.28 |
| . | . | | . | | . | | . |
| . | . | | . | | . | | . |
| 27 | 6.00 | | 48.92 | | −0.02 | | 54.90 |
| . | . | | . | | . | | . |
| . | . | | . | | . | | . |
| 34 | 6.00 | | 49.03 | | 0.01 | | 55.04 |
| . | . | | . | | . | | . |
| . | . | | . | | . | | . |
| ∞ | 6.00 | | 49.00 | | 0 | | 55.06 |

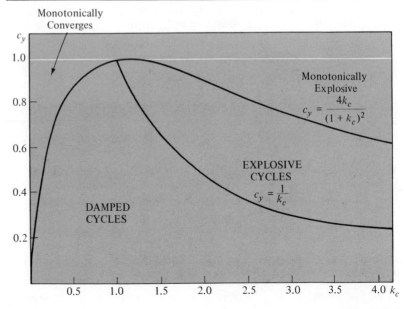

**Figure 4-1**

Stability of Multiplier-Accelerator Model—
Investment a Function of Consumption Expenditures

86

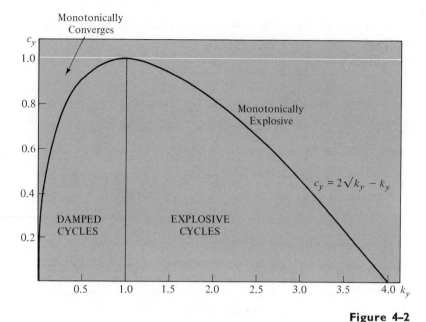

**Figure 4–2**

Stability of Multiplier-Accelerator Model—
Investment a Function of Total Expenditures

The substantial difference in the dynamic characteristics of the two models can be seen from the graphic presentations, Figures 4–1 and 4–2. Figure 4–1 presents the boundary conditions when investment is a function of consumption, and Figure 4–2 is based upon a model in which investment is a function of total income. In the latter case, stability (convergence toward equilibrium) is achieved if, and only if, the accelerator is less than unity; whereas, in the former case, convergent cycles can still be achieved with a large accelerator coefficient if the multiplier is sufficiently small. An intuitive explanation is simple. If investment is a function of the change in income, then investment depends not only on past consumption but also past investment. Thus there are two possible sources of instability in this model. If investment is a function of the change in consumption only, however, there is but one source of possible instability.

## 5. A Concluding Comment on Multiplier-Accelerator Models

First, a word on the limitations of these models. It should be obvious to the reader that the models considered here are only examples of the infinite variety of models that could be constructed by considering alternative formulations of the underlying equations and the values of the relevant parameters. A particular economy is infinitely more complex than the relatively naive models presented in the foregoing pages. No serious economist expects to find *the* multiplier-accelerator model appropriate for predicting the pattern of fluctuations in a particular economy. It has never been shown conclusively that the marginal propensity to consume or the intercept of the consumption function is stable through time, and it is felt that many more factors are involved in setting the level of consumption than total income. Further, a history of more than one or two periods is probably relevant to present activity (whether these periods are one month or one year).

On the positive side, these models do illustrate some important principles. The most general principle is that with rather simple assumptions as to the behavior patterns on the part of consumers and investors one may generate fluctuations of almost any desired magnitude and frequency. The foundation of this result is the time lag in the response of the economic decision makers. In the real world there are undoubtedly time lags; those making consumption and investment decisions do base their actions on present and past magnitudes of the relevant variables. The importance of lagged responses in the fluctuation of aggregate demand cannot be overemphasized. However, a good deal more is involved in the actual time path of aggregate demand than that which is included in a simple multiplier-accelerator model. Some of these additional complexities are the subject material for the remaining chapters of this book.

## V  SUMMARY

The change in the stock of capital resulting from investment expenditures adds to the productive capacity of the economy, while the expenditures themselves add to the current value of GNP. While many different explanations of the determinants of investment expenditures have been proposed, this chapter has examined only two basic types of investment models. The first of these, a static model, suggested that businessmen compare the expected rate of return over cost, called the marginal efficiency of capital, to the rate of interest. As long as the *MEC* is greater than the interest rate, investment is profitable. However, increasing investment lowers the expected earnings of new investment while also raising the supply price. Thus, in equilibrium, the rate of interest and the *MEC* will be equated.

The second approach is dynamic and suggests that investment expenditures depend on past changes in consumption or total expenditures. In this model, varying combinations of the multiplier and the accelerator coefficient produce different time paths for the behavior of aggregate demand.

## EXERCISES

1.  Assume that the following three equations are a simplified description of the economy:

$$C_t = c_0 + c_y Y_{t-1}$$

$$I_t = i_0 + k_y(Y_{t-1} - Y_{t-2})$$

$$Y_t = G_t + C_t + I_t$$

Suppose that the economy's behavior can be described by the following equation:

$$Y_t = G_t + 20.00 + 1.70 Y_{t-1} - 0.90 Y_{t-2}$$

a.  What is the implied numerical value of the accelerator coefficient, $k_y$?

b.  What is the implied numerical value of the marginal propensity to consume, $c_y$?

c.  What would be the cyclical behavior of this model if a change in $G_t$ moved it from an equilibrium level?

## RECOMMENDED REFERENCES

Clark, J. M., "Business Acceleration and the Law of Demand: A Technical Factor in Economic Cycles," *The Journal of Political Economy*, March 1917, pp. 217–35.

Keynes, J. M., *The General Theory of Employment, Interest, and Money*. New York: Harcourt, Brace & World, Inc., 1936, Chapter 11.

Samuelson, Paul A., "Interaction Between the Multiplier Analysis and the Principle of Acceleration," *The Review of Economics and Statistics*, May 1939, pp. 75–78.

# 5 The Commodity Market

The previous chapters have presented the behavioral relationships that separately determine expenditures on consumption and investment. In the models discussed in these chapters, however, there was nothing to indicate that separately determined consumption and saving would necessarily be consistent with separately determined investment. It is the purpose of this chapter to identify the necessary equilibrium conditions that make possible the joint determination of mutually consistent components of national income. Because the variables in this analysis refer to dollars spent on goods and services, the resulting model is often referred to as the "commodity" market, as differentiated from the "money" market. Section I discusses equilibrium in a no-government commodity market, while Section II introduces both government expenditures and taxes.

## I THE NO-GOVERNMENT MODEL

### 1. Equilibrium

Under the assumption that there is no government sector in the economy, the circular flow of income presented in Chapter 1 is very simple. GNP expenditures are made only by consumers purchasing goods and services and by businesses investing in plant and equipment. When this amount is viewed as the sum of all incomes, it becomes available for either consumption or saving since, in the absence of government, GNP is equal to disposable income. Thus, the consumption expenditures "return" to the stream of income immediately, and consumer saving may be channeled to the business sector where it is used to purchase more plant and equipment.

As pointed out in Chapter 1, the circular flow of income is a continuous process, although for bookkeeping purposes we must record the transactions that have taken place over a particular time period. The transactions that are recorded become the basis of the national income accounts. Also as pointed out earlier, total expenditures must be equal to total withdrawals from the income stream by definition. Thus, GNP may be defined in the no-government model in the two following ways:

$$Y = C + I \qquad\qquad (5\text{-}1)$$

$$Y = C + S \qquad\qquad (5\text{-}2)$$

In order to ensure that the accounts are consistent, terms used in the accounting framework are always defined so that Eqs. (5-1) and (5-2) are equal. Accordingly, by substitution,

$$S = I \qquad\qquad (5\text{-}3)$$

However, the fact that saving is equal to investment in the national income accounts does not ensure that the level of income is in equilibrium. In making the decision as to how much to invest, the businessman estimates the future behavior of consumers in predicting his stream of future returns. In making the decision to consume or save, the consumer estimates what his income for the period will be. If in fact these different groups hit upon that unique combination of behavior where everyone has guessed exactly right, then everyone will be satisfied with the decision that he has made, there will be no impetus to alter that decision in the ensuing period, and therefore the system will be in equilibrium. Consumers will have spent the amount of money that will leave investors satsified with their current level of investment. Moreover, the sum of investment and consumption will equal a total GNP that makes consumers exactly satisfied with the allocation of their incomes between consumption and saving. Finally, the desired volume of saving will exactly equal the investment made.

Because the investor and consumer groups are not composed of the same individuals, however, it is not necessary, or even likely, that the unique combination cited above will be the one actually decided upon. Producers may make an output decision based upon expectations of high consumer expenditures, but consumers in the aggregate may decide to reduce consumption in favor of increased saving. Thus, as time passes, businesses will find that their output decision was too optimistic, and unsold goods will begin to accumulate on their shelves. When the national income accounts are collected for that time period, however, recorded saving will still be equal to recorded investment since the undesired inventory accumulations are defined as investment. Conversely, if consumers had decided to spend more than the amount anticipated by businessmen, stocks would be depleted below desirable levels. In this case, however, inventory liquidation would be counted as negative investment, or disinvestment, and saving would still equal investment in the national income books.

Neither of the cases cited in the previous paragraph is an equilibrium condition. In the first case businessmen would slow production, forcing workers to accept decreased incomes. As the income levels fell below what had been anticipated by consumers, that group would cut back on saving. This process would continue until a consistent set of behavior is reached at a lower level of aggregate income. In the second case, declining inventories would cause production to be increased, thereby raising incomes above anticipated levels and therefore stimulating saving. In the language of Chapter 3, when planned or *ex ante* saving is greater than planned or *ex ante* investment, income will fall until equilibrium is obtained. When *ex ante* saving is less than *ex ante* investment, income will increase until equilibrium is obtained. Yet, realized or *ex post* saving will always be equal to realized or *ex post* investment simply because of the accounting definitions.

Thus, complete criteria for an equilibrium level of income include not merely that savings be equal to investment but that *planned* investment be equal to *planned* saving. When these two variables are defined in this manner, Eq. (5-3) is not merely an identity but an equilibrium condition.

## 2. The IS Curve

The equilibrium relationships above can be combined with the basic structural equations of Chapters 2, 3, and 4 in an attempt to build a model that simultaneously determines the equilibrium values for the variables in question. These relationships are presented below, with the variables in each case referring to planned or desired levels. For simplicity, only the linear equations are considered:

Equilibrium condition: $\quad I = S$ (5-3)

Consumption function: $\quad C = c_0 + c_y Y$ (2-5)

Investment function: $\quad I = i_0 - i_r r$ (4-10)

Accounting identity: $\quad Y = C + I$ (5-1)

Notice that the four equations contain the five endogenous variables C, S, Y, I, and r. Because there are more unknowns than independent equations, the system cannot be solved for explicit values of the five variables. However, one can reduce the system to only one equation containing just two variables. Then, if further information can be provided about either of those unknowns, the system can be solved. Because analysis of the money market will later introduce more information about the interrelationship between Y and r, it will be advantageous here to solve the commodity market equations for a single equation containing both Y and r. In this case, the solution is

$$Y = \left(\frac{1}{1 - c_y}\right)(c_0 + i_0 - i_r r) \tag{5-4}$$

or, solving explicitly for r,

$$r = \left(\frac{1}{i_r}\right)[c_0 + i_0 - (1 - c_y)Y] \tag{5-5}$$

Whether this relationship is expressed as an explicit function for $Y$ or $r$, it is called the *IS* curve since it considers only points of equilibrium between saving and investment. Verbally, this may be explained as follows: Every level of the rate of interest will have some unique volume of investment associated with it. In equilibrium, that level of investment will be equal to planned saving. Finally, that amount of saving will be generated by a unique value of national income. The *IS* curve therefore is a relationship between the rate of interest and the level of income that is necessary if planned saving is to be equal to planned investment at that rate.

The slope of the *IS* curve may be obtained by taking the derivative of Eq. (5-4) with respect to $r$:

$$\frac{dY}{dr} = - \frac{i_r}{1 - c_y} < 0 \qquad (5\text{-}6)$$

Since the marginal propensity to consume, $c_y$, is a positive fraction, the slope of the *IS* curve is negative and decreases in the rate of interest will lead to increases in income. The economic meaning of this may perhaps be more clearly observed if Eq. (5-6) is broken down into the product of $-i_r$ and $1/(1 - c_y)$. From the investment function, Eq. (4-10),

$$\frac{dI}{dr} = -i_r \qquad (5\text{-}7)$$

Moreover, from the simple equilibrium model of Chapter 3,

$$\frac{dY}{dI} = \frac{1}{1 - c_y} \qquad (3\text{-}4)$$

By substitution into Eq. (5-6),

$$\frac{dY}{dr} = \left(\frac{dI}{dr}\right)\left(\frac{dY}{dI}\right) = - \frac{i_r}{1 - c_y} \qquad (5\text{-}8)$$

In other words, the rate of change of income with respect to the rate of interest is equal to the rate of change of investment with respect to the rate of interest times the rate of change of income with respect to investment. Lower interest rates stimulate investment, and increased investment exerts a multiplied effect upon income via the investment multiplier. Thus, lower interest rates automatically lead to higher levels of income; hence the *IS* curve must be negatively sloped.

It is also interesting to know the impact on the *IS* curve of changes in parameters of the structural equations, especially changes in the slope of the marginal efficiency of capital function, $i_r$, and in the marginal propensity to consume. Taking the derivative of Eq. (5-4) with respect to $i_r$ and $c_y$,

$$\frac{\partial Y}{\partial i_r} = -\frac{r}{1 - c_y} < 0 \qquad (5\text{-}9)$$

$$\frac{\partial Y}{\partial c_y} = \frac{c_0 + i_0 - i_r r}{(1 - c_y)^2} > 0 \qquad (5\text{-}10)$$

The derivative in Eq. (5-9) is clearly negative, reflecting the fact that if investment becomes more highly interest-inelastic, national income must fall. In other words, if $i_r$ increases, *with $i_0$ held constant*, the slope of the *MEC* schedule becomes greater. As compared with the old schedule, every rate of interest will be associated with a lower level of investment than previously. Thus, by the investment multiplier, national income must decrease.

The derivative in Eq. (5-10) will usually be positive because investment, equal to $i_0 - i_r r$ in the numerator of Eq. (5-10) will generally be positive. The economic meaning of this condition is that an increase in the *MPC* will lead to a higher level of income. If the *MPC* increases, the *MPS* must necessarily decrease. Accordingly, every previous level of planned saving will now be associated with a higher level of income.

## II THE *IS* CURVE WITH A GOVERNMENT SECTOR

### 1. Equilibrium

In the previous no-government model, equilibrium consisted of the equality between planned saving and planned investment. If these two were not equal, withdrawals from the circular flow of income would not be equal to injections into the stream, and income would be either rising or falling. When a government sector is added to the model, the basic equilibrium condition remains the same: Planned withdrawals from the income stream must be equal to planned injections into it. However, a simple equality between planned saving and planned investment is not sufficient to describe the new equilibrium because the government sector will itself be making some withdrawals from and injections into the flow of income in the form of taxes and government expenditures.

As shown in Figure 1–1, GNP when viewed as expenditures on final goods and services can be broken down into consumption expenditures, investment expenditures, and government expenditures. On the other hand, when looked at from the point of view of total incomes, GNP can be broken down into how much is taxed, how much is saved, and how much is used for personal consumption expenditures. Thus, if planned injections are equal to planned withdrawals, it must be true that

$$Y = C + I + G \tag{1-6}$$

and

$$Y = C + S + T \tag{1-7}$$

and, therefore,

$$S + T = I + G \tag{5-11}$$

Equilibrium in the commodity market with a government sector requires that the sum of planned saving and taxes equal planned investment and government expenditures. With the incorporation of government into the model, it is no longer necessary that planned saving be equal to planned investment in order to ensure equilibrium. Saving may be greater than, less than, or exactly equal to investment, and equilibrium will still hold as long as taxes are, respectively, less than, greater than, or equal to government expenditures. Note, however, that the difference between saving and investment would have to be equal to the difference between government expenditures and taxes.

The reader should be careful not to overlook three immediate implications of the preceding paragraph. First, in any practical situation, deciding how much money the government will collect in taxes with a given tax rate, $t_y$, is not a simple matter. If it is desirable to raise taxes by 5 %, simply raising the tax rate by the same percentage will not do the job. As we will show later, the size of the tax rate is a key variable in determining the resulting level of income, and any change in the tax rate will hence lead to induced changes in the tax base. These secondary changes must be taken into account if actual taxes are to equal planned taxes. A similar phenomenon exists for government expenditures, as a change in the value of $G$ will lead to changes in income, and certain types of government expenditures, especially unemployment compensation payments, will be affected by the changing income. Again, planned expenditures will not be equal to actual expenditures unless these secondary or induced effects are taken into consideration. Secondly, the previous paragraph implies that the government budgetary surplus or deficit may be used as an instrument of economic policy. If planned saving is not equal to planned investment at the current level of income, the government may ensure that equilibrium will nonetheless be obtained simply by incurring a surplus or deficit that exactly offsets the difference between planned saving and planned investment. Thus, equilibrium will result at the current level of income rather than at a higher or lower value where planned saving and planned investment would be equilibrated. Finally, and less obvious, the government can not only generate equilibrium at current income but also set equilibrium at *any* desired level of income. This may be accomplished in either of two ways. Suppose, for example, that the current equilibrium income is below the level of income that is desired and that planned saving would be greater than planned investment at the desired level of income. In a no-government economy, this condition would ensure that income would fall below the desired level. In the expanded model, however, the government may stabilize income at its desired level by incurring a deficit to offset the excess saving. To push income up to the desired level, the government can increase the size of the deficit by increasing expenditures or cutting taxes. Increased government expenditures will lead to larger receipts than businessmen had expected, while decreased taxes will lead to larger consumer purchasing. In either case, income will rise. The second technique by which this might have been accomplished would have been to expand *both* taxes and expenditures, the government share in the economy being increased. By the balanced budget theorem mentioned earlier, each added increase in government expenditures, even though matched by additional taxes, will result in an additional dollar of national income.

Analysis of the implications above has led to a theory of economic policy called *functional finance*. Briefly, this theory contends that certain national economic goals may be reached if the economy operates at some particular level of national income that is sufficiently high to provide full employment but not so high as to cause rising prices. Because these are important goals, it should be national economic policy to adjust the government budget both in terms of size and degree of balance until that particular level of income is attained. Thus, the governmental budget should not be judged as to whether it is balanced or not but rather in terms of its impact on achieving the desired level of national income. More will be said about this topic in the following chapters.

## 2. The *IS* Curve

With the government sector incorporated into the model, the *IS* curve can be constructed using a consumption function, an investment function, a tax function, an equilibrium condition, and an accounting identity. Accordingly, the following five functions are presented:

Equilibrium condition:    $S + T = I + G$    (5-11)

Consumption function:    $C = c_0 + c_y(Y - T)$    (2-15)

Investment function:    $I = i_0 - i_r r$    (4-10)

Tax function:    $T = t_y Y - t_0$    (2-17)

Accounting identity:    $Y = C + I + G$    (1-6)

The five equations above contain the six endogenous variables $C$, $S$, $Y$, $T$, $I$, and $r$ and thus cannot be solved for unique values. As before, one equation in two unknowns can be obtained from this model. Solving for a relationship between $Y$ and $r$ yields

$$Y = \frac{c_0 + i_0 + G + c_y t_0 - i_r r}{1 - c_y + c_y t_y} \tag{5-12}$$

or

$$r = \frac{Y(-1 + c_y - c_y t_y) + c_0 + i_0 + G + c_y t_0}{i_r} \tag{5-13}$$

Again, note that the slope of the $IS$ curve is negative, with

$$\frac{dY}{dr} = -\frac{i_r}{1 - c_y + c_y t_y} < 0 \tag{5-14}$$

As before, it is again useful to examine the sign of the partial derivative of $Y$ with respect to some of the parameters of Eq. (5-12). Remember, the partial with respect to a parameter indicates the rate of change by which the entire curve is being shifted upward or downward. Considering the $MPC$,

$$\frac{\partial Y}{\partial c_y} = \frac{(1 - c_y + c_y t_y)(t_0) + (c_0 + c_y t_0 + i_0 - i_r r + G)(1 - t_y)}{(1 - c_y + c_y t_y)^2}$$

$$= \frac{Y - T}{1 - c_y + c_y t_y} > 0 \tag{5-15}$$

This result is very much similar to that of Eq. (5-10) of the no-government model except that disposable income has replaced total income in the numerator and the effective $MPC$ has replaced the ordinary $MPC$ in the denominator. If disposable income is positive, Eq. (5-15) will be greater than zero, so increases in the $MPC$ will lead to increases in, or outward shifts of, the $IS$ curve.

A change in the slope of the $MEC$ schedule or investment function will lead to a downward shift in the $IS$ curve, as explained in the previous no-government model. As $i_r$ increases ($i_0$ held constant), each rate of interest becomes associated with a lower level of investment than previously and, via the multiplier, income falls. Mathematically,

$$\frac{\partial Y}{\partial i_r} = \frac{-r}{1 - c_y + c_y t_y} < 0 \tag{5-16}$$

If government expenditures increase (all other parameters held constant), national income should increase, according to the functional finance argument. If investment is held constant, planned saving would have to increase in order to ensure equilibrium and the higher level of saving could be forthcoming only at a higher level of income, assuming no change in the *MPS*. The multiplier in this case is the same as derived in Chapter 3:

$$\frac{\partial Y}{\partial G} = \frac{1}{1 - c_y + c_y t_y} > 0 \qquad (5\text{-}17)$$

An increase in taxes will lower disposable income and hence also lower planned saving. This level of planned saving can only be generated in equilibrium by a lower level of national income. Therefore, an increase in the tax rate will lead to a inward shift in the *IS* curve, and the derivative of *Y* with respect to $t_y$ should be negative:

$$\frac{\partial Y}{\partial t_y} = \frac{-c_y Y}{1 - c_y + c_y t_y} < 0 \qquad (5\text{-}18)$$

## III  SUMMARY

In both of the national income models above, equilibrium is attained only when planned injections into the income stream are equal to planned withdrawals from it. In these models, however, there are fewer equations than unknowns, and the systems cannot be solved for determinant values of income, consumption, investment, saving, and the rate of interest. At this point, we reduce the model to one equation in two unknowns, income and the rate of interest. This relationship describes pairs of income levels and interest rates at which the savings-investment market is in equilibrium. Standard differentiation techniques applied to this *IS* curve show the direction in which the curve is shifted as values of the parameters are altered.

## NONMATHEMATICAL APPENDIX TO CHAPTER 5: GRAPHIC ANALYSIS

Many modern economists have employed a graphic technique to help explain the *IS* curve, an example of which is given in Figure 5–1. Graph (a) represents the investment function given by Eq. (4-10). Given some rate of

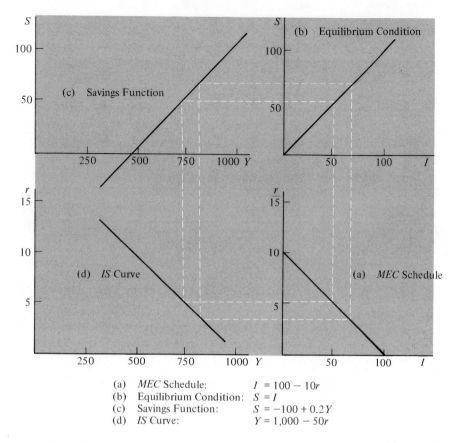

(a)   *MEC* Schedule:           $I = 100 - 10r$
(b)   Equilibrium Condition:   $S = I$
(c)   Savings Function:         $S = -100 + 0.2Y$
(d)   *IS* Curve:                 $Y = 1,000 - 50r$

**Figure 5–1**

The *IS* Curve

interest, say 5%, the amount of investment that will be forthcoming may be read off the abscissa, in this case, $50. Graph (b) represents Eq. (5-3), the equality between planned saving and planned investment. Scaling of the abscissa is the same as for graph (a). Thus, by extending a vertical line upward from graph (a) to graph (b), one can read from the ordinate in graph (b) what planned saving must be if the system is in equilibrium. For the present example, this is $50. Graph (c) plots the saving function, found by substituting the consumption function, Eq. (2-5), into the accounting identity, Eq. (1-4). For this graph, the ordinate has the same scaling as the ordinate in graph (b). By extending a horizontal line across from graph (b), we can find what level of income is necessary if planned saving is to be realized at $50. This value of income is $750. Finally, the *IS* curve may be obtained by dropping a vertical line from graph (c) and extending a horizontal from graph (a) until they meet in graph (d). The intersection of these two lines provides one point on the *IS* curve. By repeating the process for other assumed rates of interest, enough points may be determined so that the *IS* curve may be drawn. In this case since all the structural equations are linear, only two points are necessary.

Figure 5–2 illustrates what changes result in the *IS* curve when parameters in the structural equations are changed. The solid lines are the same equations as presented in Figure 5–1. The broken line in graph (a) in Figure 5–2 represents an increase in the coefficient of the *MEC* schedule from 0.10

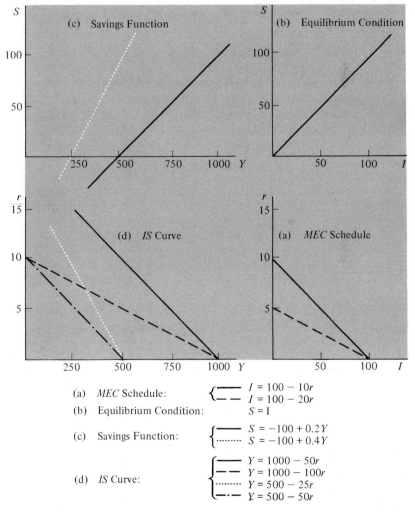

(a) *MEC* Schedule: $\left\{\begin{array}{l} I = 100 - 10r \\ I = 100 - 20r \end{array}\right.$

(b) Equilibrium Condition: $S = I$

(c) Savings Function: $\left\{\begin{array}{l} S = -100 + 0.2Y \\ S = -100 + 0.4Y \end{array}\right.$

(d) *IS* Curve: $\left\{\begin{array}{l} Y = 1000 - 50r \\ Y = 1000 - 100r \\ Y = 500 - 25r \\ Y = 500 - 50r \end{array}\right.$

**Figure 5–2**

The *IS* Curve Shifted

to 0.20. When this new *MEC* schedule is used to construct the *IS* curve, the result is the broken line in graph (d). As indicated by Eq. (5-9) above, this curve lies below the original *IS* schedule. In graph (c) the dotted line represents a decrease in the *MPC* from 0.8 to 0.6 or, alternately, an increase in the *MPS* from 0.2 to 0.4. Using the new savings function (with the original *MEC* schedule) to construct a new *IS* curve yields the dotted line in graph (d). Because the *MPC* has decreased in this case, it also lies below the original curve. As the *IS* curve constructed with *both* parameter shifts is merely the sum of each, the resulting *IS* schedule is the alternately dotted and broken line in graph (d).

As is the case with any geometric presentation, the *IS* analysis when described graphically becomes more and more complex as additional variables are brought into the model. Indeed, one compelling motivation for the mathematical format of this book is to overcome many of the difficulties

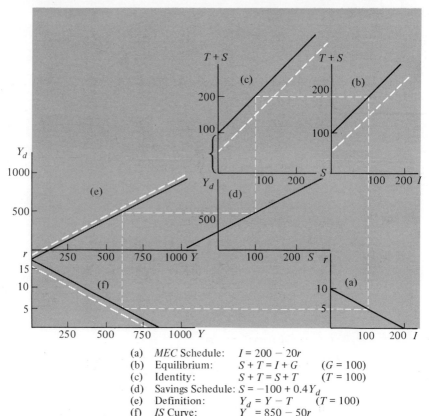

| (a) | *MEC* Schedule: | $I = 200 - 20r$ | |
| (b) | Equilibrium: | $S + T = I + G$ | $(G = 100)$ |
| (c) | Identity: | $S + T = S + T$ | $(T = 100)$ |
| (d) | Savings Schedule: | $S = -100 + 0.4Y_d$ | |
| (e) | Definition: | $Y_d = Y - T$ | $(T = 100)$ |
| (f) | *IS* Curve: | $Y = 850 - 50r$ | |

**Figure 5–3**

Commodity Market Equilibrium

of graphic analysis. However, another attempt at graphic presentation will be made here so that the reader may familiarize himself with this often used approach. The model will be somewhat restricted because a graphic presentation with taxes as a function of income is too cumbersome to serve as a teaching device. Hence, the following section assumes that taxes are fixed at some level $T$.

The $IS$ curve is derived graphically in Figure 5–3. Consider first only the bold lines. Graph (a) presents the $MEC$ schedule while graph (b) gives the equilibrium conditions described by Eq. (5-11). In this graph, the intercept on the ordinate is the value of fixed government expenditures. Graph (c) breaks the sum of saving and taxes down into its components, with the intercept in this case being the fixed level of taxes. Graph (d), immediately below graph (c), charts the level of disposable income necessary to bring about the equilibrium level of saving. Next, graph (e) describes the linear relationship between total income and disposable income, this time with taxes being the intercept on the abscissa. Finally, graph (f) is the $IS$ curve, which may be derived by initially assuming points on the $MEC$ schedule and then tracing around the equilibrium conditions by extending alternate vertical and horizontal lines to the following graphs. The equations used in this particular example are given at the top of Figure 5–3.

To demonstrate the balanced budget theorem, we need only alter the schedules in which taxes or government expenditures appear. If we consider a decrease in both taxes and expenditures the intercepts in graphs (b) and (c) both shift down by the same amount, and the intercept in graph (e) will move to the left, indicating that lower taxes increase disposable income. If a new $IS$ curve is traced out, the result is the broken line in graph (f), which lies below the original $IS$ curve. By inspection, it can be seen that the expenditures effect outweighs the tax effect.

1. Assume

$$C = 20 + 0.8(Y - T)$$
$$I = 350 - 30r$$
$$T = 0.2Y - 40$$
$$G = 42$$

   **a.**  Find the equation of the *IS* curve.
   **b.**  If the rate of interest is 10%, find the values of $C$, $I$, $T$, $Y$, and $S$.

## RECOMMENDED REFERENCES

Hicks, John R., "Mr. Keynes and the 'Classics'; A Suggested Interpretation." *Econometrica*, Vol. V, 1937, 147–59. Reprinted in Wm. Fellner and B. F, Haley, *Readings in the Theory of Income Distribution*. Homewood, Ill.: Richard D. Irwin Co., 1951.

McKenna, Joseph P., *Aggregate Economic Analysis*. New York: Holt, Rinehart and Winston, Inc., 1969, Chapter 9.

# 6 The Money Supply

# and the *LM* Curve

In the three previous chapters we have discussed changes in the level of aggregate demand resulting from changes in the expenditures of consumers, investors, and the government. Consumption was considered to be a function of income, investment to be a function of income and the interest rate, and government expenditures to be exogenously determined. It was concluded that such a system will be in equilibrium at an infinite number of compatible levels of income and interest rates. This set of equilibria, called the *IS* curve, is often said to describe the conditions of equilibrium in the "commodity market" as differentiated from the "money market," which will be considered in this chapter. As we shall see, the necessary conditions for equilibrium in the money market also generate a set of equilibria consisting of compatible levels of money income and the interest rate called the *LM* curve. The two curves interact to set a unique equilibrium level of aggregate demand and a unique interest rate.

This chapter is concerned with the influence of the money supply on aggregate demand. Section I provides a necessary set of definitions and identities, and Section II offers a simple formulation of the quantity theory of money. Section III is concerned with the development of the demand for money and construction of the *LM* curve. Since the theory developed in these sections is applicable to any modern economy, the institutional peculiarities of the United States economy and problems with the definition of money will be covered separately in Chapter 8.

## I DEFINITIONS AND IDENTITIES

Some of the more fundamental monetary variables were defined in Chapter 1. They will be repeated in greater detail in this section.

### 1. Velocity

There are a number of different concepts of the velocity of money used in economic analysis, the two most common of which are the "transactions velocity" and "income velocity." Transactions velocity, $V_T$, is defined as the average number of times that a dollar is spent during some particular accounting period. More precisely, it is the dollar total of *all* transactions taking place, $T_R$, divided by the average outstanding money stock of the period, $M$. Algebraically, the transactions velocity of money is

$$V_T = \frac{T_R}{M} \tag{6-1}$$

Income velocity is defined as the average turnover of each dollar in payment for *final goods and services*. Of course, this will be much smaller than the transactions velocity as all intermediate transactions involved in the production of the final goods and services are excluded, as are the many purely financial transactions that take place in the economy. Algebraically, income velocity is defined as

$$V_y = \frac{Y}{M} \tag{6-2}$$

## 2. Real Variables

To this point, the level of prices has not been considered. It is intuitively obvious that changes in streams of income and stocks of money or goods stated in money terms can be misleading if price levels have changed significantly. Of course, it is very difficult to define precisely what is meant by *the* price level, just as it is difficult in general to define *the* interest rate. The appropriate measure frequently depends on the problem at hand, and even in a specific case certain conceptual problems must always be solved. For present purposes, the price level may be defined as some index of the price of all goods and services produced in the economy. If the price index, $P$, is 100.0 at one point in time and 110.0 at a later point, prices are said to have increased on the average by 10 percent.

The concept of real income or output is one of some measure of total income that has been abstracted from price changes, a measure of what the dollar totals would have been if actual changes in production had taken place with no change in prices. Such "real" measures are generated by dividing the current money measure by the price level. The current measure is then said to have been "deflated" by the price index to obtain the "real" measure. Hence, real income or output, $Q$, is defined as follows:

$$Q = \frac{Y}{P} \tag{6-3}$$

Similarly, the real money stock is defined as

$$M_r = \frac{M}{P} \tag{6-4}$$

Rearrangement of the identities, Eqs. (6-3) and (6-4), gives the following relationships:

$$Y = PQ \tag{6-3'}$$

$$M = PM_r \tag{6-4'}$$

# II THE QUANTITY THEORY OF MONEY

## 1. The Quantity Equation

With the addition of a few critical assumptions, the identities given above can be used to construct a simple macroeconomic model giving a determinate price level or level of real income. Substituting the definition of $Y$ given by Eq. (6-3) into the definition of income velocity given by Eq. (6-2) gives the following identity:

$$V_y = \frac{PQ}{M}$$

or

$$MV_y = PQ \tag{6-5}$$

Obviously, if one is willing to assume that $V_y$ and $Q$ are fixed, any changes in $M$ must be reflected in a change in $P$. If one assumes prices to be absolutely rigid and thereby $P$ constant, any change in $M$ must be reflected in a change in real output, $Q$. Such assumptions have been frequent over the history of economic thought. A more precise statement of the result of such assumptions is obtained by differentiating Eq. (6-5).

$$M \, dV_y + V_y \, dM = P \, dQ + Q \, dP \tag{6-6}$$

If velocity and real output are assumed constant, then $dV_y$ and $dQ$ are equal to zero, and Eq. (6-6) reduces to

$$V_y \, dM = Q \, dP$$

or

$$\frac{dP}{dM} = \frac{V_y}{Q} \tag{6-7}$$

Equation (6-7) indicates that under these assumptions there is a constant relationship between changes in the money stock and changes in the price level. Thus, a doubling of the money stock should exactly double the price level.

Alternatively, if one assumes that the price level is rigid, and velocity is constant, then $dV_y$ and $dP$ are equal to zero, and Eq. (6-6) becomes

$$\frac{dQ}{dM} = \frac{V_y}{P} \qquad (6\text{-}8)$$

Under this set of assumptions, Eq. (6-8) indicates that there is a constant relationship between changes in the money supply and the level of real output. A doubling of the money supply under these conditions would not affect prices but would lead to twice the volume of output.

The assumptions to be applied to Eq. (6-7) have been given very much attention over the history of economic thought under the name of the quantity theory. Because they believed that output and velocity depended on population, transportation, and commercial conditions, all of which are independent of the quantity of money, many economists have argued that the simple quantity theory relating money and prices was quite realistic. Because of this, and because it provides a good starting point for more complex monetary theory, the quantity theory deserves a more detailed examination.

Returning to the assumptions that velocity and the level of output are constant, we can observe from Eq. (6-5) that the relationship between the price level and the money supply is linear and, graphically speaking, passes through the origin. A rearrangement of Eq. (6-5) will make this clear.

$$P = \frac{V_y}{Q} M \qquad (6\text{-}5)$$

With $V_y$ and $Q$ constant, this equation is linearly homogeneous in $P$ and $M$. In other words, the elasticity of the price level with respect to the money supply is unity at all levels. This can be demonstrated quite simply. The formula for this coefficient of elasticity is

$$\eta_{P,M} = \frac{dP}{dM} \frac{M}{P} \qquad (6\text{-}9)$$

Substituting Eq. (6-7) into the definition in Eq. (6-9) yields

$$\eta_{P,M} = \frac{V_y}{Q} \frac{M}{P} \qquad (6\text{-}10)$$

Next, substituting Eq. (6-2) into (6-10) gives

$$\eta_{P,M} = \frac{1}{Q}\frac{Y}{M}\frac{M}{P} = \frac{Y}{PQ} = 1.00 \qquad (6\text{-}11)$$

A unitary elasticity means each percentage change in the money supply is matched by an equal percentage change in the price level. Thus, again we see the primary conclusion of the "quantity theory" that the price level is set by and is proportional to the quantity of money.

**Illustration:**

Let $V_y = 4.00$  $Q = \$4000$  $M = \$1000$
From Eq. (6-5),

$$P = \left(\frac{V_y}{Q}\right)M \quad \text{or} \quad 1.00 = \left(\frac{4.00}{\$4000}\right)\$1000$$

In general, $P = (1/1000)M$
If $M$ is increased by 50% to \$1500, then $P$ must go to 1.50.
Thus,

$$P = \left(\frac{1}{1000}\right)(1500) = 1.50$$

The assumption that the price level is fixed and that the quantity of money circulating at a fixed velocity determines the level of output is methodologically symmetrical to the argument above, but it has not been a popular argument historically. Such assumptions if made would yield a linearly homogeneous relationship between the money supply and real output. Again, the implication would be that a given percentage increase in the money supply would yield the same percentage increase in real output and income.

## 2. The Cash Balances Approach

Another formulation of fixed relationships among the money supply, prices, and output is the so-called "cash balances approach." Under assumptions similar to that for the quantity theory, it gives identical results. This approach is based upon the identification of the "Cambridge $k$" which is the fraction of total income which the economy as a whole chooses to keep in the form of cash balances, or money. Thus, $k = m_y$ may be defined as

$$m_y = \frac{M}{Y} \qquad (6\text{-}12)$$

When Eq. (6-12) is compared to the definition of income velocity given by Eq. (6-2), it can be seen immediately that $m_y$ is merely the reciprocal of $V_y$, the income velocity.

$$m_y = \frac{1}{V_y} \tag{6-13}$$

Substitution of Eq. (6-3) into (6-12) yields

$$\frac{M}{m_y} = PQ \tag{6-14}$$

Taking the total differential of Eq. (6-14),

$$\frac{(m_y)\,(dM) - (M)\,(dm_y)}{m_y^2} = (P)\,(dQ) + (Q)\,(dP) \tag{6-15}$$

Under the assumptions that $m_y$ and $Q$ are constants, both $dm_y$ and $dQ$ are equal to zero, and Eq. (6-15) reduces to

$$\frac{dM}{m_y} = (Q)\,(dP)$$

or

$$\frac{dP}{dM} = \frac{1}{m_y Q} \tag{6-16}$$

As with the quantity theory, this approach implies a constant linear relationship between the money supply and the price level.

If prices instead of output are assumed constant, a constant linear relationship between the money supply and output is implied as given in Eq. (6-17).

$$\frac{dQ}{dM} = \frac{1}{m_y P} \tag{6-17}$$

## III THE DEMAND FOR MONEY AND THE LM CURVE

### 1. The Demand for Money

More recent monetary theory approaches the role of money in the economy more from the point of view of the microeconomic tools of supply and demand analysis than from the viewpoint of just velocity or cash balances, although these latter concepts are employed.

Let us assume that the supply of money is set exogenously by governmental or monetary authorities and explore the demand for money. Of course, in equilibrium, the quantity demanded must be equal to the quantity supplied. The demand for money must be distinguished from the desire for wealth. Wealth refers to the entire array of physical and financial assets, while money is just one particular form of wealth. Thus, the demand for money is the desire to hold a part of one's wealth in the form of cash balances. If everyone in the economy attempted to convert all his assets into money, everyone would be a seller of assets, but there would be no buyers. Velocity would fall to zero, desired cash balances would be infinitely greater than the available stock of money, the price level would move toward zero, and presumably real output would likewise move toward zero. The converse is also true. If suddenly the demand for money went to zero, everyone in the economy would be attempting to get rid of their money by buying other assets. Since there would be no sellers, however, velocity would move toward infinity, desired cash balances would be zero, and the price level would increase. In fact, either of these extremes is unlikely. Thus, the problem of this chapter is to discuss what determinants cause individuals to seek specified finite levels of cash balances.

Economists have long struggled with questions concerning the demand for money. In the process, they have developed a wide variety of overlapping motivations for holding cash, but most of them can be put in two broad classifications: the demand for money to conduct immediate or impending transactions, and the demand for money as a financial investment.

### THE TRANSACTIONS DEMAND

The imperfect synchronization of incomes and expenditures requires that individuals keep on hand a certain amount of cash balances so that they can carry out their ordinary transactions during the pay period. Since this demand for cash is likely to be a fairly stable fraction of income, the demand for transactions balances, $M_t$, can be written as being directly proportional to GNP, as given by Eq. (6-18).

$$M_t = m_y Y \qquad (6\text{-}18)$$

### THE INVESTMENT DEMAND

The second category, the demand for money as a financial investment, is more complex and likely to be more volatile. The utility of money as an investment is that its price is always the same and that it is always acceptable as a means of exchange. In other words, money represents pure "liquidity." Although money itself provides no interest return, it is delightful to possess when a lucrative investment opportunity or an unexpected expense presents itself. Moreover, since money earns no interest, its price cannot change when interest rates change. Bonds, however, offer fixed interest payments, and their prices therefore vary inversely with the market rate of interest. Thus, an investor who expects interest rates to be rising in the future would rather hold cash than bonds to avoid the potential capital loss from holding the bonds.

It must be pointed out that the utility of holding cash is not cost free since the money could have been used to purchase an interest-bearing asset. Thus, the cost of holding money is the return sacrificed on alternative financial investments. The higher the return on these other investments, the less desirable idle cash balances become. Thus, the implication of this section is that the investment demand for cash balances varies inversely with the rate of interest. At high rates of interest, not only is the cost of holding money very great, but also it may be expected that future interest rates will be declining, so that the owner of other financial assets will reap capital gains. At low rates of interest, the cost of holding money is low, and investment in any other asset may bring future capital losses. Accordingly, the investment or speculative demand for money, $M_s$, may be written as a decreasing function of the rate of interest.

$$M_s = m_0 - m_r r \tag{6-19}$$

In the past few years, the concept of speculative balances has received considerable criticism. The critics argue that the rational investor would not hold cash while awaiting a rise in interest rates as long as low-risk, short-term investment opportunities are available, such as open market paper and U.S. Treasury bills. The wise investor would invest his speculative balances in this type of asset, earn some rate of return, and yet liquidate easily when he wanted to shift to longer-term investments. In that case, speculative cash balances would be zero, and the demand for money would consist entirely of the transactions demand. However, this criticism, if true, would not mean that the demand for money would be completely insensitive to the market rate of interest. James Tobin has pointed out that if it is wise to invest speculative balances in short-term investments, it would also be wise to invest transactions balances in short-term investments.[1] Ideally, the entire receipts from any pay period would be invested immediately in financial assets. Then, as transactions were made, the assets would be sold to meet the amount of the transaction. In this manner, there is a perfect synchronization

[1] James Tobin, "The Interest Elasticity of the Transactions Demand for Cash," *Review of Economics and Statistics*, August 1956.

between the availability of cash and the making of expenditures. The purchase of financial assets is not cost free, however, since brokers' fees and other charges have to be paid. If the rate of interest is quite high, the rate of return on the investments might be great enough to justify selling a bill whenever a transaction has to be made. As the rate of interest decreases, however, the practice of selling assets as need dictates becomes unprofitable so the investor will make larger, periodic sales of bills and keep transactions balances on hand in cash in the interim periods. The lower the rate of interest, the fewer the sales, and the larger the transactions balances. In that case, the average level of transactions balances will be inversely related to the interest rate, and the transactions demand might be written as

$$M_t = m_0 + m_y Y - m_r r \qquad (6\text{-}20)$$

## 2. The LM Curve

If the money market is to attain equilibrium, the demand for money must be equated to the supply of money. If the total money supply is exogenously determined by the monetary authorities, this means that some combination of income and the rate of interest must be generated such that individuals want to hold in cash balances exactly as much as is being supplied. In terms of the symbols defined above,

$$M = M_t + M_s \qquad (6\text{-}21)$$

Substituting Eqs. (6-18) and (6-19) into (6-21) yields[2]

$$M = m_0 - m_r r + m_y Y \qquad (6\text{-}22)$$

which may be written in terms of $r$ or $Y$ as

$$Y = \frac{M + m_r r - m_0}{m_y} \qquad (6\text{-}23)$$

and

$$r = \frac{m_y Y - M + m_0}{m_r} \qquad (6\text{-}24)$$

[2] Note that if Eqs. (6-18) and (6-20) had been substituted into Eq. (6-21) instead of Eqs. (6-18) and (6-19), the form of Eq. (6-22) would not have been changed substantially.

Relevant partial derivatives from Eqs. (6-22) and (6-23) are given as follows:

$$\frac{\partial Y}{\partial M} = \frac{1}{m_y} > 0 \tag{6-25}$$

$$\frac{\partial Y}{\partial r} = \frac{m_r}{m_y} > 0 \tag{6-26}$$

$$\frac{\partial r}{\partial M} = -\frac{1}{m_r} < 0 \tag{6-27}$$

$$\frac{\partial r}{\partial Y} = \frac{m_y}{m_r} > 0 \tag{6-28}$$

Equations (6-23) and (6-24) indicate that once the money supply is fixed, the *LM* curve is defined as a straight line in the $r,Y$ plane. Both Eqs. (6-26) and (6-28) indicate that the line is positively sloped. The upward slope of the line can be explained intuitively by considering the impact in the money market of a change in the rate of interest. If the interest rate is increased, Eq. (6-19) indicates that less cash balances will be held for speculative demands. With the money supply held constant, the smaller speculative balances necessarily dictate larger transactions balances. If the ratio between transactions balances and income is constant, the larger transactions balances are consistent only with a larger level of income. Thus, *in equilibrium* (in the money market), an increase in the rate of interest implies an increase in the level of income.

The signs of Eqs. (6-25) and (6-27) indicate the impact on income and the interest rate in the money market from a change in the exogenous money supply. For example, an increase in the money supply means that more money is available for both transactions balances and speculative balances. For larger transactions balances to be demanded, equilibrium income must increase and, therefore, the sign of Eq. (6-25) is positive. On the other hand, speculative balances will be demanded in larger quantities only if the interest rate falls. Accordingly, the sign of Eq. (6-27) is negative.

The *LM* curve can also be derived from a velocity approach as well as the cash balances approach just used since one necessarily implies the other. The same rationale applied to holding smaller cash balances when interest rates are high can be phrased in terms of the public increasing the velocity of money in times of high interest rates, as easily shown by manipulation of previous equations. Dividing Eq. (6-22) by $M$ gives

$$1 = \frac{m_0 - m_r r}{M} + m_y V_y$$

or

$$V_y = \frac{M - m_0 + m_r r}{M m_y}$$

and

$$\frac{\partial V_y}{\partial r} = \frac{m_r}{M m_y} > 0$$

More simply, if we did not want to be absolutely consistent with the algebraic construction of our cash balances model, we could merely hypothesize that the equilibrium velocity is a positive, linear function of the rate of the interest as follows:

$$V_y = v_0 + v_r r = \frac{Y}{M} \qquad (6\text{-}22v)$$

Results analogous to those previously derived with the cash balances approach are as follows:

$$M = \frac{Y}{v_0 + v_r r} \qquad (6\text{-}22v)$$

$$Y = M(v_0 + v_r r) \qquad (6\text{-}23v)$$

$$r = \frac{Y}{M v_r} - \frac{v_0}{v_r} \qquad (6\text{-}24v)$$

$$\frac{\partial Y}{\partial M} = v_0 + v_r r = V_y > 0 \qquad (6\text{-}25v)$$

$$\frac{\partial Y}{\partial r} = M v_r > 0 \qquad (6\text{-}26v)$$

$$\frac{\partial r}{\partial M} = -\frac{Y}{v_r M^2} = -\frac{V_y}{v_r M} < 0 \qquad (6\text{-}27v)$$

$$\frac{\partial r}{\partial Y} = \frac{1}{M v_r} > 0 \qquad (6\text{-}28v)$$

In the following chapters, we shall utilize the cash balances formulation of the LM curve for its somewhat greater algebraic simplicity, but the student should be aware of the velocity approach, as much empirical research is conducted in terms of the velocity of money.

## 3. The "Liquidity Trap"

The argument in the previous paragraphs ignores an interesting possibility to which economists have given a great deal of attention. Equation

(6-27) indicates that the rate of interest varies inversely with the money supply because, in equilibrium, increased speculative balances will rise to absorb part of the increase in the money supply only if the interest rate is forced downward. However, it is possible that at some point in time the interest rate might be so low that it would be impossible to force it any lower. For example, the cost of writing a loan might be so great to a bank that it would be impossible for the bank to offer loans below a rate of interest of, say 2%. Moreover, if individuals feel that the only possible future course for the interest rate is upward, they will not be willing to purchase financial assets for fear of incurring capital losses. In this situation, any increase in the money supply will simply be "hoarded," or added to idle speculative balances. Thus, any increase in the money supply when the interest rate is at this minimum level will have no further impact on the interest rate.

The converse phenomenon might occur when interest rates are at such a high level that individuals believe they can go no higher. In this case, any decrease in the money supply will have to come out of transactions balances, as speculative balances are already at the absolute minimum, which might well be zero. No one wants to hold cash as a speculation, since it is believed that interest rates must fall and bond prices rise.

When we combine these two possibilities with the material developed earlier in this section, the relationship between speculative balances and the rate of interest is (as shown in Figure 6–1)

$$r = r_{\min} \qquad \text{when} \quad M_s > M_s^* \tag{6-29}$$

$$M_s = M_{s,\min} \qquad \text{when} \quad r > r^* \tag{6-30}$$

$$M_s = m_0 - m_r r \quad \text{when} \quad r^* > r > r_{\min}$$

$$M_s^* > M_s > M_{s,\min} \tag{6-19}$$

The corresponding $LM$ equations are therefore (as shown in Figure 6–2)

$$r = r_{\min} \quad \text{when} \quad Y < Y^* \tag{6-31}$$

$$Y = \frac{M}{m_y} - \frac{M_{s,\min}}{m_y} \quad \text{when} \quad Y = Y_{\max} \tag{6-32}$$

$$Y = \frac{(M + m_r r - m_0)}{m_y} \quad \text{when} \quad Y^* < Y < Y_{\max} \tag{6-23}$$

Over the range covered by Eq. (6-31), the interest rate is always equal to its minimum value, no matter what the level of income. In Eq. (6-32), once the money supply is known, income is equal to a constant that is determined by the total money supply and the minimum level of speculative balances but it is not determined even partially by the rate of interest.

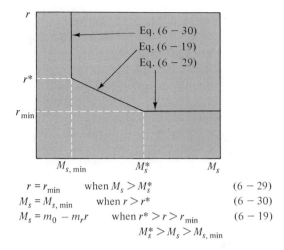

$$r = r_{min} \quad \text{when } M_s > M_s^* \tag{6-29}$$

$$M_s = M_{s,min} \quad \text{when } r > r^* \tag{6-30}$$

$$M_s = m_0 - m_r r \quad \text{when } r^* > r > r_{min} \tag{6-19}$$

$$M_s^* > M_s > M_{s,min}$$

**Figure 6–1**

Numerical examples of segmented curves of this type are given in the appendix to this chapter.

Equation (6-32) depicts a situation in which a "*modified* quantity theory of money" is applicable. In this less restricted version of the quantity theory, the money supply does not necessarily set the price level (or the level of output) but rather the level of total expenditures or national income. The level of total expenditures is set at what is indicated as $Y_{max}$ on the graph. If the

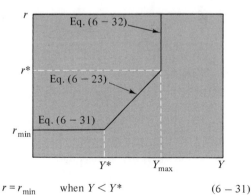

$$r = r_{min} \quad \text{when } Y < Y^* \tag{6-31}$$

$$Y = \frac{M}{m_y} - \frac{M_{s,min}}{m_y} \quad \text{when } Y = Y_{max} \tag{6-32}$$

$$Y = \frac{M + m_r r - m_0}{m_y} \quad \text{when } Y^* < Y < Y_{max} \tag{6-23}$$

**Figure 6–2**

supply of money is changed, this vertical *LM* curve will be shifted accordingly—to the right for an increase in the money supply and to the left for a decrease. Differentiating Eq. (6-32) with respect to the money supply, we obtain

$$\frac{dY}{dM} = \frac{1}{m_y}$$

Using this result to obtain the elasticity of total expenditures with respect to the money supply gives

$$\eta_{Y,M} = \left(\frac{dY}{dM}\right)\left(\frac{M}{Y}\right) = \left(\frac{1}{m_y}\right)\left(\frac{M}{M/m_y - M_{s,\min}/m_y}\right)$$

$$= \frac{M}{M - M_{s,\min}} > 1$$

(6-33)

If

$$M_{s,\min} = 0, \qquad \eta_{Y,M} = 1.00 \tag{6-34}$$

Equation (6-33) indicates that if the minimum level to which speculative balances have been driven by high interest rates is greater than zero, a given percentage change in the money supply will result in a larger percentage change in total expenditures. Equation (6–34) indicates that for changes in total expenditures to be exactly proportional to changes in the money supply, the speculative demand for money would have to be driven to zero.

## IV  FURTHER REFINEMENTS IN THE THEORY OF MONEY

The impact of a change in the money supply or a change in the public's desire to hold money is twofold. If the stock of money is increased, or if people decide that they want to hold less money, they may either (1) spend it on goods and services, increasing *Y*, or (2) buy financial assets with their excess cash balances, driving down *r*. Conversely, a decrease in the money supply or an increase in "liquidity preference" (a desire to hold larger cash balances) will be reflected in either (1) a decrease in the purchase of goods and services, decreasing *Y*, or (2) the sale of financial assets, which will drive interest rates up.

An important distinction is that the interest rate is the price of credit and can be thought of as depending on whether individuals choose to trade money for bonds (and drive rates down) or trade bonds for money (and drive rates up) as the system moves toward equilibrium. The aggregate price level $P$ is the inverse of the price of money as an economic good and, insofar as the money market is concerned, can be thought of as depending on whether the public chooses to shift from money into goods (driving $P$ up and the price of money down) or to shift from goods into money (driving $P$ down and the value of money up). These interest rate and price effects are parallel to (1) and (2) in the previous paragraph. Without knowledge of the magnitudes of the parameters $m_0$, $m_y$, and $m_r$, we cannot determine whether the effect of a change in the desire to hold cash balances or a change in the money supply will be dominated by a change in the rate of interest or a change in income.

A change in liquidity preference or the desire to hold cash balances implies that the parameters may shift, even if the money supply remains constant. The impacts of such possible shifts can be obtained by partial differentiation of Eqs. (6-22), (6-23), and (6-24). These derivatives show that an increase in $m_0$, the autonomous demand for cash balances, will increase interest rates but decrease the level of total expenditures. Changes in $m_r$ are accompanied by changes in income in the same direction, and interest rate changes in the opposite direction. Finally, a change in $m_y$ will cause income to move in the opposite direction and the interest rate to move in the same direction. This consideration of shifts in the parameters implies that the demand for cash balances and thus the velocity of money may not be stable functions. Although some empirical research has isolated the interest rate as a major factor in determining the demand for cash balances,[3] other more subjective factors such as price and interest rate *expectations* are also believed to be important.[4]

The concern over the stability of the parameters in the equations in this and other chapters has been the centerpiece of a recent controversy in economic literature. The analysis presented in Chapter 3 was based upon a model in which national income or total expenditures was a function of autonomously determined investment and government expenditures. In that model, it was shown that a change in autonomous expenditures would lead to a change in income that was a multiple of the change in autonomous expenditures. The value of the multiplier depended only on the value of the marginal propensity to consume. The more stable the *MPC*, the more exact is the empirical relationship between income and autonomous expenditures. An updated variant of the quantity theory of money described earlier suggests

---

[3] Henry A. Latane, "Cash Balances and the Interest Rate: A Pragmatic Approach," *Review of Economics and Statistics*, November 1954. Also, E. I. Whalen, "An Extension of the Baumol-Tobin Approach to the Transactions Demand for Cash," *Journal of Finance*, March 1968.

[4] J. M. Keynes, *The General Theory* (New York: Harcourt, Brace & World, Inc., 1936), Chapter 15.

a role for money that is very similar to the role played by autonomous expenditures described above. Consider Eq. (6-5):

$$MV_y = PQ = Y \tag{6-5}$$

If the velocity of money is constant, and the money supply changes, then

$$\frac{dY}{dM} = V_y$$

In that case, the money multiplier is equal to the velocity of money, and the level of national income would be directly proportional to the level of the money supply. Empirically, we would then expect changes in national income to correspond closely with changes in the stock of money. As a matter of fact, the modern quantity theory does not suggest that velocity is constant but merely that it is more stable than the autonomous expenditures multiplier. For example, differentiation of the previous Eq. (6-5) yields

$$dY = V_y \, dM + M \, dV_y$$

Then

$$\frac{dY}{dM} = V_y + M \frac{dV_y}{dM}$$

In essence, the modern quantity theorists argue that the term on the right-hand side of the previous equation is less variable than the marginal propensity to consume in the autonomous expenditures multiplier. Thus, the relationship among national income, autonomous expenditures, and the money supply in these two simple models depends on the stability of the underlying parameters. If velocity is more stable than the *MPC*, or if the determinants of velocity are more stable than the determinants of the *MPC*, then the modern quantity theory should give better predictions of national income than the autonomous expenditures theory. If velocity or its determinants are less stable than the *MPC* or its determinants, then the modern quantity theory should give worse predictions.[5]

Another important factor in the effect of changes in the money supply on the economy concerns lagged responses in the system. Some economists

---

[5] Milton Friedman, leading proponent of the modern quantity theory, and David Meiselman concluded from a study in the early 1960's "that as far as these data go, the widespread belief that the investment multiplier is stabler than the monetary velocity is an invalid generalization from the experience or three or four years. It holds for neither later nor earlier years." *Stabilization Policies*, prepared for the Commission on Money and Credit (Englewood Cliffs, N.J.: Prentice-Hall, Inc., 1963). See the comments by Ando and Modigliani and by DePrano and Mayer in the *American Economic Review*, September 1965.

who have built monetary models analytically similar to the multiplier-accelerator models of Chapter 4 contend that a long and variable lag exists before changes in the money supply result in changes in income, employment, and the interest rate. Because of this, they suggest that government's manipulation of the money supply has tended to destabilize the economy rather than to stabilize it. As an alternative, they suggest that the government forego short-run stabilization policy and instead merely increase the money stock each year by a percentage that will accommodate economic growth.[6]

A careful analysis of the problems and issues posed by the modern quantity theory is beyond the scope of this book. In fact, a deeper analysis would first call for consideration of alternative definitions of the money supply, the role of "near-monies," and appropriate means of empirical investigation. It should be noted here, however, that in most current empirical work *both* the autonomous expenditures approach and the monetary approach are incorporated into multi-equation models as important components. Chapter 7 makes the same type of incorporation and leaves the issue of stability of the underlying parameters of each to empirical research.

## NONMATHEMATICAL APPENDIX TO CHAPTER 6: GRAPHIC ANALYSIS

It may be helpful to develop a graphic explanation of the *LM* curve in much the same manner as the *IS* curve. Such a presentation is given by Figure 6–3. The graph in the lower right-hand corner represents the transactions demand for money and is given by the following equation:

$$M_t = 0.20\,Y$$

The upper left-hand graph represents the demand for speculative balances. The equation used here was

$$M_s = 250 - 2000r$$

The graph in the lower left-hand corner of Figure 6–3 depicts all possible ways in which the money supply may be divided among transactions and speculative balances. The bold line is constructed for a money supply of $200.

---

[6] See two more works of Milton Friedman: "A Monetary and Fiscal Framework for Economic Stability," *American Economic Review*, June 1948; and "The Lag in the Effect of Monetary Policy," *Journal of Political Economy*, October 1961. [For a reconsideration of some of his earlier views, see "The Optimum Quantity of Money," in *The Optimum Quantity of Money and Other Essays* (Chicago: Aldine Publishing Company, 1969).]

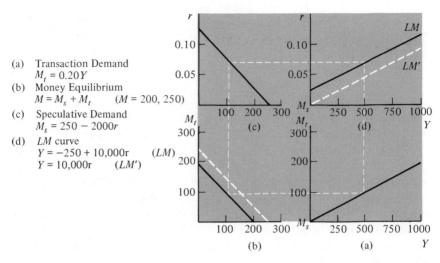

(a)  Transaction Demand
     $M_t = 0.20Y$
(b)  Money Equilibrium
     $M = M_s + M_t$      $(M = 200, 250)$
(c)  Speculative Demand
     $M_s = 250 - 2000r$
(d)  *LM* curve
     $Y = -250 + 10{,}000r$    $(LM)$
     $Y = 10{,}000r$          $(LM')$

**Figure 6–3**

As in the case of the graphic presentation of the *IS* curve, the scaling is the same for each of the graphs for any pair of adjoining vertical or horizontal axes. In order to construct the *LM* curve, any arbitrary starting point may be selected. For example, pick some income level (e.g., $Y = 500$) on the transactions demand in graph (a). After finding from graph (a) what transactions balances are called for by that income level, move horizontally to the left to graph (b) to see how much would be left for speculative balances (100) if that amount of transactions demand was subtracted from the fixed money supply of \$200. Then, move vertically upward to graph (c) to determine what interest rate (7.5%) will bring forth that speculative demand. Finally, the resulting interest rate and the original income starting point may be joined in graph (d) to form one point ($Y = 500$, $r = 7.5$) on the *LM* curve. The process may then be repeated enough times to find points sufficient in number to sketch in the *LM* curve. In this case, since only linear equations are employed, only two points will be necessary. The resulting curve is the bold line in graph (d).

In order to demonstrate the impact of a change in the money supply, a second *LM* curve has been added to Figure 6–3 for an increased money supply of \$250. As seen, the resulting *LM* curve is the broken line in graph (d) to the right of the bold line, demonstrating the validity of Eqs. (6-25) and (6-26).

Figure 6–4 shows the effect of incorporating Eqs. (6-29) and (6-30) into the model. For example, let

$$r_{\min} = 0.05 \quad \text{when } M_s > 150 \tag{6-29}$$

(a)   Transaction Demand
$M_t = 0.20Y$
(b)   Monetary Equilibrium
$M = M_s + M_t (M = 200, 250)$
(c)   Speculative Demand
$M_s = 50 \qquad r \geqslant 0.10 \ (c')$
$r = 0.05 \ (c'')$
$M_s = 250 - 2000r$
$0.05 < r < 0.10 \ (c''')$
(d)   LM curve
$M = 200$
$Y = 750 \qquad r \geqslant 0.10 \ (d')$
$r = 0.05 \ (d'')$
$Y = -250 + 10,000r$
$0.05 < r < 0.10 \ (d''')$
$M = 250$
$Y = 1000 \qquad r \geqslant 0.10$
$r = 0.05$
$Y = 10,000r$
$0.05 < r < 0.10$

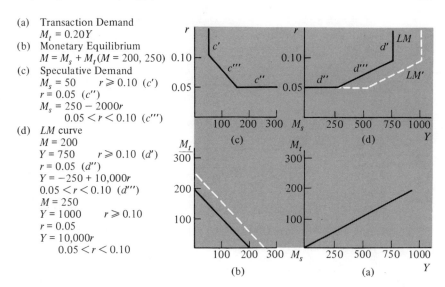

Figure 6–4

and

$$M_{s,\min} = 50 \qquad \text{when } r > 0.10 \qquad (6\text{-}30)$$

Thus, graph (c) in Figure 6–4 depicts three distinct portions of the demand for speculative balances. For rates of interest above 0.10, speculative balances are perfectly inelastic at a level of 50. Below an interest rate of 0.05, speculative balances are perfectly elastic.

Graph (d) in Figure 6–4 is the resulting $LM$ schedule after the inclusion of Eqs. (6-29) and (6-30). As long as the interest rate is set equal to 0.05, the minimum value, any level of income up to \$250 is possible. For interest rates greater than 0.10, the level of income remains fixed at \$750. The upward-sloping line between these two sections has the same equation as in Figure 6–3.

The broken line in Figure 6–4 indicates the result of an increase in the money supply to a level of 250. As seen, the entire $LM$ curve is shifted to the right by a constant amount, with the horizontal and vertical sections of the curve both remaining.

**EXERCISES**

1. Assume

$$M_t = 0.333\,Y$$

$$M_s = 150 - 10r$$

$$M = 180$$

    **a.** Find the equation of the *LM* curve.
    **b.** If the rate of interest is 10%, find the values of $Y$, $M_t$, $M_s$.

2. Using Eqs. (6-23) and (6-24), calculate the partial derivatives of $Y$ and $r$ each with respect to $m_0$, $m_r$, and $m_y$.

## RECOMMENDED REFERENCES

Ando, Albert, and Franco Modigliani, "The Relative Stability of Monetary Policy and Investment Multipliers," *The American Economic Review*, September 1965, pp. 693–728.

Boston Federal Reserve Bank, *Controlling Monetary Aggregates* (1969).

Brunner, Karl, and Allan H. Meltzer, "Predicting Velocity: Implications for Theory and Policy," *The Journal of Finance*, May 1963, pp. 319–59.

Culbertson, John M., "Friedman on the Lag in Effect of Monetary Policy," *The Journal of Political Economy*, December 1960, pp. 617–21.

DePrano, Michael, and Thomas Mayer, "Tests of the Relative Importance of Autonomous Expenditures and Money," *The American Economic Review*, September 1965, pp. 729–52.

Friedman, Milton, "A Monetary and Fiscal Framework for Economic Stability," *The American Economic Review*, June 1948, pp. 245–64.

———, "The Lag in Effect of Monetary Policy," *The Journal of Political Economy*, October 1961, pp. 447–66.

———, ed., *Studies in the Quantity Theory of Money*. Chicago: The University of Chicago Press, 1956.

———, and David Meiselman, "The Relative Stability of Monetary Velocity and the Investment Multiplier in the United States," in E. C. Brown *et al.*, *Stabilization Policies*. Englewood Cliffs, N.J.: Prentice-Hall, Inc., 1965.

Heller, H. R., "The Demand for Money: The Evidence of the Short-Run Data," *The Quarterly Journal of Economics*, May 1965, pp. 291–303.

Keynes, J. M., *The General Theory of Employment, Interest, and Money*. New York: Harcourt, Brace & World, Inc., 1936, Chapter 15.

Latane, Henry A., "Cash Balances and the Interest Rate: A Pragmatic Approach," *Review of Economics and Statistics*, November 1954, pp. 456–60.

Tobin, James, "The Interest Elasticity of the Transactions Demand for Cash," *Review of Economics and Statistics*, August 1966.

Whalen, E. L. "An Extension of the Baumol-Tobin Approach to the Transaction Demand for Cash," *Journal of Finance*, March 1968, pp. 113–34.

# 7 The Equilibrium Level of Aggregate Demand

Chapters 2, 3, and 4 have presented the basic structural relationships that make up the demand for goods and services at the macroeconomic level. These relationships, translated into equilibrium values, were then combined into a single equation, the *IS* curve, which expressed possible equilibrium values between national income and the rate of interest. Chapter 4 analyzed the nature of equilibrium between the supply of and the demand for money. This also led to a single equation, called the *LM* curve, expressing possible equilibrium values between income and the rate of interest. It is the purpose of this chapter to examine the simultaneous solution of both the *IS* and *LM* curves, at which point the commodity market and the money market will both be in equilibrium.

Section I is concerned with the simple algebraic statement of the equilibrium, while Section II analyzes changes in equilibrium resulting from shifts in the parameters in the underlying structural equations. Section III investigates how monetary and fiscal policy can be implemented to shift the equilibrium. Section IV is concerned with the dynamics of moving from one equilibrium position to another. Throughout the chapter, linear relationships will be assumed.

The results derived from our presentation of "aggregate demand theory" will be used with the theory of "aggregate supply" of Chapter 9 to present a theory of the equilibrium levels of output, prices, and employment in Chapter 10.

# I SIMULTANEOUS EQUILIBRIUM IN THE MONEY AND COMMODITY MARKETS

To repeat some of the analysis of previous chapters, the *IS* curve presents all possible combinations of national income and the rate of interest for which planned withdrawals from the income stream (saving and taxes) will be equal to planned injections into it (investment and government expenditures). In Chapter 5, this equation was obtained by the simultaneous solution of the consumption function, Eq. (2-15); the investment function, Eq. (4-10); a tax function, Eq. (2-17); an equilibrium condition, Eq. (5-11); and an accounting identity, Eq. (1-6). The resulting equation in two variables could then be expressed with income as an explicit function of the rate of interest or with interest as a function of the level of income. These were given in Eqs. (5-12) and (5-13):

$$Y = \frac{c_0 + c_y t_0 + i_0 + G - i_r r}{1 - c_y + c_y t_y} \tag{5-12}$$

$$r = \frac{c_0 + c_y t_0 + i_0 + G - (1 - c_y + c_y t_y)Y}{i_r} \tag{5-13}$$

For the money market, the LM curve presents all possible combinations of national income and the rate of interest for which the supply of money, determined exogenously by the monetary authorities, is equal to the total demand for money. The demand for money was determined in Chapter 6 by adding together the transactions demand, Eq. (6-18), and the speculative demand for cash balances, Eq. (6-19). Equating that sum with the fixed money supply yielded the LM curve, again with either income or the rate of interest serving as the dependent variable, [Eqs. (6-23) or (6-24)].

$$Y = \frac{M + m_r r - m_0}{m_y} \tag{6-23}$$

$$r = \frac{m_y Y - M + m_0}{m_r} \tag{6-24}$$

It seems intuitively obvious that if the economy as a whole is to be in equilibrium, each of the component markets must be in equilibrium as well. Moreover, the nature of the aggregate equilibrium will of course also require that the equilibrium levels of income and the rate of interest in each market be the same. In a single economy, there cannot be two different levels of national income prevailing simultaneously. Thus, the equilibrium level of national income may be found by solving the IS and LM equations simultaneously. The solution for national income may be found by setting Eq. (5-13) equal to Eq. (6-24), since both are equal to the rate of interest. Solving the resulting equation for $Y$ yields

$$Y = \frac{m_r(c_0 + i_0 + c_y t_0 + G) + i_r(M - m_0)}{m_r(1 - c_y + c_y t_y) + i_r m_y} \tag{7-1}$$

If the values for the parameters of the structural equations are known, and if levels of government spending and the money supply are given, then Eq. (7-1) can be solved for a determinate numerical value of national income that will be consistent with both the money and commodity markets.

The equilibrium value of the rate of interest may be found by setting Eq. (5-21) equal to Eq. (6-23). The solution for $r$ is

$$r = \frac{m_y(c_0 + i_0 + c_y t_0 + G) - (1 - c_y + c_y t_y)(M - m_0)}{m_r(1 - c_y + c_y t_y) + i_r m_y} \tag{7-2}$$

Again, the resulting value for the rate of interest will lead to equilibrium in both markets.

The attainment of simultaneous equilibrium in both markets can be demonstrated by referring to Figure 7–1. Suppose, for example, that an original level of income is set at $Y_1$ and a rate of interest at $r_1$, so that the commodity market is in equilibrium at point $A$. However, the money market

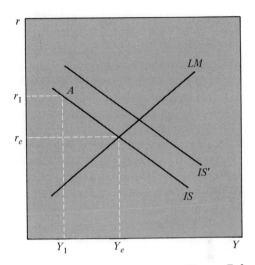

**Figure 7–1**

Simultaneous Equilibrium

is in disequilibrium. At the level of $Y_1$, very little cash is needed for trans-actions purposes, which frees a considerable amount for speculative balances. At the high rate of interest, however, the demand for speculative balances is also quite low, and people are not willing to hold that much. Thus, they attempt to reduce their balances by purchasing financial assets, which drives the rate of interest down. As the rate of interest falls, investment is stimulated via the marginal efficiency of investment schedule, and income is thus pushed upward via the multiplier. As income increases, more money is needed for transactions balances, which helps to eliminate the disparity between the demand for and the supply of money. The entire process continues until the rate of interest has fallen to $r_e$ and the level of income has increased to $Y_e$, at which point both markets are in equilibrium. Of course, this explanation is very much oversimplified and other explanations for the attainment of equilibrium may be given. A more complete discussion of the dynamics of attaining equilibrium will be given in Section IV of this chapter.

## II AUTONOMOUS CHANGES IN THE PRIVATE SECTOR

The equilibrium levels of national income and the rate of interest given by Eqs. (7-1) and (7-2) are conditional in the sense that they are dependent on the values of the parameters in the underlying structural equations. It is the purpose of this section to examine the impact of changes in these parameters upon the resulting equilibrium values. The net effect of these changes can be deduced from the two previous chapters and Figure 7-1. In Chapter 5, it was demonstrated that an increase in the *MPC* shifted the *IS* curve to the right. In Figure 7-1 this may be seen as a shift from *IS* to *IS'*. Since the upward-sloping *LM* curve has not shifted, the higher level of income demands more cash for transactions balances, leaving less for speculative demands. In order to increase the transaction balances, financial assets are liquidated, which has the impact of increasing the rate of interest, which in turn tends to restrict private investment. Again, the decrease in private investment exerts a contractionary influence on national income. The net result of all these changes is that a shift of the *IS* curve to the right raises income (but not by an amount as large as indicated in Chapter 5) and the rate of interest. It is left to the reader to demonstrate for himself why a rightward shift of the *LM* curve increases income but lowers the rate of interest.

More complete analysis of parameter shifts are presented in the following sections.

## I. Changes in the Consumption Function

The impact on national income and the rate of interest of a change in the consumption function can be assessed by evaluating the sign of the partial derivatives of Eqs. (7-1) and (7-2) with respect to $c_y$ (the marginal propensity to consume):

$$\frac{\partial Y}{\partial c_y} = \frac{m_r t_0}{m_r(1 - c_y + c_y t_y) + i_r m_y}$$
$$+ \frac{[m_r(c_0 + i_0 + G + c_y t_0) + i_r(M - m_0)]m_r(1 - t_y)}{[m_r(1 - c_y + c_y t_y) + i_r m_y]^2}$$
$$= \frac{m_r t_0 + m_r Y(1 - t_y)}{m_r(1 - c_y + c_y t_y) + i_r m_y}$$
$$= \frac{m_r(Y - T)}{m_r(1 - c_y + c_y t_y) + i_r m_y} > 0 \tag{7-3}$$

$$\frac{\partial r}{\partial c_y} = \frac{[m_y t_0 + (M - m_0)(1 - t_y)] - r(m_r t_y - m_r)}{m_r(1 - c_y + c_y t_y) + i_r m_y}$$
$$= \frac{m_y t_0 + (1 - t_y)(M - m_0 + m_r r)}{m_r(1 - c_y + c_y t_y) + i_r m_y}$$
$$= \frac{m_y(Y - T)}{m_r(1 - c_y + c_y t_y) + i_r m_y} > 0 \tag{7-4}$$

Since all coefficients in this book have been assigned positive values, the denominators of Eqs. (7-3) and (7-4) will be positive as long as the standard assumption is met that $1 - c_y + c_y t_y$ is greater than zero. The bracketed term in the numerator is merely disposable income, which will also be positive. Thus, an increase in the *MPC* will result in higher equilibrium values of income and the rate of interest.

## 2. Changes in the Investment Function

It was demonstrated in Chapter 5 that an increase in $i_r$, the interest rate coefficient in the investment function, will move the *IS* curve to the left. Interaction of this change with the money market should therefore lower the levels of both income and the rate of interest. By differentiation of Eqs. (7-1) and (7-2) with respect to $i_r$,

$$\frac{\partial Y}{\partial i_r} = \frac{M - m_0 - m_y Y}{m_r(1 - c_y + c_y t_y) + i_r m_y}$$

$$= \frac{-m_r r}{m_r(1 - c_y + c_y t_y) + i_r m_y} < 0 \qquad (7\text{-}5)$$

$$\frac{\partial r}{\partial i_r} = \frac{-m_y r}{m_r(1 - c_y + c_y t_y) + i_r m_y} < 0 \qquad (7\text{-}6)$$

The derivatives, Eqs. (7-5) and (7-6), are clearly negative, which proves the previous statement. If the value of $i_r$ increases, the intercept $i_0$ remaining constant, both income and the rate of interest will fall.

## 3. Changes in the Demand for Money

Alterations in the structural coefficients in the money market will also have impacts on national income and the rate of interest. These changes can come about through changes in the value of $m_y$ that reflects the income motives for holding cash or in the value of $m_r$ that is related to the interest motives for holding cash.

### CHANGES IN $m_y$

A change in the value of $m_y$ can come about for several reasons. First, transportation or banking improvements might increase the velocity of money and therefore reduce the value of $m_y$. Or, the use of credit cards and overdraft privileges might cause individuals to reduce the average balances in their checking accounts. Whatever the reason for the change, the net impact can be gauged by partial differentiation of Eqs. (7-1) and (7-2) with respect to $m_y$.

$$\frac{\partial Y}{\partial m_y} = \frac{-i_r Y}{m_r(1 - c_y + c_y t_y) + i_r m_y} < 0 \qquad (7\text{-}7)$$

$$\frac{\partial r}{\partial m_y} = \frac{(c_0 + c_y t_0 + G + i_0) - i_r r}{m_r(1 - c_y + c_y t_y) + i_r m_y} > 0 \qquad (7\text{-}8)$$

Since $i_r$ is positive, the numerator of Eq. (7-7), and therefore the entire term, is less than zero. Accordingly, an increase in $m_y$ lowers the level of national income. Since Eq. (7-8) is positive, however, the same increase in $m_y$ will increase the rate of interest.

### CHANGES IN $m_r$

An increase in the value of $m_r$, other things remaining constant, means that for any level of the rate of interest less cash will be demanded for speculative balances than was previously demanded at that rate of interest. Thus, the attempt to reduce speculative balances by investment in financial assets should reduce the rate of interest and therefore increase national income. By partial differentiation,

$$\frac{\partial Y}{\partial m_r} = \frac{(c_0 + c_y t_0 + G + i_0) - Y(1 - c_y + c_y t_y)}{m_r(1 - c_y + c_y t_y) + i_r m_y}$$

$$= \frac{i_r r}{m_r(1 - c_y + c_y t_y) + i_r m_y} > 0 \qquad (7\text{-}9)$$

$$\frac{\partial r}{\partial m_r} = \frac{-(1 - c_y + c_y t_y)r}{m_r(1 - c_y + c_y t_y) + i_r m_y} < 0 \qquad (7\text{-}10)$$

Again, Eq. (7-9) is obviously positive, while Eq. (7-10) is negative, indicating the truth of the previous statement.

## III  CHANGES IN POLICY VARIABLES

The variables examined in the previous section are structural parameters that are determined by the aggregate behavior of individuals. They are the result of individual habits, propensities, and desires, as well as of the entire social, political, and economic institutions of the system. Accordingly, they are not given to easy or straightforward manipulation by governing bodies.

Thus, if regulatory agencies are to be able to exert some control or guidance over the behavior of national income and the rate of interest, they must look elsewhere. A cursory examination of Eqs. (7-1) and (7-2) indicates that the variables which are subject to regulation are $M$, the money supply; $G$, the level of government expenditures; and $t_y$, the tax rate. Control over the money supply falls under the heading of *monetary policy*, while adjustments in the level of government spending and the tax rate are said to constitute *fiscal policy*.

Section I below examines some aspects of fiscal policy while Section II is addressed to monetary policy. Section III is concerned with some interesting interrelationships between the two types of policy.

## I. Fiscal Policy—Changes in G and $t_y$

The impact on the economy of changes in the level of governmental expenditures or the tax rate can be examined exactly in the same manner as employed in the previous section, by partial differentiation of Eqs. (7-1) and (7-2).

$$\frac{\partial Y}{\partial G} = \frac{m_r}{m_r(1 - c_y + c_y t_y) + i_r m_y} > 0 \tag{7-11}$$

$$\frac{\partial r}{\partial G} = \frac{m_y}{m_r(1 - c_y + c_y t_y) + i_r m_y} > 0 \tag{7-12}$$

$$\frac{\partial Y}{\partial t_y} = \frac{-m_r c_y Y}{m_r(1 - c_y + c_y t_y) + i_r m_y} < 0 \tag{7-13}$$

$$\frac{\partial r}{\partial t_y} = \frac{-[c_y(M - m_0) - m_r c_y r]}{m_r(1 - c_y + c_y t_y) + i_r m_y}$$

$$= \frac{-c_y(M - m_0 + m_r r)}{m_r(1 - c_y + c_y t_y) + i_r m_y}$$

$$= \frac{-c_y m_y Y}{m_r(1 - c_y + c_y t_y) + i_r m_y} < 0 \tag{7-14}$$

The signs of Eqs. (7-11) through (7-14) indicate that an increase in government expenditures increases both national income and the rate of interest, while an increase in the tax rate lowers both. Thus if governmental authorities desire to stimulate the level of national income, they may do so either by increasing expenditures or decreasing the tax rate. Which technique should be employed depends on what effects upon the *composition* of national output are desired. If more public goods such as roads or schools are desired, the proper approach would be to augment government spending in these areas. If it is desirable that the private sector should increase its role in the economy, however, the increase in income should be sought by lowering the tax rate. Of course, the two could be used in combination.

The balanced budget theorem has been mentioned several times in previous chapters, each time in a slightly different context. As stated before, the crux of this theorem is that if a change in government expenditures is offset by an opposite change in taxes, there will still be a resulting change in national income. Considering the commodity market only, it was shown that the resulting change in income would be equal to the change in government expenditures.

When consideration of the money market is added to the balanced budget theorem, the basic conclusion is altered slightly. In this case, an increase in government spending that is offset by increased taxes will still lead to increased national income, but the increase will not be so large as the increase in government spending. The reason for this is that the increase in income requires larger balances for transactions purposes. As shown above, this increase can be generated only by smaller speculative balances and hence, a higher rate of interest. Thus the increase in income will be constrained by decreased private investment. The results can be demonstrated algebraically:

$$dT = t_y\,(dY) + Y\,(dt_y) = dG$$

$$dt_y = \frac{dG - t_y\,(dY)}{Y}$$

$$dY = \frac{\partial Y}{\partial G}\,(dG) + \frac{\partial Y}{\partial t_y}\,(dt_y)$$

$$= \frac{\partial Y}{\partial G}\,(dG) + \frac{\partial Y}{\partial t_y}\left[\frac{dG - t_y\,(dY)}{Y}\right]$$

$$= \frac{m_r\,(dG) - m_r c_y\,(dG) + t_y m_r c_y\,(dY)}{m_r(1 - c_y + c_y t_y) + i_r m_y}$$

$$dY\left[1 - \frac{m_r c_y t_y}{m_r(1 - c_y + c_y t_y) + i_r m_y}\right] = dG\left[\frac{m_r(1 - c_y)}{m_r(1 - c_y + c_y t_y) + i_r m_y}\right]$$

which simplifies to

$$dY = \left[\frac{m_r(1 - c_y)}{i_r m_y + m_r(1 - c_y)}\right] dG$$

$$dY = \left[\frac{1}{1 + i_r m_y/m_r(1 - c_y)}\right] dG \qquad (7\text{-}15)$$

since

$$0 < \frac{1}{1 + i_r m_y / m_r (1 - c_y)} < 1.00 \qquad dY < dG$$

## 2. Monetary Policy—Changes in $M$

Regulatory authorities can also affect the level of national income and the rate of interest by changing the money supply, $M$. Since it has previously been shown that an increase in the money supply has the effect of shifting the $LM$ curve to the right, it can be deduced that the consequence of this policy would be to increase national income and lower the rate of interest. Again, this can be demonstrated by partial differentiation of Eqs. (7-1) and (7-2).

$$\frac{\partial Y}{\partial M} = \frac{i_r}{m_r(1 - c_y + c_y t_y) + i_r m_y} > 0 \qquad (7\text{-}16)$$

$$\frac{\partial r}{\partial M} = \frac{-(1 - c_y + c_y t_y)}{m_r(1 - c_y + c_y t_y) + i_r m_y} < 0 \qquad (7\text{-}17)$$

Exactly how the money supply is to be changed is of no particular concern at this point. Chapter 8 is devoted to an examination of the money supply and the banking system. What matters here is that *if* the money supply is increased, equilibrium will only be reattained when the demand for cash balances increases to equal the new money supply. The adjustment mechanism in this case will be that after the increase in the money supply, individuals find that aggregate cash balances are larger than their desired balances. Thus, they try to lower their actual balances by investing in financial assets, thereby driving down the interest rate. The effect of this is to stimulate investment and increase the level of income to the point where the larger transactions and speculative balances equal the new money supply.

## 3. The Interaction between Fiscal Policy and Monetary Policy

The previous two sections treat fiscal policy and monetary policy as though they might be employed independently of each other. While this is of course possible, it is much more reasonable that they should be used in conjunction with each other. Some examples of possible interactions between these policies are given below.

### A Constant Interest Rate

As an example of the joint utilization of monetary policy and fiscal policy, consider the problems posed by a large increase in government expenditures, say to finance a national emergency. If an increase in taxes is not feasible at the time, the increased expenditures will result in increased income and a higher rate of interest. However, it may be contrary to national social policy to allow the interest rate to increase at that time, so monetary policy could be employed to keep the interest rate constant. Manipulation of Eq. (7-2) may be used to illustrate what relationship is required between the increase in government expenditures and the increase in the money supply in order to maintain the constant interest rate. Assuming that the tax rate remains constant ($dt_y = 0$), the total differential of Eq. (7-2) is

$$dr = \frac{m_y\,(dG) - (1 - c_y + c_y t_y)\,(dM)}{m_r(1 - c_y + c_y t_y) + i_r m_y}$$

For $dr$ to be zero,

$$\frac{dM}{dG} = \frac{m_y}{1 - c_y + c_y t_y} \tag{7-18}$$

If $c_y = 0.8$, $t_y = 0.25$, and $m_y = 0.25$, then

$$\frac{dM}{dG} = \frac{0.25}{0.40} = \frac{5}{8}$$

In other words, if the money supply is increased by \$5 for every increase in government expenditures of \$8, then the rate of interest will be held constant. Of course, since the money supply is increased, it will also be true that income will expand beyond what would have been generated by an increase in government expenditures alone. The reader may verify for himself that the resulting change in income is the same in this case as it would have been had the *IS* curve alone been examined.

Equation (7-18) can also be looked upon as the ratio of two multipliers. Let $1/(1 - c_y + c_y t_y)$ be designated as $(\partial Y/\partial G)IS$, which is the government-spending multiplier for the *IS* curve, the rate of interest remaining constant. Analogously, $1/m_y = (\partial Y/\partial M)LM$ may be called the money supply multiplier for the *LM* curve, the rate of interest remaining constant. Note that these are merely derivatives from Eqs. (5-12) and (6-23). Then Eq. (7-18) can be written as

$$\frac{dM}{dG} = \left(\frac{\partial Y}{\partial G}\right)IS \div \left(\frac{\partial Y}{\partial M}\right)LM \qquad \text{when} \quad dr = 0 \tag{7-19}$$

In other words, the ratio of the change in the money supply to the change in government expenditures must be equal to the ratio of their multipliers.

### A CONSTANT LEVEL OF AGGREGATE DEMAND

There are also occasions when governmental authorities might seek interest changes without wanting to affect the level of total expenditures in the economy. For example, it may be proper policy to attempt to increase the interest rate in hopes of improving a balance of payments position. In order to negate the impact of the rising rate of interest on investment expenditures and thus upon national income, governmental expenditures would have to increase. If there is to be no net change in income, the total differential of Eq. (7-1) must again be zero.

$$dY = \frac{m_r(dG) + i_r(dM)}{m_r(1 - c_y + c_y t_y) + i_r m_y} = 0$$

or

$$\frac{dM}{dG} = -\frac{m_r}{i_r} \tag{7-20}$$

If $i_r = 1.20$ and $m_r = 0.20$,

$$\frac{dM}{dG} = -\frac{0.20}{1.20} = -\frac{1}{6}$$

Government expenditures would have to increase by $6 for every dollar decrease in the money supply if a given level of income was to be maintained. Analogous to the previous section, Eq. (7-20) can be rewritten in terms of interest rate multipliers taken from Eqs. (5-13) and (6-24).

$$\frac{dM}{dG} = \left(\frac{\partial r}{\partial G}\right) IS \div \left(\frac{\partial r}{\partial M}\right) LM \quad \text{when} \quad dY = 0 \tag{7-21}$$

As above, the ratio of the change in the money supply to the change in government expenditures must be equal to the ratio of their multipliers.

### THE BALANCED BUDGET THEOREM

Section III–1 of this chapter has demonstrated that in the combined commodity and money markets an increase in government expenditures matched by an equal increase in taxes does not lead to an increase in GNP equal to the increase in government expenditures. If the money supply remains constant, the increased rate of interest will force private investment expenditures to decrease and thereby dampen the rising income. This section addresses itself to the problem as to what monetary policy must be employed if the interest rate is to be held constant so that the familiar "unit multiplier" for the balanced budget can be obtained.

Total differentiation of Eq. (7-2), allowing $G$, $T$, and $M$ to vary, yields

$$dr = \frac{m_y(dG) - (1 - c_y + c_y t_y)(dM) - c_y m_y Y(dt_y)}{D} \tag{7-22}$$

where

$$D = m_r(1 - c_y + c_y t_y) + i_r m_y$$

Setting $dr$ equal to zero,

$$dM = \frac{m_y (dG) - m_y c_y Y (dt_y)}{1 - c_y + c_y t_y} \tag{7-23}$$

If the change in government expenditures is to be equal to the change in taxes,

$$dt_y = \frac{dG - t_y dY}{Y} \tag{7-24}$$

Finally, the change in income resulting from changes in expenditures, taxes, and the money supply can be assessed by looking at the total differential of Eq. (7-1).

$$dY = \frac{m_r (dG) - m_r c_y Y (dt_y) + i_r (dM)}{D} \tag{7-25}$$

Substitution of Eqs. (7-23) and (7-24) into (7-25) gives:

$$dY = \frac{m_r}{D} dG - \left(\frac{m_r c_y Y}{D}\right) \left(\frac{dG - t_y dY}{Y}\right) + \frac{i_r}{D} m_y dY$$

$$dY \left(1 - \frac{m_r c_y t_y + i_r m_y}{D}\right) = \frac{(1 - c_y) m_r dG}{D}$$

$$dY[m_r(1 - c_y + c_y t_y) + m_y i_r - m_r c_y t_y - i_r m_y] = (1 - c_y) m_r dG$$

$$dY[m_r(1 - c_y)] = m_r(1 - c_y) dG$$

$$dY = dG \tag{7-26}$$

Thus, the money supply must be increased by an amount given by Eq. (7-23) if the change in national income is to be equal to the change in government expenditures.

## 4. Two Extreme Cases

The analysis to this point has assumed that the $LM$ curve is an upward-sloping relationship between total expenditures $Y$ and the interest rate $r$. Important modifications of the previous analysis result, however, when the possible horizontal and vertical sections of the $LM$ curve are considered.

First, consider the equilibrium level of aggregate demand when the *IS* curve intersects a horizontal section of the *LM* curve, called the *liquidity trap*. The solution to this question is given by simultaneous solution of Eqs. (5-12) and (6-29), presented in Eq. (7-27).

$$Y = \frac{c_0 + c_y t_0 + G + i_0 - i_r r}{1 - c_y + c_y t_y} \tag{5-12}$$

$$r = r_{\min} \tag{6-29}$$

$$Y = \frac{c_0 + c_y t_0 + G + i_0 - i_r r_{\min}}{1 - c_y + c_y t_y} \tag{7-27}$$

Notice that the money supply variable, $M$, does not appear in Eq. (7-27). Thus,

$$\frac{\partial Y}{\partial M} = 0$$

The conclusion here is that when interest rates are at the minimum possible level, any increase in the money supply will be added to idle speculative balances, since at the minimum interest rate the demand for money is infinitely elastic with respect to the rate of interest. Therefore, no downward pressure on the interest rate is possible, and no new investment will be induced by the larger money supply. The level of aggregate demand is unaffected. However, aggregate demand is still sensitive to both the level of government expenditures, $G$, and the tax rate, $t_y$, with government expenditures and the tax multipliers given by Eqs. (3-15) and (5-26). The obvious implication for government policy here is that when the economy is to be stimulated and interest rates are abnormally low, monetary policy is likely to be less effective than fiscal policy.

A second extreme case results when the *IS* curve intersects a vertical segment of the *LM* curve; this is given by Eq. (6-32).

$$Y = \frac{M - M_{s,\min}}{m_y} \tag{6-32}$$

As mentioned earlier, this phenomenon could result when interest rates are so high that speculators almost universally believe that they will be falling shortly. Thus, speculative balances are at a minimum, $M_{s,\min}$, as investors anticipate that large capital gains can be made on substantial bond holdings. In this case, as shown in Eq. (6-32), aggregate demand is a function only of $M$, $M_{s,\min}$, and $m_y$ but not $r$. Thus, when the three values on the right-hand side of Eq. (6-32) are given, aggregate demand is known and constant.

Nothing in the commodity market will affect its value. Accordingly,

$$\frac{\partial Y}{\partial G} = \frac{\partial Y}{\partial t_y} = 0$$

This case is obviously the reverse of the previous example. Fiscal policy is totally ineffective upon aggregate demand, whereas the money supply still exerts an impact. The money multiplier is given by Eq. (7-28).

$$\frac{\partial Y}{\partial M} = \frac{1}{m_y} \tag{7-28}$$

The two examples presented here are often cited as the "Keynesian" and "classical" cases because of the widely differing views of John M. Keynes and an earlier group of British economists often referred to as classical in their beliefs. The student should guard against the careless use of these labels, however, as other "Keynesian-classical" differences are also quite prominent, the more important of which will be considered in Chapters 9 and 10.

## IV DYNAMICS AND PROBLEMS OF ADJUSTMENT

The model described in the immediately previous sections is a static one. For any given set of values of the parameters and policy variables, the equilibrium solution can be determined, and a new equilibrium can be found if any of those parameters or variables are changed. However, such a model completely ignores the problems associated with the process of adjustment to the new equilibrium. This section attempts to look at some of the simpler concepts of such adjustment.

### 1. A Simple Adjustment Model

The investment function described in the previous model, Eq. (4-10), is unrealistic because it does not allow investment to increase unless the rate of interest falls. In fact, however, investment increases are often accompanied by rising interest rates, so some relevant variable is probably omitted from Eq. (4-10). In view of the fact that increasing income probably increases business optimism about future profits, many economists argue that national income should be included as a determining variable in the investment function. For simplicity, we shall assume that the relationship between investment and its determinants is a simple linear function, as given by Eq. (7-29).

$$I_t = i_0 - i_r r_t + i_y Y_t \tag{7-29}$$

Thus, investment is a simple function of the rate of interest and the level of income.

Incorporating Eq. (7-29) into the commodity market yields the following equation for the *IS* curve:[1]

$$Y_t = \frac{i_0 + c_0 + G_t - i_r r_t}{1 - i_y - c_y + c_y t_y} \tag{7-30}$$

Note that the slope of the *IS* curve, $dr_t/dY_t$, is given by

$$\frac{dr_t}{dY_t} = \frac{1 - i_y - c_y + c_y t_y}{-i_r} \tag{7-31}$$

This slope may be either positive or negative, depending on the relationship between $i_y$ and $1 - c_y(1 - t_y)$. If $1 - c_y(1 - t_y)$ is less than $i$, then the *IS* curve will have a positive slope, contrary to usual expectations.

Using the framework developed so far in this section, we may now trace out some of the adjustment processes to see if a shift in one of the parameters automatically produces a movement to a new equilibrium. Specifically, let us suppose that there is an increase in the money supply. Furthermore, let us also assume that, in the adjustment process, the rate of interest always adjusts instantaneously to changes in the money market but that there is a one-period lag before the level of income responds. Additionally, suppose that the amount of adjustment in income depends on the difference between planned investment and planned saving in the previous period. If that difference was zero, the earlier period was an equilibrium period, and there should be no further adjustments beyond that. If investment was greater than saving, income should increase. Thus, let

$$Y_t - Y_{t-1} = \alpha(I_{t-1} - S_{t-1}) \quad \text{where} \quad \alpha > 0 \tag{7-32}$$

By substitution of the investment function and savings function into Eq. (7-32),

$$Y_t - Y_{t-1} = \alpha[i_0 - i_r r_{t-1} + i_y Y_{t-1} + c_0 - (1 - c_y + c_y t_y) Y_{t-1}] \tag{7-33}$$

[1] For purposes of this discussion the tax function is assumed to be $T = t_y Y$.

Substituting Eq. (6-23) into (7-33) to remove $r_{t-1}$ gives

$$Y_t - Y_{t-1} = \alpha \left[ i_0 - \frac{i_r}{m_r}(m_y Y_{t-1} - M + m_0) + i_y Y_{t-1} \right.$$

$$\left. + c_0 - (1 - c_y + c_y t_y)Y_{t-1} \right] \quad (7\text{-}34)$$

which simplifies to the form

$$Y_t = A + BY_{t-1} \quad (7\text{-}35)$$

where

$$A = \alpha \left[ i_0 + c_0 + \left( \frac{i_r}{m_r} \right)(M - m_0) \right]$$

$$B = 1 + \alpha \left[ i_y - \left( \frac{i_r}{m_r} \right)m_y - (1 - c_y + c_y t_y) \right]$$

The general solution to Eq. (7-35) is

$$Y_t = \frac{A(1 - B^t)}{1 - B} + B^t Y_0 \quad (7\text{-}36)$$

An equilibrium position $Y_t = Y_{t-1} = Y_{t-2} = Y_e$ will be reached only if $B^t$ approaches zero as $t$ gets very large. This will occur only if $B$ is a fraction. Thus,

$$-1 < B < 1$$

or

$$-1 < 1 + \alpha \left[ i_y - \left( \frac{i_r}{m_r} \right)m_y - (1 - c_y + c_y t_y) \right] < 1 \quad (7\text{-}37)$$

Examining the right-hand inequality of Eq. (7-37) to determine if the expression is less than unity,

$$\alpha \left[ i_y - \left( \frac{i_r}{m_r} \right)m_y - (1 - c_y + c_y t_y) \right] < 0$$

Since $\alpha$ is positive,

$$i_y - \frac{i_r}{m_r}m_y - (1 - c_y + c_y t_y) < 0$$

or

$$\frac{m_y}{m_r} > \frac{1 - c_y + c_y t_y - i_y}{-i_r} \quad (7\text{-}38)$$

Eq. (7-38) implies that the slope of the *LM* curve must be greater than the slope of the *IS* curve if the adjustment process is to lead to a stable equilibrium. Such a condition will be met if the *IS* curve has a negative slope, as normally assumed, or if a positively sloped *IS* curve is less steeply sloped than the positively sloped *LM* curve. The following cases serve to illustrate this point.

### Case 1

*IS* is negatively sloped. Figure 7–2 illustrates the conventional *IS* and *LM* curves. Let point *S* be the original equilibrium determined by $IS_1$ and $LM_1$. Then, allow the money supply to increase so that $LM_2$ becomes the appropriate curve. The new equilibrium will be at point $U(r_2, Y_2)$, but that point will not be reached immediately. The first response to the increased money supply will be the instantaneous reaction by the rate of interest, as it falls to the lower level of $r_3$. At the lower rate of interest, however, income is still at $Y_1$, private investment will increase and rise above saving. Thus, income will be forced up and saving will respond to the increased income. As income rises, more money is needed for transactions purposes that reduces the amount available for speculative balances and thus causes the rate of interest to increase. The adjustment process continues as long as the rate of interest is below $r_2$. When the rate has finally risen to $r_2$, planned

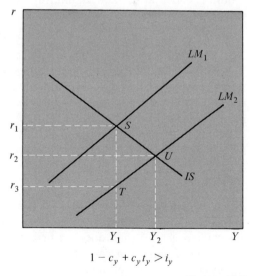

$$1 - c_y + c_y t_y > i_y$$

**Figure 7–2**

Attainment of Equilibrium—Case 1

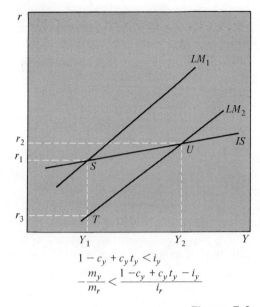

$$1 - c_y + c_y t_y < i_y$$

$$-\frac{m_y}{m_r} < \frac{1 - c_y + c_y t_y - i_y}{i_r}$$

**Figure 7-3**

Attainment of Equilibrium—Case 2

saving and planned investment are again equated, and the adjustment procedure is ended at the new equilibrium level.

### CASE 2

*IS* is positively sloped, but less steep than *LM*, as illustrated in Figure 7-3. In this case, the adjustment process is very much the same as in Case 1. An increase in the money supply initially causes the rate of interest to fall to $r_3$, which causes investment to increase. The increased investment causes income and saving to rise in turn, and the demand for transactions balances forces the interest rate upward. The only real difference is in the final equilibrium since $r_2$ will be higher than $r_1$ even though the money supply increased.

### CASE 3

As illustrated in Figure 7-4, *IS* is positively sloped and steeper than *LM*. In this case the second equilibrium position occurs at both lower income and lower interest rates than does the first. However, there is no way by which the second equilibrium can be reached. The initial increase in the money supply forces the rate of interest down to a level of $r_3$ but investment and income again start to rise after that, always moving away from the new equilibrium, $r_2$. In other words, investment is so sensitive to the level of income

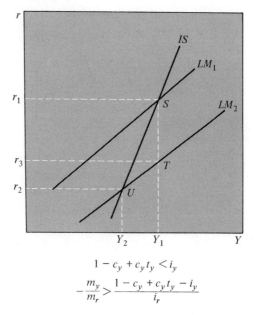

$$1 - c_y + c_y t_y < i_y$$

$$-\frac{m_y}{m_r} > \frac{1 - c_y + c_y t_y - i_y}{i_r}$$

**Figure 7–4**

Attainment of Equilibrium—Case 3

($i_y$ is large) that investment always increases more rapidly than saving does. Thus the gap between the two constantly increases and income must perpetually increase also. The equilibrium here is unstable.

## EXERCISES

**1.** Using your solutions to Problem 1 of Chapter 5 and Problem 1 of Chapter 6, solve for equilibrium values of $Y$, $r$, $M_s$, $M_t$, $C$, $S$, $I$, and $T$.

## RECOMMENDED REFERENCES

McKenna, Joseph P., *Aggregate Economic Analysis*. 3rd ed. New York: Holt, Rinehart and Winston, Inc., 1969.

# 8 The Banking System

# and Money Creation

## I WHAT IS MONEY?

A platitude as true as it is trite is that "money is as money does." Money is whatever happens to be the generally accepted means of exchange in a particular economic system. Historically it has been everything from rocks to cattle. Economists generally list a few or many of the whole host of characteristics that are desirable in the particular tangible good to be used as money. These characteristics include such things as high value to weight, easy identifiability, and durability. Typically a number of additional monetary functions are given besides the "medium of exchange" function, such as serving as a store of value, as a means of deferred payment, and as a means of comparing the market value of heterogeneous goods. Any commodity that is generally acceptable in exchange for other goods will necessarily be useful in these roles as well. The prime requisite of money is that it be generally acceptable in exchange for other goods at an exchange ratio that has some degree of certainty.

NOTE: Those not desiring an introduction to monetary theory and its relationship to contemporary money and banking arrangements in the United States may skip this chapter without detriment to their comprehension of the following chapters.

The requirement that money be readily acceptable in exchange for other goods at an exchange ratio (or price) that has some degree of certainty is merely to say that money has what economists have come to call "liquidity." Of course, all goods with some economic value have *some* liquidity and thereby some degree of "moneyness." Everything from real estate to a pile of iron ore has some value in exchange and can serve as a store of value through time. Most goods have a low degree of liquidity since they are not widely acceptable in exchange. You must find someone who wants to barter for them; or, more realistically, you must first sell these goods for money and then buy the goods for which you desire to exchange. It is obvious that even though real estate and iron ore can be used in exchange and can serve as a store of value, they are not money. The distinguishing characteristic of the social invention called money (it would be of no use to Robinson Crusoe) is that it serves no other purpose than to provide liquidity to the economy. The real estate and the iron ore have economic value based on something other than the small amount of liquidity they may provide; pure money has no other value.

The fact that liquidity is the essence of moneyness makes the definition of what constitutes the money supply at any historical point in time subject to a certain amount of arbitrary judgment. We can exclude real estate and iron ore easily enough and include paper currency; but what about a savings deposit, a government bond due to mature tomorrow, or an insurance policy with immediately available cash value? These last named items are certainly very liquid assets. There is the whole panorama of economic assets, real and financial, each of which provides its owner with some degree of liquidity. As a matter of convention, most economists define the money supply to include only currency and demand deposits. For some particular empirical studies, savings deposits are also included. For the remainder of this chapter, we shall use the "demand deposits plus currency" definition of money, although the last section will give some consideration to the other very liquid assets called "near moneys."

## II MONEY CREATION UNDER A "100% RESERVE CURRENCY SYSTEM"

### I. Under a Full Commodity Standard

The creation of the money supply in an economy has varied historically and varies substantially throughout the world today. The money supply in any advanced country must, however, to a greater or lesser degree be administered by a central government. In early stages of economic development this was not always the case. In some instances, where gold was the money supply, the amount in circulation was set by how much was dug out of the ground, and the citizens devised their own ways to guarantee the purity and weight of what they gave and received in payment. Coins apparently came into use as a result of the guarantee of the government that they contained a certain weight of precious metal of a specified purity. Without belaboring the historical development, it should be apparent to the reader that but a short step was required for the government to start holding the precious metal or other commodity "in reserve" and issuing a paper note stating that the government held a certain amount of the commodity on deposit that would be available to the holder of the note on demand. The paper money was more convenient than the commodity so few people ever redeemed it as long as their faith in the government held up.

In this presentation we shall use "gold" as our commodity. The reader should remember that this is strictly for illustrative purposes. Many other commodities have historically been used, and in principle *any* economic good could similarly be adopted.

With the government holding the commodity on reserve and the notes circulating as currency (but rarely being redeemed for gold), there was always the temptation for the government to violate the "100% reserve" rule and issue notes in excess of the amount of the commodity held. As we are for the moment speaking of 100% reserve currency systems, however, let us assume that government note issue is strictly limited by the amount of gold presented to it in exchange for notes. This means that the money supply in the hands of the public, $M$, is equal to the face value of the notes in circulation, $N$, plus whatever gold may be held by the public and circulating as currency, $G_p$.

$$M = N + G_p \qquad (8\text{-}1)$$

Under the 100% reserve rule the maximum amount of notes that can be issued is equal to the gold held by the government, $G_g$:

$$N_{\max} = G_g \qquad (8\text{-}2)$$

Therefore, the maximum amount of money in the system is equal to the total amount of gold in the system $G$:

$$M_{\max} = N_{\max} + G_p = G_g + G_p = G \qquad (8\text{-}3)$$

As a result, Eq. (8-1) defining the money supply at any point in time must be constrained by the following inequality:

$$M \leq M_{\max} = G \qquad (8\text{-}4)$$

If the government always issues the maximum amount of notes available to it, the actual money supply will always equal the maximum money supply and we need only look at the total amount of gold in the system to determine the money supply. The dynamics are very simple since changes in the gold stock coming about through domestic production and consumption or gains or losses through foreign trade will change the publicly held supply dollar for dollar.

$$\frac{dM_{\max}}{dG} = 1.00 \qquad (8\text{-}5)$$

However, the government can draw money out of the private economy by taxing, $T$, or borrowing, $B$, to a greater extent than it spends, $E$, during any particular time period.

$$\Delta M_t = E_t - T_t - B_t \qquad (8\text{-}6)$$

Conversely, the government can increase the privately held money supply up to the maximum by allowing its expenditures in any given time period to exceed the amount of money it withdraws through taxing and borrowing from the public. These increases must of course not exceed previous decreases. That is,

$$\Delta M_t \leq \sum_{i=0}^{t-1} (T_i - E_i + B_i) \qquad (8\text{-}7)$$

Making Eq. (8-6) subject to the constraint of Eq. (8-7) indicates that the government may decrease the money supply by taxing or borrowing money out of circulation virtually without limit (down to a zero money supply), but it can only increase the money supply by an amount equal to the excess of its previous tax revenues and borrowings over its previous expenditures.

The mechanics of the system remain unchanged if we modernize it a bit by including a banking system and demand deposits. The government can, and historically did, charter one or more banks to accept the gold and issue the bank notes. If, instead of bank notes, the banks choose to issue demand deposits redeemable in gold, the system is unchanged as long as the 100% reserve requirement remains in effect. The interrelationships among government spending, taxing, and borrowing and the money supply stand as presented above. One need only change $N$ for notes to $D$ for demand deposits in the foregoing equations.

## 2. Under a Fiat Money System

We continue our discussion of a 100% reserve currency system, but we remove the requirement for gold or some other commodity reserves. We refer to such a system as a "fiat" money system because we are discussing money that is money simply because the government says it is. This is not the place to argue whether government fiat is sufficient to make the item the generally accepted means of exchange, so we shall only point out that making fiat money the acceptable means of payment for taxes and the only satisfactory payment for "debts public and private" to be enforced by the courts goes a long way toward that end.

How does such money get into circulation? The government must spend it or lend it into circulation or give it away. The difference between a fiat money system and the commodity reserve system is that rather than monetizing a particular commodity upon presentation the government merely monetizes its own expenditures by having no offsetting taxation. Since the government has an infinite supply of fiat money, it can control the money in the hands of the public in either a positive or negative direction as indicated by Eq. (8-6), and the constraint of inequality (8-7) setting the maximum money supply no longer applies.

At this time we should point out why this chapter has concerned itself with the money supply in the hands of the public and not considered the government's stock of money also. Although the concept of the government's stock of money has some meaning under a commodity reserve currency, in a fiat money system the publicly held money supply is the *only* relevant money supply. The government can issue its notes at will. The money comes into existence when spent by the government, and it ceases to exist when received by the government in payment of taxes or as the proceeds of borrowing from the public. Under a fiat money system the concept of the government's stock of money ceases to have any relevance.

Returning to the consideration of the modern form of the banknote, the demand deposit, let us set up a government agency to make sure that the banks do not issue more demand deposits than they have in reserves, which are the original fiat money issued by the government. We shall call this agency the Federal Reserve System, or the "Fed" for short. The Fed will, in accordance with the 100% reserve requirement, require that each bank have on deposit with it an amount of reserves, $R$, equal to the total amount owed to the public in the form of demand deposits, $D$. We shall also allow for some of the fiat money not to be converted to demand deposits but to remain in the hands of the public and circulate as currency, $C$. Our complete monetary system is made up of the following set of identities (and various others which can be generated from these):

$$M = D + C$$

The money supply is made up of demand deposits plus currency.

(8-8)

$$\Delta M = \Delta D + \Delta C$$

Changes in the money supply must come about through changes in demand deposits or currency.

(8-9)

$$D = R$$

The banks must keep reserves on deposit with the Fed equal to their demand deposit liability.

(8-10)

$$\Delta R + \Delta C = E - T - B$$
$$= \Delta M$$

Changes in bank reserves and currency must equal the net cash outflow (or inflow) of the government that equals the change in the money supply.

(8-11)

Every net expenditure of the government must go either into the hands of the public as currency in circulation or into the Fed as reserves for demand deposits. In this system the money supply will change dollar for dollar in response to fiscal policy, an increase in the money supply resulting from a deficit and a decrease resulting from a surplus. The money supply will also change dollar for dollar in response to government borrowing activities or "monetary policy" as it has come to be called. If the government borrows from the public, the money supply will be reduced. If the government pays off maturing debt or buys it in the open market, the money supply will be increased accordingly.

In a 100% reserve system with fiat money reserves, the government sets the money supply, the public decides the division of the money supply between currency and demand deposits, and the banks have no influence on either. The banking system creates no addition to the money supply as in some systems we shall consider below. The two outstanding features of this system are that with no upper limit the government has complete discretion in setting the money supply and the linkages between government action and the money supply are direct and dollar for dollar. No cooperation is required from the private sector.

## III MONEY CREATION UNDER A FRACTIONAL RESERVE SYSTEM

### 1. Gold or Other Commodity Standard

As implied by the subtitle, the basic difference between the monetary system to be discussed here and that discussed under the 100% reserve heading is that reserves of something less than 100% are required. We assume that the government or the banks are no longer restricted in their issuance of notes (currency) or demand deposits to the amount that is backed dollar for dollar by gold or some other commodity. In this particular monetary system it is of no consequence whether we are talking about banknotes partially backed by gold or demand deposits with the same reserve requirement. To simplify matters, we shall ignore the banknotes and merely use demand deposits as a proxy for banknotes plus demand deposits.

Under a required reserve of $K$, with $K$ assumed to be less than unity, the maximum amount of demand deposits that can be issued is

$$D_{\max} = \frac{G_b}{K} \qquad K < 1.00 \tag{8-12}$$

where $G_b$ is the gold on deposit with the banks. For example, if $K = \frac{1}{2}$, the total amount of demand deposits that could be created is twice the amount of gold reserves held by the banking system.

This system allows the banking system to create demand deposits for lending to private borrowers or the government and thereby create more money than it has commodity reserves, but there is an absolute ceiling on what the total demand deposits can be. That ceiling is proportionately related to the commodity reserves in the hands of the banking system as indicated by Eq. (8-12).

This situation is not just the 100% reserve commodity case with a higher ceiling, however. A basic difference is that the public now has a hand in setting the ceiling on the money supply. A dollar's worth of gold or other commodity in the hands of the public is just a dollar in the money supply; however, if it is deposited in a bank, it can serve as reserves for $1/K$ dollars of demand deposits. Conversely, if a citizen exercises his right under such a system to demand payment in gold for his demand deposit, he reduces the maximum demand deposits by a factor of $1/K$ and the maximum total money supply by $1/K - 1$. In the limit, if the citizens demand all the gold reserves held by the banking system, there will be no demand deposits, the money supply will equal the supply of gold, and we are back to 100% reserve currency.

Not only does the private citizen have a role in setting the maximum level of the money supply under this system but also a role in determining its actual level below this maximum through his borrowing activities. For the banking system to create more demand deposits than they have given in exchange for commodity reserves placed with them, the banks must create demand deposits by lending to the public or government. If neither wants to borrow, the demand deposits will not be created. Whether or not the banking system actually does the maximum amount of lending allowable under the reserve requirement and the available gold reserves is a critical question. This system can be considered as two somewhat different monetary systems depending on whether the banking system has used all its reserves and is "loaned up" or whether the banks have "excess reserves" on hand. While we shall consider each of these situations separately, the reader should remember that the "loaned up" situation is really just a constraint within which the "excess reserves" system operates.

### COMPLETE UTILIZATION OF RESERVES, BANKS "LOANED UP"

Under the assumption that the banking system does in fact utilize each dollar of commodity reserves available to it to provide reserves for $1/K$ dollars in demand deposits, our monetary system is composed of the following relationships:

$$M = G_p + D$$

The money supply is composed of the gold held by the public and the demand deposits.

(8-13)

$$D = \frac{G_b}{K}$$

Total demand deposits are equal to the gold reserves held by the banks divided by the reserve requirement.

(8-14)

or

$$G = G_p + G_b$$

$$G_b = G - G_p$$

The total gold in the system is the sum of that held by the public and that held by the banks.

(8-15)

Substituting Eqs. (8-14) and (8-15) into (8-13) gives

$$M = G_p + \frac{G - G_p}{K} \tag{8-16}$$

If the total amount of the commodity in the system, $G$, is assumed constant and the amount circulating as money is subject to change as a result of the public withdrawing it from the banking system in exchange for bank deposits or vice versa, the following relationship would hold:

$$\frac{\partial M}{\partial G_p} = 1 - \frac{1}{K} < 0 \tag{8-17}$$

Since $K < 1.00$, $1 - 1/K$ must be negative; that is, an increase in the gold holdings of the public taken from the gold reserves of the banks will result in a net reduction in the money supply. Conversely, if the public deposits some of its gold holdings in the banking system in exchange for demand deposits, there will be a net increase in the money supply.

If, on the other hand, we assume the public's gold holdings, $G_p$, are fixed and the total amount of gold in the system, $G$, changes (and thereby changes the banks' reserves accordingly), the following relationship would follow from the partial differentiation of Eq. (8-16):

$$\frac{\partial M}{\partial G} = \frac{1}{K} > 0 \tag{8-18}$$

With $K$ less than one, this is a multiple change in the money supply resulting from gold production or consumption within the economy or gains and losses in foreign trade. This is on the assumption that the entire change in the gold stock is reflected in a change in the gold reserves of the banks. To the extent that a change in an economy's gold stock results in a change in the amount of gold held as currency by the public, its effect on the money supply will be exactly equal to the change in the gold stock.

INCOMPLETE UTILIZATION OF RESERVES; BANKS HAVE
"EXCESS RESERVES"

If we consider a more realistic system in which the commodity reserves are not fully utilized, we must examine in greater detail the process of the utilization of bank reserves. At this point let us consider the banking system as one large bank with many branches. If $100 worth of the monetary commodity, say gold, is deposited in the bank in exchange for a $100 demand deposit, the money supply is not immediately affected, as gold money is substituted for deposit money. The bank is required to hold only some percentage, $K$, in reserves, however, and for this $100 of deposits it now has a 100% reserve in gold. If the reserve requirement is 50% and thereby $K = 0.5$, the bank has $50 in "excess reserves" as that term is ordinarily used. Actually, the banking system has $100 of unused money creating power since the $100 worth of gold can support $200 of demand deposits with a required reserve of 50%. The bank could lend this additional $100 to a businessman by giving him a demand deposit in that amount in exchange for his promissory note for $100 and still be within the rules of the game. If, however, loan demand were weak or for some other reason the bank did not lend the full $100, the additional demand deposits simply would not be created. For example, if the bank lent only $50, the money supply accruing from this $100 addition to the bank's reserves would result in only a $50 addition to the money supply. The important point here is that lending by the banking system to the public (or to the government) is absolutely necessary to the money creation process. Conversely, a reduction in bank loans results in a reduction in the money supply.

Algebraically our monetary system under these conditions can be expressed by the following relationships:

$$M = G_p + D$$ The money supply consists of the gold held by the public plus demand deposits.

(8-13)

$$D = G_b + B_{bp} + B_{bg}$$ Demand deposits are equal to the commodity reserves held by the banking system plus borrowing from the banks by the public ($B_{bp}$) and by the government ($B_{bg}$).

(8-19)

$$G_b = G - G_p$$ The commodity reserves held by the banks equal the total commodity in the system less that held by the public.

(8-15)

Substituting the definition of $G_b$ given in Eq. (8-15) into (8-19) and then substituting the resulting definition of $D$ into Eq. (8-13) gives the following relationship between the money supply and the other relevant variables:

$$M = G + B_{bp} + B_{bg}$$

The total money supply equals the supply of the monetary commodity plus the total borrowings from banks by the public and the government.

(8-20)

This relationship differs significantly from Eq. (8-16), which assumed that the banks always found enough borrowers to utilize all their commodity reserves. The amount of gold in circulation, $G_p$, is no longer a factor in setting the total money supply; only the total gold in the system, $G$, is relevant. In this situation there is a one-for-one correspondence between the money supply and changes in the gold in the system and between the money supply and changes in the borrowing from the banks by the public or the government:

$$\frac{\partial M}{\partial G} = \frac{\partial M}{\partial B_{bp}} = \frac{\partial M}{\partial B_{bg}} = 1.00 \qquad (8-21)$$

One further important difference in this system from those previously discussed is that it makes a difference whether the government finances a deficit by borrowing from the nonbank public or from the banking system. If it borrows demand deposits from the nonbank public and spends the full amount, the money supply will be unchanged. If, however, the government finances a deficit by borrowing from the banking system, it induces money creation through the utilization of excess reserves adding dollar for dollar to the money supply as indicated in Eqs. (8-20) and (8-21) above.

## 2. A Fiat Money System

A fractional reserve fiat money system is basically what we have in the United States. However, since there are a great many features of this system which are peculiar to this country, specific discussion of the United States monetary system as such will be reserved for the next section. This section will be confined to a discussion of the characteristics common to any system of this type. Again, we have the problem of whether the banking system is fully utilizing its reserves to generate demand deposits or whether it has excess reserves. Let us consider each of these in turn, remembering that the former is a constraint within which the latter must operate.

## BANKS "LOANED UP"; NO EXCESS RESERVES

In a fiat money system the reserves are, of course, made up of fiat money, that is, claims on the government or central bank. These reserves can come into being only when the government runs a deficit or pays off its outstanding indebtedness to the banks or the public. This money can circulate as currency, in which case it does not serve as bank reserves. It is only when this fiat money is deposited in a bank that it becomes usable as reserves.

Let us assume, as before, that by law the banking system must have a claim against the central government (reserves) equal to a fraction, $K$, of its demand deposit liability. If the banking system has no reserves in excess of those required for its current level of demand deposits, we can be sure that

$$D = \frac{R}{K}$$ 
Demand deposits equal the available reserves divided by the fractional reserve requirement.

(8-22)

Defining the money supply as demand deposits plus currency, we obtain the following relationships:

$$M = D + C \tag{8-23}$$

$$M = \frac{R}{K} + C \tag{8-24}$$

resulting from the substitution of Eq. (8-22) into (8-23). This maximum level of the money supply is set by the level of reserves held by the banking system, $R$, and the currency held by the public, $C$. However, the public has the right to demand currency for its demand deposits and the option of depositing currency to gain a demand deposit. Such flows of currency in and out of the banking system affect the reserves available to the banking system and thereby the total stock of money. Assuming the government does nothing to change the level of total fiat money outstanding, $F$, the sum of bank reserves plus the currency held by the public must equal that amount:

$$R + C = F \quad \text{or} \quad R = F - C \tag{8-25}$$

Substituting the definition of $R$ given in the second formulation of Eq. (8-25) into (8-24) gives

$$M = \frac{F - C}{K} + C \tag{8-26}$$

Taking the partial derivative of the money supply with respect to the currency in the hands of the public gives

$$\frac{\partial M}{\partial C} = 1 - \frac{1}{K} < 0 \qquad (8\text{-}27)$$

which is negative since $K$ is less than unity. Equation (8-29) indicates that the money supply will change in the opposite direction of changes in the currency in the hands of the public with the magnitude of the change dependent on the required reserve ratio, $K$. For example, if the required ratio is 20%, $K = 0.2$, $1/K = 5$, and a \$1 increase in the currency held by the public (drawn out of the banks) will require that \$5 of demand deposits cease to exist. The net effect is a \$4 decrease in the money supply as demand deposits are reduced \$5 and currency in circulation is increased by \$1.

Let us now consider the government's role in setting the total amount of currency and bank reserves in the economy, $F$. Any net cash inflow or outflow in the government's accounts will change $F$ on a dollar-for-dollar basis, and such a net flow must necessarily change the sum of bank reserves plus currency in circulation accordingly. This relationship, discussed earlier under the 100% reserve system as Eq. (8-11), must now be changed to read

$$\Delta F = \Delta R + \Delta C$$
$$= E - T - B \neq \Delta M$$

A change in the total fiat money outstanding will result in an equal change in the sum of bank reserves plus currency and can only come about by a net cash outflow (or inflow) of the government; but it will not necessarily equal the change in the money supply.

$$(8\text{-}28)$$

The effect of such a change in $R + C$ will, as indicated by Eq. (8-24), depend on the division of this fiat money outflow between that which circulates as currency and that which finds its way into the banking system in exchange for demand deposits. Assuming the currency in circulation holds constant, we may differentiate Eq. (8-26) with respect to $F$ and obtain

$$\frac{\partial M}{\partial F} = \frac{1}{K} \qquad (8\text{-}29)$$

Equation (8-29) indicates that as $F$ is changed and thereby $R$ (assuming $C$ is held constant), there will be a change in the same direction by some multiple thereof, $1/K$, since $K$ is less than unity but greater than zero. For example, assume $K = 0.2$. If in a particular period the government spent \$100 more than it took in via taxes and borrowing, the potential increase in the money supply resulting from the full utilization of the reserves so created would be $500; (1/0.2)($100) = $500.

Except for changes in the desire of the public for currency holdings (which in some cases turn out to be relatively stable, or at least predictable), the government under this system could set bank reserves about where it wanted them via fiscal policy ($E$ and $T$) and monetary policy ($B$). If, as we have been assuming, the banks consistently utilized all these reserves for deposit creation, the government would have rather firm control over the total money supply. Unfortunately, the full utilization of bank reserves at all times does not describe the performance of any particular economy, so we must now consider the situation in which there is incomplete utilization of reserves.

### INCOMPLETE UTILIZATION OF RESERVES; BANKS HAVE "EXCESS RESERVES"

This system differs from the commodity fractional reserve system with excess reserves only in the respect that gold or some other commodity does not provide the bank reserves but instead claims on the government are used as reserves. As noted in the commodity reserve system, the banking system creates demand deposits in two ways: by accepting a deposit of something usable as reserves or by making a loan to the public or to the government. As a result,

$$D = R + B_{bg} + B_{bp}$$

Total demand deposits equal bank reserves plus borrowing from the banks by the government, $B_{bg}$, plus borrowing from the banks by the public, $B_{bp}$.

$$(8\text{-}30)$$

As noted earlier, all fiat money injected into the system by the government must either be deposited in the banks to create an equal amount of bank reserves or be held by the public as currency in circulation:

$$F = C + R \quad \text{or} \quad R = F - C \qquad (8\text{-}25)$$

Substituting the definition of $R$ given in Eq. (8-25) into (8-30) gives

$$D = F - C + B_{bg} + B_{bp} \leq \frac{F - C}{K} \qquad (8\text{-}31)$$

Since, as noted by Eq. (8-23), the money supply is defined as demand deposits plus currency or $M = D + C$, we may now substitute the factors determining demand deposits as given by Eq. (8-31) for $D$ and obtain the following statement of the determinants of the money supply when excess reserves are available:

$$M = F + B_{bg} + B_{bp}$$

$$\leq C + \frac{F - C}{K}$$

The money supply is equal to the total fiat money (currency and reserves) plus the government's borrowing from the banks plus the public's borrowing from the banks.

(8-32)

An alternative formulation is

$$M = C + R + B_{bg} + B_{bp} \tag{8-33}$$

The dynamics of changes in the money supply under this system are somewhat more complex. Taking first differences of Eq. (8-33) gives

$$\Delta M = \Delta C + \Delta R + \Delta B_{bg} + \Delta B_{bp} \tag{8-34}$$

The total supply of fiat money in the system (currency plus bank reserves) can only be changed by a net cash flow into or out of the government; that is,

$$E - T - B = \Delta F$$

$$= \Delta C + \Delta R$$

In any given period the sum of government expenditures minus tax receipts minus net borrowings will equal the change in the supply of fiat money that will equal the change in currency in circulation plus the change in reserves.

(8-28)

The term $B$ used in Eq. (8-28) is a *flow* of money to the government resulting from borrowings over a given period of time. The $B_{ij}$ terms used in Eq. (8-33) are *stocks* of outstanding borrowings that have resulted from a flow of money from $i$ to $j$. The first differences of these variables are, however, *flows* for a particular time period. The first difference of borrowings from the banks by the government, $\Delta B_{bg}$, and from the banks by the public, $\Delta B_{bp}$, is a flow of money for a given accounting period. The flow of borrowing of the government from the economy, $B$, can be divided into borrowings from the banks, $\Delta B_{bg}$, and government borrowings from the nonbank public, $\Delta B_{pg}$:

$$B = \Delta B_{bg} + \Delta B_{pg}$$

For any period, government borrowing is the sum of borrowings from the banks by the government and borrowings from the public by the government.

(8-35)

Substituting Eq. (8-35) into (8-28) gives

$$E - T - \Delta B_{bg} - \Delta B_{pg} = \Delta F = \Delta C + \Delta R \tag{8-36}$$

Substituting Eq. (8-36) for $(\Delta C + \Delta R)$ in Eq. (8-34) gives us the mechanics of the changes in the stock of money:

$$\Delta M = E - T - \Delta B_{pg} + \Delta B_{bp}$$

The change in the money stock in any given period will equal government expenditures minus tax receipts minus net borrowings from the public by the government plus net borrowings from the banks by the public.

(8-37)

The money supply will be increased dollar for dollar in accordance with government expenditures and increases in indebtedness to the banks by the public. The money supply will be reduced dollar for dollar with tax collections and the borrowings of the government from the nonbank public. The government's borrowings from the banks, $B_{bg}$, is not a determinant of the money supply in this model because such action causes an equal number of dollars to be created in demand deposits by the act of borrowing from the banks and to be withdrawn from circulation as the government removes them from the private sector. We are assuming that the government keeps all of its balances on deposit with itself (or in a government central bank). If, however, the government immediately spent the proceeds of such a loan from (or sale of securities to) the commercial banking system, government expenditures, $E$, would increase and thereby increase the money supply accordingly. On the other hand, if the government financed an increase in expenditures by borrowing from the nonbank public, $\Delta B_{pg}$ and $E$ would have equal and offsetting values and the money supply would remain unchanged.

## IV THE MONETARY MECHANISM OF THE UNITED STATES

The reader is warned that this section gives only a skeletal outline of the monetary mechanism of the United States and will not enable him to fully utilize the detailed monetary statistics available from government and private sources any more than Chapter 1 made him an analyst of the national income accounts.

The monetary system of the United States is basically a fractional reserve fiat money system, the last one considered in the previous section of this chapter. All the results derived above are, generally speaking, applicable to the present-day system of the United States. There is one notable exception, the creation of additional fiat money (bank reserves) by the central bank lending directly to commercial banks, called "discounting."

## I.  Required Reserves, Excess Reserves, and Net Free Reserves

The three terms given in the subheading are institutional terms peculiar to the U.S. banking structure. To understand them, we must consider the practice in this country of the government (specifically, a regional Federal Reserve Bank) lending reserves directly to individual banks. Let us designate the stock of reserves so created as $R_d$ as it is termed "discounting." The terminology comes from the fact that it was originally set up to allow the individual bank to "discount" or sell business loans to the central bank. Most such discount loans today are secured by U.S. government securities rather than business loans.

Allowing for these discount loans by the central bank to the banking system, we must now change Eq. (8-25) that stated that total reserves, $R$, is the total amount of fiat money created in the system minus the currency in circulation, $R = F - C$. If we wanted to count this lending by the Federal Reserve to the banking system as negative government borrowing and thereby to be included in the fiat money creation, $F$, no change would be required; but our present purposes will be better served if we differentiate between the reserves obtained through discount operations of the Federal Reserve and reserves coming into the banking system through other means. This requires that we restate Eq. (8-25) as

$$R = F - C + R_d$$

Total reserves equal total fiat money from government spending, taxing, and borrowing activities minus currency in circulation plus reserves made available through Federal Reserve discount loans to banks.

(8-38)

The three terms "required reserves," $R_r$; "excess reserves," $R_x$; and "free reserves" or sometimes "net free reserves," $R_f$, are defined as follows:

$$R_r = KD$$

Required reserves equal the legal required percentage reserve, $K$, times the total demand deposits.

(8-39)

$$R_x = R - R_r$$

Excess reserves equal the total reserves in the banking system minus those required by the current level of demand deposits.

(8-40)

$$R_f = R_x - R_d$$

Free reserves equal the excess reserves minus those reserves obtained by borrowing directly from the Federal Reserve System, i.e., by "discounting."

(8-41)

The levels of these particular items are frequently discussed in the literature on money and banking as important guides to the state of the economy and the results of governmental policies. Therefore, it is useful to go behind the definitions to find the determinants of each of these items. We have discussed in some detail the determinants of total reserves accruing from the government's creation of fiat money. The possibility of the banks borrowing from the central bank merely introduces a new source of funds and, of course, total bank reserves will vary on a one-for-one basis with reserves made available through discounting. Also, we need spend no further time on the level of required reserves as it is simply the legal reserve ratio times the deposit level and we have previously discussed the determinants of the level of demand deposits. Therefore, let us turn to the determinants of the level of excess reserves. Substituting Eqs. (8-38) and (8-39) into (8-40) gives

$$R_x = F - C + R_d - KD \qquad (8\text{-}42)$$

We can now substitute the equation

$$D = F - C + B_{bg} + B_{bp} \qquad (8\text{-}31)$$

into Eq. (8-42) and obtain

$$R_x = (1 - K)(F - C) + R_d - K(B_{bp} + B_{bg}) \qquad (8\text{-}43)$$

Partial differentiation of Eq. (8-43) reveals some important properties:

$$\frac{\partial R_x}{\partial K} = -(F - C) -$$
$$(B_{bp} + B_{bg}) < 0$$

Excess reserves vary inversely with the reserve requirement.

(8-44)

$$\frac{\partial R_x}{\partial F} = 1 - K > 0$$

Excess reserves vary directly with the amount of fiat money put into the system by the government if the amount of currency held by the public does not change.

(8-45)

$$\frac{\partial R_x}{\partial C} = K - 1 < 0$$

Excess reserves vary inversely with holdings of currency by the public, assuming the total fiat money in the system does not change.

(8-46)

$$\frac{\partial R_x}{\partial R_d} = 1.00$$

The level of excess reserves varies dollar for dollar with the amount of reserves made available by discounting.

(8-47)

$$\frac{\partial R_x}{\partial B_{bp}} = \frac{\partial R_x}{\partial B_{bg}} = -K < 0$$

Borrowing from the banks by either the public or the government reduces excess reserves by $K on the dollar since required reserves are increased by that percentage of the borrowing.

(8-48)

The last relationship given, Eq. (8-48), requires that we not assume as we have previously that the government keep all its money on deposit with itself but rather requires that we assume that the proceeds of government borrowing from the banks be either left on deposit with the commercial banking system or spent. If the assumption is made that the government borrows the money and removes it from the economy, total reserves are reduced by a like amount, and the effect is shown by Eq. (8-45) minus Eq. (8-48), or unity; that is, excess reserves are reduced dollar for dollar as a result of such borrowing activity.

Since free reserves, $R_f$, is defined as excess reserves minus discounts, $R_d$, by Eq. (8-41), an expanded definition of free reserves can be obtained from Eq. (8-43) by merely subtracting $R_d$ from both sides:

$$R_f = (1 - K)(F - C) - K(B_{bp} + B_{bg})  \qquad (8-49)$$

Taking partial derivatives of Eq. (8-49) to determine the effect of changes in various factors upon the level of free reserves will yield identical results with those obtained for the level of excess reserves, differentiating Eq. (8-43), with one exception. The one exception is, of course, that the level of free reserves is independent of the level of reserves made available by discounting. Instead of Eq. (8-47), we have

$$\frac{\partial R_f}{\partial R_d} = 0  \qquad (8-50)$$

### 2. The Creation of Demand Deposits: The Individual Bank and the Banking System

We have previously noted that the level of demand deposits is dependent on the amount of lending by the banks to the nonbank public and to the government. Banks do indeed *create* new demand deposits each and every time they increase their loans; however, some students of economics are amazed to find that many bankers are unaware of this fact and those bankers that are aware of it find such information generally irrelevant to the operation of an individual bank. This is so because an individual bank may only lend an amount equal to its excess reserves if it is to be certain of meeting its legal reserve requirements. If the bank is operated on the reasonable assumption that money loaned may well be withdrawn and paid to a depositor of another bank, when the checks are cleared, the first bank will lose (and the second bank will gain) an amount of reserves equal to the amount loaned. As a result, the following somewhat paradoxical statement is a true description of the U.S. banking scene: An individual bank may lend only such amounts as are deposited with it, while the banking system as a whole may lend some multiple of the total fiat money made available to it by the government.

With the help of a couple of simplifying assumptions, let us trace the mechanics of this process. Let us assume first that each bank loans all its excess reserves as soon as they become available and second that all loans are withdrawn from the lending bank and deposited with another bank. This latter assumption could reflect the fact that when the borrower spent the money, the recipients just happen to do their banking at another institution. Let us begin the process by assuming an initial infusion of fiat money (bank reserves) by the government, $\Delta F$, which might well be the result of an additional government expenditure not offset either by a tax increase or by borrowing from the banks or the nonbank public. This infusion of fiat money from the federal government would, of course, result in an immediate increase in some particular bank's deposits and reserves by an equal amount; i.e.,

$$\Delta F = \Delta D_1 = \Delta R_1 \qquad (8\text{-}51)$$

An individual bank's excess reserves are, by definition, the difference between its total reserves, $R_1$, and its required reserves, which equal the product of the reserver equirement, $K$, and its demand deposits, $D_1$:

$$R_{x1} = R_1 - KD_1 \qquad (8\text{-}52)$$

To obtain the effect of the net injection of fiat money by the government on the level of excess reserves of this particular bank, we may take first differences of Eq. (8-52) and obtain

$$\Delta R_{x1} = \Delta R_1 - K\,\Delta D_1 \qquad (8\text{-}53)$$

Equation (8-51) indicates that we may substitute $\Delta F$ for both $\Delta R_1$ and $\Delta D_1$ in Eq. (8-53) with the result that

$$R_{x1} = (1 - K)\,\Delta F \qquad (8\text{-}54)$$

At this point demand deposits have been increased only by the amount of the injection of fiat money by the government as indicated by Eq. (8-51).

Let us now assume that bank No. 1 lends an amount equal to its excess reserves, $(1 - K)\Delta F$, by accepting a businessman's note and creating a demand deposit. This is the point at which the individual bank has *created money*—in this case, in the amount of $(1 - K)\Delta F$. The demand deposit is immediately withdrawn, leaving bank No. 1 with no further increase in demand deposits and no excess reserves. Its total reserves now equal $K$ times its demand deposits. The first bank initially received a deposit of $\Delta F$ that increased its reserves accordingly. It lent $(1 - K)\Delta F$ and lost an equivalent amount in reserves, leaving it with $K\Delta F$ in new reserves to cover its new deposits of $\Delta F$.

Somewhere in the banking system a bank (or banks) has received the deposit withdrawn from bank No. 1 and had a corresponding increase in its reserves. Let us designate this bank as bank No. 2.

$$\Delta D_2 = \Delta R_2 = (1 - K)\Delta F \qquad (8\text{-}55)$$

Repeating Eq. (8-53) with appropriate subscripts,

$$\Delta R_{x2} = \Delta R_2 - K\Delta D_2 \qquad (8\text{-}53)$$

we can obtain the change in bank No. 2's excess reserves. By substituting Eq. (8-55) into (8-53), we can obtain an expression for the excess reserves available to bank No. 2 for lending in terms of $\Delta F$ as follows:

$$\Delta R_{x2} = (1 - K)^2 \Delta F \qquad (8\text{-}56)$$

This equation gives the change in excess reserves of bank No. 2 and thereby the amount that would be received in new deposits by a third bank as a result of bank No. 2's lending activities; that is,

$$\Delta D_3 = (1 - K)^2 \Delta F \qquad (8\text{-}57)$$

We could keep this example going indefinitely, but by now the pattern should be clear. To reiterate,

$$\Delta D_1 = \Delta F(1 - K)^0 \qquad (8\text{-}51)$$

$$\Delta D_2 = \Delta F(1 - K)^1 \qquad (8\text{-}55)$$

$$\Delta D_3 = \Delta F(1 - K)^2 \qquad (8\text{-}57)$$

or, in general,

$$\Delta D_n = \Delta F(1 - K)^{n-1} \qquad (8\text{-}58)$$

If this expansion of demand deposits were to keep up until all the net injection of fiat money were "used up," $(1 - K)^{n-1} \to 0$, we would obtain a total expansion of deposits equal to the sum of an infinite geometric expansion:

$$\Delta D = \sum_{i=1}^{\infty} D_i = \Delta F \sum_{j=0}^{\infty} (1 - K)^j = \Delta F \left( \frac{1}{K} \right) \quad \text{assuming} \quad K < 1.00 \quad (8\text{-}59)$$

An infinite number of banks are not, of course, required since the mechanics are the same even if we come back to the first bank again. If one wanted to reach the absolute maximum expansion of demand deposits with a given injection of reserves, however, an infinite number of transactions would be required under our assumptions. It is to be noted that this result is the same as that previously obtained under a fractional reserve fiat money system under the assumption of "Complete Utilization of Reserves, Banks 'Loaned Up.'" There Eq. (8-29) indicated that the money supply would change by a factor of $1/K$ times the change in the fiat money in the system.

### 3. The Tools of Monetary Policy

There are three specific categories of monetary policy tools in the United States. We shall consider each in turn.

#### OPEN MARKET OPERATIONS

This tool of monetary policy is the purchase or sale of securities by the Federal Reserve Bank of New York for the specific purpose of adding to or subtracting from the total reserves available to the banking system. The mechanics of the operation are fairly simple. If the Federal Reserve (the Fed) buys a security, it pays for it with a check drawn on itself. When this check is deposited in a commercial bank, the bank presents it to the Federal Reserve Bank and has its reserve account increased by the amount of the open market purchase. Since this bank gained reserves without any other bank losing reserves, the total reserves in the system have been increased by the amount of the transaction. A sale of securities by the Fed sets up an opposite set of transactions ending with the reserve account of some commercial bank being decreased when the check drawn on it to pay for the securities is cleared through the Federal Reserve System.

The effect on the money supply of such an increase (by the purchase of securities) or decrease (by the sale of securities) in total reserves depends in part on whether the banks are fully utilizing their reserves. If the banks are "loaned up" and if we assume that they remain so, Eq. (8-24) is appropriate:

$$M = \frac{R}{K} + C \quad (8\text{-}24)$$

The effect of a change in reserves is

$$\frac{\partial M}{\partial R} = \frac{1}{K} > 1.00$$

A change in bank reserves via open market operations will cause a multiple change in the money supply when bank reserves are being fully utilized.

(8-60)

If the banks have excess reserves, then Eq. (8-33) is the appropriate definition of the money supply.

$$M = C + R + B_{bg} + B_{bp}$$        (8-33)

In this case, we must make the further distinction as to whether the Fed buys the security from or sells it to a commercial bank or buys it from or sells it to the nonbank public. Specifically, does this transaction change $B_{bg}$ (borrowings from the banking system by the government) as well as $R$ in Eq. (8-33)? If the Fed buys or sells the security to a commercial bank, then $R$ and $B_{bg}$ will change in opposite directions by an equal amount. If the security is bought from or sold to the nonbank public, only $R$ will be changed. We can distinguish between these results by first taking the total derivative of Eq. (8-33), assuming that $dC$ and $dB_{bp}$ equal zero:

$$dM = \left(\frac{\partial M}{\partial R}\right) dR + \left(\frac{\partial M}{\partial B_{bg}}\right) dB_{bg}$$        (8-61)

If only the nonbank public is involved, $dB_{bg}$ is zero, and

$$\frac{dM}{dR} = 1.00$$

A change in reserves via open market operations with the nonbank public will change the money supply dollar for dollar if the banks have excess reserves.

(8-62)

If the security is bought from or sold to the commercial banks, then $dR = -dB_{bg}$. That is, a sale of securities to the banks will decrease reserves by the amount of the transaction and will increase the government's borrowing from the commercial banking system by an equal amount. The borrowing will create an equal and offsetting amount of demand deposits. Algebraically,

$$dM = \left(\frac{\partial M}{\partial R}\right) dR + \left(\frac{\partial M}{\partial B_{bg}}\right) dB_{bg}$$        (8-61)

If $dR = -dB_{bg}$, then

$$\frac{dM}{dR} = 1 - 1 = 0$$

Open market operations via the purchase and sale of securities from and to commercial banks with excess reserves will have no effect on the money supply.

(8-63)

As noted above, in practice, at any point in time some banks in the system will be fully utilizing their reserves and others will have excess reserves. The actual effect of open market operations falls somewhere between the theoretical extremes given above. The system as a whole is more fully utilizing available reserves in periods of "tight money" and high interest rates and has substantial excess reserves in periods of "easy money" and low interest rates. The actual results of open market operations vary accordingly. For example, if the banks have large amounts of excess reserves (as was the case in 1934), the creation of additional reserves via open market operations will have no effect, as indicated by Eq. (8-63), or will only expand the money supply on a one-for-one basis as indicated by Eq. (8-62). On the other hand, in a period of strong loan demand, a multiplicative effect will result from each injection of reserves via open market operations, as indicated by Eq. (8-60).

Open market operations are the most important area of the application of monetary policy by the government, and the purchase and sale of securities is closely watched by experts in the money and capital markets. However, the student must be warned that simply determining whether the Fed is buying or selling does *not* indicate whether the government is attempting to expand or contract the money supply. In fact, most open market operations are undertaken simply to offset other factors influencing the total reserves available to the banking system, such as changes in the holdings of currency by the public, a highly seasonal factor.

CHANGES IN RESERVE REQUIREMENTS

The effect of a change in reserve requirements also depends on whether or not we assume that the banks are fully utilizing the reserves available to them. If we assume that the banks are always fully "loaned up," the appropriate equation is

$$M = \frac{R}{K} + C \qquad (8\text{-}24)$$

The effect of a change in the reserve requirement ratio is

$$\frac{\partial M}{\partial K} = -\frac{R}{K^2} < 0$$

If the banking system has no excess reserves available, a change in the reserve requirement will cause the money supply to move in the opposite direction.

(8-64)

On the other hand, if the banks have excess reserves, Eq. (8-32) is appropriate, and a change in the reserve requirement ratio has no effect on the money supply but only on excess and free reserves.

$$M = F + B_{bg} + B_{bp} \tag{8-32}$$

$$\frac{\partial M}{\partial K} = 0$$

When banks have excess reserves, a change in the reserve requirement will have no effect on the money supply.

$$\tag{8-65}$$

### Discount Window Policy

We have already discussed the practice of the Fed lending reserves directly to the individual commercial banks in our definition of net free reserves above. In the case of this policy tool, we could also examine the results under the two alternative assumptions regarding the complete or incomplete utilization of reserves; but, in the United States, commercial banks borrow from the Fed with some reluctance, and it is thus realistic to assume that reserves are only borrowed when banks plan to utilize these reserves. As a result, Eq. (8-24) is again the appropriate definition of the money supply.

$$M = \frac{R}{K} + C \tag{8-24}$$

Defining reserves to include discounting separately, as above,

$$R = F - C + R_d \tag{8-38}$$

Substitution of Eq. (8-38) into (8-24) yields

$$M = \frac{F + R_d}{K} + C\left(1 - \frac{1}{K}\right) \tag{8-66}$$

The effect of making reserves available via discounting is mechanically no different from making reserves available by any other means. Thus, simple differentiation yields

$$\frac{\partial M}{\partial R_d} = \frac{\partial M}{\partial F} = \frac{1}{K} > 1.00$$

Making reserves available via discounting is the same as increasing the stock of fiat money in the system in some other fashion and will have a multiplicative effect on the money supply.

$$\tag{8-67}$$

The interest rate charged the banks on their borrowings from the discount window was expected to be a prime tool of monetary policy when the Federal Reserve System was first organized. However, the discount rate, as it is called, is no longer a rate at which banks can borrow all the money that they think will contribute to profits. In fact, banks do not have a "right" to borrow, and current regulations explicitly state that borrowing from the Fed is a "privilege" to be granted at the discretion of the regional Federal Reserve Banks. This is the reason for stressing above that making more or less reserves available via discounting is strictly a policy decision.

Changes in the discount rate have come to exert a significant impact on money and capital markets through what is called the "announcement effect." An upward change in the discount rate has come to be a signal by the monetary authorities that they foresee the beginning or continuation of a restrictive monetary policy. Conversely, a decrease in the rate signals the beginning or continuation of an expansionary monetary policy. Such changes have come to mean more than just an indication of a change in policy regarding only reserves to be made available through discounting. A change in the discount rate is usually followed by active open market operations in the indicated direction.

OTHER TOOLS OF MONETARY POLICY

There are a number of other more or less direct controls on money and credit which have been important at various times in this economy. At this writing, Regulation Q, which is the Federal Reserve's regulation setting the maximum rates of interest that member banks may pay on time and savings deposits, is an important part of monetary policy. The Federal Reserve System also has the right to set "margin requirements," the percentage of the total price that a buyer of common stock must put up if he wants to borrow the remainder from a member bank. Direct controls such as these change from time to time in both legal form and the extent to which they are used. The interested student should consult an up-to-date Federal Reserve publication for further explanation.

### 4. Using Net Free Reserves as an Indicator of Monetary Conditions[1]

The use of free reserves as an indicator of how "tight" or "easy" the supply of funds is in the economy is common in professional writings and in the financial press. Such a use of this indicator seems to rest on the assumption that the bankers have a desired level of free reserves that is a negative

---

[1] The reader is cautioned at the outset to take note of the dangers inherent in the use of free reserves as an indicator of monetary conditions presented at the conclusion of this section, for methodologically speaking these dangers are substantial.

function of the level of interest rates. When rates are high, the banks will push free reserves to a low, usually a negative, level through such activities as lending excess funds to business and to each other and obtaining the maximum amount of funds from the central bank through rediscounting. When interest rates are low, the banks are satisfied with a relatively high level of free reserves since the cost (lost interest) of not utilizing these funds is less. For illustrative purposes we shall use a simple linear functional relationship between the desired level of free reserves, $\hat{R}_f$, and the interest rate, $r$, although identical results would be achieved with any relationship the first derivative of which is negative.

$$\hat{R}_f = a - br$$

The "desired" level of free reserves is a negative function of the level of interest rates.

(8-68)

If the equilibrium position of the money market is defined as being a situation in which the desired level of free reserves is equal to the actual level of free reserves, we can study the comparative statics of the system by recalling our previously stated determinants of free reserves:

$$R_f = (1 - K)(F - C) - K(B_{bp} + B_{bg}) \qquad (8\text{-}49)$$

Setting the expression for $R_f$ in Eq. (8-49) equal to the expression for $\hat{R}_f$ in Eq. (8-60) and solving for the equilibrium level of interest rates, $\hat{r}$, gives

$$\hat{r} = \frac{1}{-b}[(1 - K)(F - C) - K(B_{bp} + B_{bg}) - a] \qquad (8\text{-}69)$$

Implications as to the effect on the equilibrium level of interest rates of a change in one of the determinants of free reserves may be obtained by taking partial derivatives with respect to Eq. (8-69).

$$\frac{\partial \hat{r}}{\partial K} = \frac{1}{-b}[-(F - C)$$

The level of interest rates and the legal percentage reserve requirement will vary in the same direction.

$$- (B_{bp} + B_{bg})] > 0$$

(8-70)

$$\frac{\partial \hat{r}}{\partial F} = (1 - K)\frac{1}{-b} < 0$$

The level of interest rates and the amount of fiat money (bank reserves) put into the system will vary inversely.

(8-71)

$$\frac{\partial \hat{r}}{\partial C} = (K - 1)\frac{1}{-b} > 0$$

A change in the amount of currency held by the public will move the level of interest rates in the same direction.

(8-72)

$$\frac{\partial \hat{r}}{\partial B_{bp}} = \frac{\partial \hat{r}}{\partial B_{bg}} = \frac{K}{b} > 0$$

A change in total loans by the banking system either to the nonbank public or to the government will result in a move in interest rates in the same direction.

(8-73)

Reliance on the changes in free reserves as an indicator of what is happening in the money market can be misleading as it implies that

$$\frac{\partial \hat{r}}{\partial R_d} = 0$$

The equilibrium of interest rates is unaffected by the amount of funds available to banks by discounting with the central bank.

(8-74)

This can be misleading in many circumstances. Although the banks pay interest on borrowings from the central bank, in the United States the rate is usually below what the banks might earn on this money. How much is made available is a question of Federal Reserve policy. If the central bank as a matter of policy were to make a large amount of funds available to the commercial banking system via discount loans and this led, as might be expected, to a substantial increase in loans to business by banks, $B_{bp}$, free reserves would have fallen, indicating that interest rates should be rising. In truth, the rediscounting is keeping rates lower than they otherwise would be. This result is not the fault of the use of static rather than dynamic analysis but is inherent in the definition and use of free reserves for this purpose.

### 5. "Near Moneys" and Their Creation

As pointed out at the beginning of this chapter, the definition of the money supply as currency in circulation plus demand deposits is necessarily an arbitrary one since there are many other assets having a high degree of "moneyness" or liquidity. We shall first consider the near money most commonly included in an expanded definition of the money supply, time and savings deposits created by (on deposit with) commercial banks.

#### TIME AND SAVINGS DEPOSITS CREATED BY COMMERCIAL BANKS

Savings deposits held by commercial banks are subject to a reserve requirement just as demand deposits are, but the percentage reserve on time and savings deposits, $K_s$, is typically less than the reserve requirement applicable to demand deposits, $K_d$.

Including savings deposits, the maximum total deposits that can be created by the banking system with a fixed amount of reserves is set by the linear constraint

$$K_d D + K_s S \leq R \tag{8-75}$$

or, assuming full utilization of reserves,

$$K_d D + K_s S = R \tag{8-76}$$

If savings deposits are included in the money supply, the money supply can be increased with no increase in reserves if savings deposits (with their lower reserve requirement) are substituted for demand deposits. The relevant analytical question as to the importance of this effect is: What happens to the maximum $(D + S)$ as the mix of $D$ and $S$ is changed? Solving Eq. (8-68) for $(D + S)$ gives

$$(D + S) = \frac{R}{K_d} + S\left(1 - \frac{K_s}{K_d}\right) \tag{8-77}$$

Differentiating Eq. (8-69) to obtain the derivative of $(D + S)$ with respect to $S$ gives

$$\frac{\partial(D + S)}{\partial S} = 1 - \frac{K_s}{K_d} > 0 \quad \text{since} \quad K_s < K_d \tag{8-78}$$

For example, if the reserve requirement on savings deposits were only half that applicable to demand deposits (say 5 versus 10%), a decline in demand deposits of $1 would allow for an expansion of savings deposits of $2 with *one-half* of the increase in savings deposits being a net increase in the combined total of savings plus demand deposits $[1 - (0.05/0.10) = \frac{1}{2}]$.

The transformation from demand deposits to time and savings deposits can lead to a substantial expansion of the total assets of the banking system (assuming bank reserves are constant). However, from the point of view of the individual banker this provides very little incentive to encourage this sort of transfer. As noted above, the individual banker necessarily thinks in terms of being able to lend only his excess reserves. As a result, in the example above, $1 moved from demand deposit status to savings deposit status would set free only $0.05 of extra lending ability, $1(0.10 - 0.05) = $0.05. In addition the banker must pay interest on time and savings deposits and is generally prohibited from so doing on demand deposits. It is the danger of losing the entire deposit to a competitor (or the hope of gaining new deposits not otherwise obtainable) that causes bankers to encourage savings deposits and not the lower reserve requirement.

### OTHER LIQUID ASSETS

Under the institutional arrangements prevailing in the United States, institutions other than commercial banks create financial assets for the public and liabilities for themselves that are virtually identical to savings deposits created by commercial banks. Specifically, the deposits of mutual savings banks and the "share accounts" of savings and loan associations are such liquid assets. Such deposits are not subject to a legal reserve requirement exactly comparable to those imposed by the Federal Reserve System on the deposits of member commercial banks. As a practical matter, however, since all transactions are conducted with demand deposits held by commercial banks or with cash, the rate of growth of these other liquid assets is closely correlated with the growth of the supply of cash and demand deposits. A close control of the growth of currency and demand deposits can significantly influence the growth of these other assets. The degree of this effect or the desirability of changing institutional arrangements lies beyond the scope of this book.

There are a whole host of other liquid assets such as immediate cash value of life insurance policies, shares of common stock and in mutual funds, and corporate and government bonds that contribute to the total liquidity of the economy. As noted at the beginning of this chapter, when the economist refers to the effect of changes in the "money supply," he is seeking a proxy for changes in total liquidity of the economy. For some purposes demand deposits plus currency in circulation is satisfactory; for many problems the whole range of liquid assets must be considered.

The effect of liquid assets other than currency and demand deposits on various macroeconomic behavioral relationships is the subject of much contemporary research and debate. There are as yet no simple mechanical relationships found to hold that can be reported to the student at this time.

## EXERCISES

**1.** Assume a fractional reserve, fiat money banking system. The required reserve ratio is 0.20 and the banking system keeps all reserves fully employed (banks always "loaned up"). Evaluate the effect on the money supply of an increase in government expenditures financed by

    **a.** increased taxes;

    **b.** borrowing from commercial banks;

    **c.** creation of fiat money.

**2.** Work problem 1, but assume that banks always have excess reserves (banks not "loaned up").

**3.** Assume that the Federal Reserve buys $1 million worth of government securities on the open market. Evaluate the effect on the money supply if

    **a.** The banking system has substantial amounts of excess reserves.

    **b.** The banking system is at all times fully utilizing its reserves.

**4.** Evaluate the effect of the open market purchase described in Problem 3 with a reserve requirement of 100%.

## RECOMMENDED REFERENCES

Board of Governors of the Federal Reserve System, *The Federal Reserve System: Purposes and Functions* (Washington, D.C., 1963).

Chandler, L. V., *The Economics of Money and Banking*. 5th ed., New York: Harper & Row, Pub., Inc., 1969.

Federal Reserve Bank of Chicago, *Modern Money Mechanics* (Chicago, 1961).

Polakoff, Murray E. *et al.*, *Financial Institutions and Markets*. Boston, Mass.: Houghton Mifflin Co., 1970.

# 9  Aggregate  Supply

# Relationships

Thus far we have discussed the equilibrium level of aggregate demand or total money expenditures in the economy. In our generalized model we have not as yet considered the determination of the price level, but the equilibrium level of total expenditures alone is not sufficient for this and many other macroeconomic problems. One might like to know, for example, how much of an increase in total expenditures will be reflected in an increase in the real output of the economy and how much will be reflected in a general increase in prices.

In the preceding chapters we have described orthodox neo-Keynesian macroeconomic theory. In this chapter we shall attempt as nearly as possible to continue this practice. Concerning aggregate supply relationships (and capital theory in general), however, there apparently is no widely accepted contemporary orthodoxy. In this chapter an illustrative model is presented and developed to bring forth the most widely used concepts in this area, but the reader should be aware that this area of macroeconomics is not nearly so "standardized" as the aggregate demand portion of the model. Many macroeconomic textbooks have slightly different approaches to the inter-action of aggregate demand and aggregate supply and the determination of the equilibrium levels of prices and real output.

The productive capacity of the economy given by its stock of labor and capital goods will be our main concern in this chapter. It should be noted, however, that there is a more complex dimension to the problem that can only be treated by dynamic models. In general, the division of a change in aggregate demand between price changes and changes in real output is sensitive to the rapidity, or the time dimension, of the increase. For example, if aggregate demand is increased very rapidly in a wartime emergency, the resulting rise in prices is likely to be greater than it would have been if the same increase in total expenditures had come about more slowly, giving output more time to adjust to the new demand conditions.

## I  AGGREGATE SUPPLY AND "FULL EMPLOYMENT"

The aggregate supply function is simply some unique relationship between two variables: the price index, $P$, and the measure of the quantity of real output, $Q$. As a matter of definition, total money expenditures must equal the quantity of real output times its price level. In equilibrium, aggregate demand will equal the equilibrium price level times the equilibrium level of real output. In other words, the following equation is a simple identity, *ex post*, and an equilibrium condition or behavioral relationship, *ex ante*:

$$Y = PQ$$

Aggregate demand, $Y$, is equal to the product of a comprehensive price index, $P$, and some quantitative measure of real output, $Q$.

(9-1)

The equilibrium level of $Y$ has been discussed in previous chapters; the question now is: With a given $Y$, what are the equilibrium magnitudes of $P$ and $Q$? There are an infinite number of combinations of price and output that will equal a given level of total expenditures. These possible combinations, when graphed on a $P,Q$ plane, will describe a rectangular hyperbola. Higher levels of total expenditures will shift the *aggregate demand curve* (combinations of price and quantity that equal the equilibrium level of total expenditures) to the right. In Figure 9–1, $Y_1$, $Y_2$, $Y_3$, and $Y_4$ depict successively higher levels of aggregate demand.

The most naive sort of model for aggregate supply can be built on the assumption that increases in aggregate demand will be totally reflected in increases in real output up to the point of "full employment" of labor and other resources, at which point one will begin to get only price increases. Figure 9–1 shows such an aggregate supply relationship labeled $S$. A shift in aggregate demand from a level of $Y_1$ to a higher level, $Y_2$, would increase

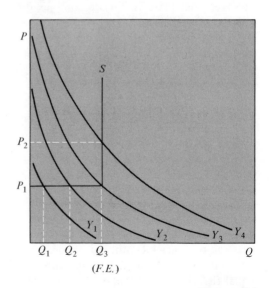

(F.E.)

**Figure 9–1**

the output of real goods and sevices from $Q_1$ to $Q_2$ but leave the price level unchanged at $P_1$. If the quantity of output had reached the full employment level, $F.E.$, and aggregate demand were increased from $Y_3$ to $Y_4$, prices would rise from $P_1$ to $P_2$ while output held constant at $F.E.$

As noted above, an aggregate supply curve of the form shown in Figure 9–1 is rather naive. It is now generally accepted that in a modern industrialized economy full employment is not a discrete point. The resources of the economy can be to a greater or lesser degree unemployed and an increase in aggregate demand will typically bring forth *both* an increase in output and a price increase. If there is a high degree of unemployment of labor and other resources, the increase in output will be relatively large and the increase in prices relatively small. Conversely, if the economy is operating at near capacity, an increase in aggregate demand will be primarily reflected in increased prices and will increase output only slightly. We shall now consider an aggregate supply function that will allow for this more realistic state of affairs.

## II  AN ILLUSTRATIVE AGGREGATE SUPPLY FUNCTION

Let us assume an aggregate supply function of the following form:

$$P = AQ^{a-1} \qquad a \geq 1.00$$

The price level is a function of the level of output in such a way that with a change in output the price level will either increase or hold constant.

(9-2)

The constraint on $a$ must be added to Eq. (9-2) since if $a$ were less than 1.00, prices would fall as output is increased. Figure 9–2 shows three possible shapes for this aggregate supply function.

If Eq. (9-1) is an equilibrium condition for aggregate supply to equal aggregate demand, it can be combined with Eq. (9-2) to obtain the following relationship between total expenditures and real output:

$$Y = AQ^a \quad \text{or} \quad Q = \left(\frac{Y}{A}\right)^{1/a} \tag{9-3}$$

The parameter $a$ in Eqs. (9-2) and (9-3) we shall hereafter refer to as the "inflation coefficient" since, as we shall discuss below, the larger this parameter, the greater the amount of inflation the economy must endure to obtain a given increase in output.

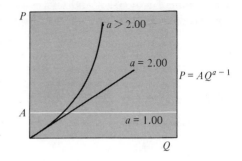

**Figure 9-2**

The combination of Eqs. (9-1) and (9-2) can also be utilized to generate the following relationship between total expenditures and the price level:

$$Y = \left(\frac{P^a}{A}\right)^{1/(a-1)} \quad \text{or} \quad P = (Y^{a-1}A)^{1/a} \tag{9-4}$$

## III ELASTICITIES OF OUTPUT AND PRICE WITH RESPECT TO CHANGES IN AGGREGATE DEMAND

The foregoing equations as presented do not tell us much of interest. Most of the interesting questions are concerned with rates of change, in either absolute or percentage terms. Let us formulate our questions in terms of percentage changes using the concept of elasticity, that is, in terms of the ratio of the percentage change in one variable to the percentage change in another. First, the elasticity of output, $Q$, with respect to aggregate demand, $Y$, can be defined as follows:

$$\eta_{Q,Y} = \frac{dQ}{Q} \div \frac{dY}{Y} = \frac{dQ}{dY}\frac{Y}{Q} \qquad$$

The elasticity of output with respect to aggregate demand is equal to the percentage change in output divided by the percentage change in aggregate demand.

$$\tag{9-5}$$

Differentiating Eq. (9-3) to obtain $dQ/dY$, we find

$$\frac{dQ}{dY} = \frac{1}{a}\left(\frac{Y}{A}\right)^{1/a-1}\frac{1}{A} \tag{9-6}$$

Combining Eqs. (9-3), (9-5), and (9-6), we obtain the following expression for the elasticity of output with respect to aggregate demand:

$$\eta_{Q,Y} = \frac{1}{a}$$

A 1% increase in aggregate demand will bring forth a $(1/a)\%$ increase in real output.

(9-7)

Let us now consider the response of the price level to a change in aggregate demand:

$$\eta_{P,Y} = \frac{dP}{P} \div \frac{dY}{Y} = \frac{dP}{dY}\frac{Y}{P}$$

The elasticity of the price level with respect to aggregate demand is defined as the percentage change in the price level divided by the percentage change in aggregate demand.

(9-8)

Differentiating Eq. (9-4) gives $dP/dY$:

$$\frac{dP}{dY} = A^{1/a}\left(\frac{a-1}{a}\right)Y^{-1/a} = \frac{a-1}{a}\left(\frac{A}{Y}\right)^{1/a}$$

(9-9)

Combining Eqs. (9-3), (9-8), and (9-9), we obtain the following expression for the elasticity of price with respect to aggregate demand:

$$\eta_{P,Y} = 1 - \frac{1}{a} = 1 - \eta_{Q,Y}$$

The elasticity of prices with respect to aggregate demand is equal to unity minus the elasticity of output with respect to aggregate demand.

(9-10)

From Eqs. (9-7) and (9-10) it is obvious that these two elasticities must sum to unity, which is merely to say that the percentage change in total expenditures is, over the range of small changes, equal to the sum of the percentage change in prices and the percentage change in output. Alternatively, this can be demonstrated by taking the total differential of Eq. (9-1),

$$dY = dQ(P) + dP(Q)$$

and dividing the left-hand side of this expression by $Y$ and each of the terms in the right-hand side by $PQ$ and obtaining

$$\frac{dY}{Y} = \frac{dQ}{Q} + \frac{dP}{P}$$

The percentage change in total expenditures equals the sum of the percentage change in output and the percentage change in the price level.

(9-11)

Similar information about the aggregate supply function can be presented in the form of two alternative elasticities. These are the elasticities of prices and output with respect to each other. By algebraic manipulations similar to those through which we obtained the previous elasticities, it can be shown that

$$\eta_{Q,P} = \frac{1}{a-1} \tag{9-12}$$

and that

$$\eta_{P,Q} = a - 1 = \frac{1}{\eta_{Q,P}} \tag{9-13}$$

In other words, the elasticity of quantity with respect to price is the reciprocal of the elasticity of price with respect to quantity, and the latter is equal to the exponent, $a - 1$, of the basic aggregate supply equation, Eq. (9-2).

To summarize the relationships derived thus far in this chapter:

$$Y = PQ \tag{9-1}$$

$$P = AQ^{a-1} \tag{9-2}$$

$$\eta_{Q,Y} = \frac{1}{a} \tag{9-7}$$

$$\eta_{P,Y} = 1 - \frac{1}{a} = 1 - \eta_{Q,Y} \tag{9-10}$$

$$\eta_{P,Q} = a - 1 \tag{9-12}$$

$$\eta_{Q,P} = \frac{1}{a-1} = \frac{1}{\eta_{P,Q}} \tag{9-13}$$

Some numerical examples may serve to put the interrelationships among these concepts into focus:

| $a$ | $\eta_{Q,Y}$ | $\eta_{P,Y}$ | $\eta_{Q,P}$ | $\eta_{P,Q}$ |
|-----|------|------|------|------|
| 1 | 1.00 | 0 | $\infty$ | 0 |
| 2 | 0.50 | 0.50 | 1.00 | 1.00 |
| 3 | 0.33 | 0.67 | 0.50 | 2.00 |
| $\infty$ | 0 | 1.00 | 0 | $\infty$ |

It should be intuitively obvious that the relationship among aggregate demand, the price level, and real output for a contemporary economy would in reality have to be a much more complicated function than that implied by Eq. (9-2). The first line of the table above ($a = 1$) might describe a situation of vast unemployed resources in the economy. A 1% rise in aggregate demand would give rise to a 1% increase in real output and no increase in prices. At the other extreme, the last line of the table ($a \to \infty$) is descriptive of an economy that is truly at "full employment." A 1% increase in aggregate demand will only serve to raise prices and not increase output. Of course the economy is typically between these two extremes, closer to $a = 1$ in depression and to a very large inflation coefficient, $a$, in wars and threats of wars.

In addition, to be realistic, there should be the explicit inclusion of the time variable since, as noted in the introduction to this chapter, the aggregate supply relationship is probably altered by the rapidity with which aggregate demand is changed. In our present terminology, the elasticity of output with respect to aggregate demand, $\eta_{Q,Y}$, is probably higher the longer the period allowed for the change in quantity to take place.

A further complication is that, in most modern economies, prices apparently rise much easier in response to a rise in aggregate demand than they fall as aggregate demand falls. In other words, $\eta_{P,Y}$ is probably larger (and $\eta_{Q,Y}$ smaller) when $dY > 0$ than when $dY < 0$. We shall have more to say on this later when wage and price flexibility is discussed in connection with the stabilization problem.

## IV SOME CONCEPTS UNDERLYING THE AGGREGATE SUPPLY RELATIONSHIP

We shall now consider some of the relationships that shape the aggregate supply function we have been discussing above. Rather than discuss these concepts in the abstract, we shall work with a specific model of each. The student should keep in mind that there are many alternative formulations of each of these, and our selection of a particular one is based upon both its frequency in the literature of economics and its usefulness for purposes of illustration.

### 1. The Aggregate Production Function

How the real output of the economy responds to a change in aggregate demand depends, among other things, on the relationship between the factors of production and the output of goods and services. The relationship between inputs (land, labor, capital, entrepreneurship, etc.) and outputs (goods and services) is called an *aggregate production function*.

There are, of course, an infinite number of conceivable aggregate production functions. The most common one in the literature and the one that has been subject of many attempts at empirical estimation is called the *Cobb-Douglas* production function. Algebraically it is of the following form:[1]

$$Q = K^b L^c \qquad 0 < b, c < 1.00$$

Real output, $Q$, is a function of the inputs capital, $K$, and labor, $L$, and the parameters $b$ and $c$ that are positive but less than unity.

$$(9\text{-}14)$$

To examine the relationships between changes in the amount of the factors of production, capital and labor in this case, and output, we can derive the elasticities of output with respect to each input. We define these partial elasticities (changing one factor while holding the other constant) as follows:

$$\eta_{Q,K} = \frac{\partial Q}{\partial K} \frac{K}{Q}$$

$$\eta_{Q,L} = \frac{\partial Q}{\partial L} \frac{L}{Q}$$

By taking the appropriate derivatives in Eq. (9-14), it can be shown that

$$\eta_{Q,K} = b \qquad (9\text{-}15)$$

and that

$$\eta_{Q,L} = c \qquad (9\text{-}16)$$

The elasticity of output with respect to each of the factors of production is equal to the exponent of that factor in the Cobb-Douglas production function of the form in Eq. (9-14).

Another attribute of the Cobb-Douglas production function is that, mathematically speaking, it is "homogeneous" to the $(b + c)$ degree; that is, if the quantity of each input is changed by some multiple, $m$, total output will be changed by $m^{(b+c)}$. This can be illustrated as follows:

$$Q_1 = K_1^b L_1^c \qquad K_2 = mK_1 \qquad L_2 = mL_1$$

$$Q_2 = K_2^b L_2^c = (mK_1)^b (mL_1)^c = m^{(b+c)} K_1^b L_1^c$$

$$Q_2 = m^{(b+c)} Q_1$$

---

[1] For $Q$ to be output measured in constant dollars (say GNP in 1958 prices), Eq. (9-14) should include a dimensioning coefficient, say $D$, to convert units of capital and labor into dollar units. Thus, $Q = DK^b L^c$. For simplicity, we shall assume that $D = 1$. Chapter 11 expands on some of the mathematical properties of aggregate production functions.

For a number of reasons, some of which will be discussed below, it is frequently assumed that the two parameters sum to unity ($b + c = 1.00$). Such a function is then "homogeneous to degree one" or "linearly homogeneous." In such a case, if there is a given percentage change in both factors of production, there will be the same percentage change in output. Such a production function is said to have the characteristic of *constant returns to scale*.

## 2. Marginal Product and Total Factor Payments

*Marginal product* is a microeconomic concept meaning the incremental contribution to output made by an additional unit of a factor of production, assuming the amounts of all other factors of production are held constant. Mathematically, the marginal product of a factor of production is the partial derivative of output with respect to that factor of production.

If one assumes a linearly homogeneous production function, the marginal productivity of each factor changes only as the factor ratios change. In our case, this means that one has the same marginal products as long as the ratio of labor to capital (or vice versa) remains unchanged. This can be demonstrated as follows:

$$MP_K = \frac{\partial Q}{\partial K} = bK^{b-1}L^c = bK^{-(1-b)}L^c = b\left(\frac{L}{K}\right)^c \tag{9-17}$$

$$MP_L = \frac{\partial Q}{\partial L} = cK^bL^{c-1} = c\left(\frac{K}{L}\right)^b \tag{9-18}$$

The equations above indicate that the marginal productivities of capital and labor ($MP_K$ and $MP_L$) are insensitive to the absolute level of output as long as the "factor proportions" or the ratio of one to the other is unchanged. This is an implication of the "constant returns to scale" property of a linearly homogeneous production function.

Under the rather restrictive assumption that the entire economy is operating under conditions of "pure competition," cost minimization by firms implies that the price paid for each unit of capital and labor will be equal to the value of its marginal product. Examining the second-order partial derivatives will indicate the effect upon the marginal productivity, and therefore factor prices in a competitive economy, of each factor as a result of a change in the amount of a particular factor utilized.

$$\frac{\partial MP_K}{\partial K} = -\frac{cbL^c}{K^{c+1}} < 0$$

$$\frac{\partial MP_L}{\partial L} = -\frac{cbK^b}{L^{b+1}} < 0$$

The marginal productivity of a factor will vary inversely with the amount of it employed.

$$\frac{\partial MP_K}{\partial L} = \frac{cbL^{c-1}}{K^c} > 0$$

$$\frac{\partial MP_L}{\partial K} = \frac{cbK^{b-1}}{L^b} > 0$$

The marginal productivity of a factor will vary directly with the amount of other factors being employed.

If each factor of production is paid at a rate per unit equal to its marginal product, the total income to a factor will be the product of its marginal product and the quantity of the factor used, as follows:

$$\text{Total payment to capital} = \frac{\partial Q}{\partial K} \cdot K = bK^bL^c = bQ$$

$$\text{Total payment to labor} = \frac{\partial Q}{\partial L} \cdot L = cK^bL^c = cQ = (1 - b)Q$$

From the foregoing it is obvious that the share of total output on which capital has a claim is $b$ and that the share going to labor will be $c$. The assumption of constant returns to scale ($b + c = 1.00$) ensures that the payments to the factors of production will exactly equal output—that income will equal production; that is,

$$Q = MP_K \cdot K + MP_L \cdot L$$

Total output will equal the sum of each factor's marginal product times the quantity of that factor employed.

(9-19)

Equation (9-19) results from a general characteristic of linearly homogeneous production functions regardless of the number of factors. Mathematically it is known as "Euler's theorem" and in economics variously as the "sum of shares," "adding up," or "exhaustion of product" theorem.

### 3. Factor-Output Ratios

Another aggregate supply concept to which we shall return later in our discussion of economic growth (Chapter 11) is the *capital-output ratio*, $K/Q$.

Assuming the same production function we have been using, Eq. (9-14), we can replace $Q$ with $K^b L^c$ and obtain

$$\frac{K}{Q} = \frac{K^{1-b}}{L^c} \tag{9-20}$$

If we assume the production function to be linearly homogeneous ($b + c = 1.00$),

$$\frac{K}{Q} = \left(\frac{K}{L}\right)^c \tag{9-21}$$

Moreover, by the same process, the labor-output ratio can be expressed as

$$\frac{L}{Q} = \left(\frac{L}{K}\right)^b \tag{9-22}$$

With such a production function the factor-output ratios, like the marginal productivities of the factors of production, remain constant as long as the ratio of the factors of production remains unchanged.

## 4. The Demand for Labor

On the basis of the assumption that individual firms will attempt to maximize their profits, it is implied that in equilibrium labor will be employed in an amount that will equalize the value of its marginal product and the wage rate. For present purposes we state this in the form that the "real" wage rate (the money wage rate, $W$, divided by the price level, $P$) equals the marginal physical product of labor; although equating the money wage with the *value* of the marginal physical product (marginal product, $\partial Q/\partial L$, times the price level, $P$) would amount to the same thing. Using the linearly homogeneous Cobb-Douglas production function, the equality of the real wage rate and marginal product implies that

$$\frac{W}{P} = \frac{\partial Q}{\partial L} = c\left(\frac{K}{L}\right)^b \tag{9-23}$$

Solving Eq. (9-23) for $L$ gives the demand function for labor.

$$L_d = c^{1/b} K \left(\frac{W}{P}\right)^{-1/b} \qquad \text{The demand for labor is a function of the amount of capital being employed, } K; \text{ the price level, } P; \text{ and the money wage rate, } W \tag{9-24}$$

Using Eq. (9-24), let us investigate the effect of changes in the other variables on the demand for labor under our assumption that the real wage rate will equal the marginal productivity of labor.

$$\frac{\partial L_d}{\partial (W/P)} = -\left(\frac{1}{b}\right) c^{1/b}$$

The demand for labor varies inversely with respect to the real wage rate.

$$\times K \left(\frac{W}{P}\right)^{-[(1+b)/b]} < 0$$

$$(9\text{-}25)$$

$$\frac{\partial L_d}{\partial W} = -\left(\frac{1}{b}\right) c^{1/b}$$

The demand for labor varies inversely with respect to the money-wage rate.

$$\times \frac{K}{P}\left(\frac{W}{P}\right)^{-[(1+b)/b]} < 0$$

$$(9\text{-}26)$$

$$\frac{\partial L_d}{\partial P} = \frac{1}{b} c^{1/b} \frac{K}{P}\left(\frac{W}{P}\right)^{-1/b} > 0$$

The demand for labor varies directly with respect to the price level.

$$(9\text{-}27)$$

$$\frac{\partial L_d}{\partial K} = c^{1/b}\left(\frac{W}{P}\right)^{-1/b} > 0$$

The demand for labor varies directly with changes in the amount of capital.

$$(9\text{-}28)$$

All the foregoing relationships are fairly obvious, with the possible exception of the last one. The reason that the demand for labor will be increased with an increase in the capital being utilized is that, as indicated by Eq. (9-18), as the ratio of capital to labor rises, the marginal productivity of labor, and thereby the demand for labor, is increased.

Similar relationships for factors of production other than labor can be developed. In our example the only other factor is capital. We would find, of course, that the demand for capital varies inversely with its real and money price and directly with the general price level and the amount of labor being utilized.

It is important to keep in mind that we have been deriving relationships by taking *partial* derivatives of functions based on an assumed aggregate production function. This means we have been holding all other variables constant and ignoring aggregate demand effects. For example, an increase in money wages will decrease demand for labor if nothing else changes. In fact, however, wages are incomes to their recipients as well as costs to the firms, and the resulting increase in aggregate demand may increase the price level, therefore increasing the demand for labor.

To determine the unique equilibrium amount of labor and capital to be employed, we must not only consider the level of aggregate demand but introduce, in one way or another, supply schedules of labor and capital. We shall expand our model to consider simultaneous aggregate supply and demand effects in Chapters 10 and 11. At this point let us turn to the problem of the supply schedule for labor.

## 5. The Supply of Labor and Equilibrium in the Labor Market

The supply of labor is a schedule of the amount of labor that will be offered at different wage rates. The literature of economics is filled with debate as to whether the supply of labor changes in response to changes in the money wage rate, $W$, or the real wage rate, $W/P$.

The argument over real versus money-wage rate can be phrased in terms of whether the workers behave as if they were subject to a "money illusion." If workers are responsive to changes in the money wage, regardless of what happens to the price level and to the real wage, they are said to suffer from a money illusion. If they are *not* subject to the money illusion, there will be no more labor supplied, when wages and prices increase by the same percentage, leaving the real wage unchanged.

Graph (a) of Figure 9–3 depicts the equilibrium level of employment with the supply of labor as a function of the real wage. Graph (b) depicts the equilibrium level of employment with the supply of labor a function of the money wage. Note that in each case in Figure 9–3 the demand for labor is a function of the real wage. In Graph (b) there is a different demand curve for each price level since it is generally assumed that employers are not subject to a money illusion—that their demand for labor responds only to the real value of the wages they are paying. As above, the demand for labor is derived by setting the marginal product of labor equal to the real wage and the latter depends on the price level.

The equilibrium levels of employment shown in Graphs (a) and (b) are equilibrium levels in that the amount supplied equals the amount demanded at the going wage rate. There is no "involuntary unemployment." A distinction to which we shall devote more time in the following chapter is between a "classical" and a "Keynesian" system. In the classical system, the labor market must be in equilibrium if the rest of the economy is in equilibrium. In a Keynesian system, it is possible for the economy as a whole to be in equilibrium with the labor market in a disequilibrium position such that the supply of labor at the existing wage rate is greater than the demand for it at that rate. Involuntary unemployment does indeed exist in such a situation since there must be workers seeking jobs at the existing wage rate and unable to find work. One circumstance under which this can occur is when money wages are not flexible downward and thereby fixed at some level, say $W_0$ on Graph (c). With a price level of, say 2, and if wages were flexible downward, the competition among the unemployed would presumably force the money

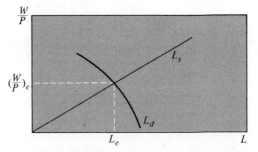

(a)   Supply of Labor as a Function of the Real Wage

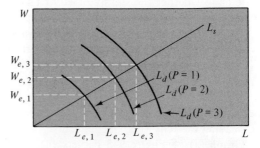

(b)   Supply of Labor as a Function of the Money Wage

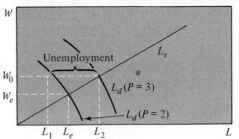

(c)   Unemployment as a Result of Fixed Money Wage, $W_0$

**Figure 9–3**

wage down to $W_e$ at which level employment would be $L_e$. Given our assumption of wage rigidity, however, wages cannot fall to $W_e$ but will hold at $W_0$. Hence, $L_1$ represents the "equilibrium" level of employment under these conditions with unemployment equal to the distance from $L_1$ to $L_2$.

The assumption of a fixed money wage at a level where supply exceeds demand implies that the supply of labor is perfectly elastic at the prevailing money wage. Graphically, the supply curve is effectively horizontal over the range zero to $L_2$ in Graph (c). The amount of labor that is demanded at the prevailing real wage will be the amount employed. If the demand curve is shifted to the right for any reason, such as an increase in the price level from $P = 2$ to $P = 3$ as illustrated, an equal increase in employment will take place.

## V DERIVING SOME ILLUSTRATIVE
## AGGREGATE SUPPLY RELATIONSHIPS

We have discussed and illustrated graphically the equilibrium condition in the labor market when the supply of labor depends on the real wage rate, when the supply of labor depends on the money-wage rate, and when because of a fixed money wage unemployment exists. Each of these models has implications for the aggregate supply function. We shall now derive an aggregate supply function from each of these conditions assuming that the demand for labor results from business employing that amount of labor that will equalize the real wage rate and the marginal productivity of labor derived from a linearly homogeneous Cobb-Douglas production function. All these derivations assume that the quantity of capital is fixed.

### 1. The Aggregate Supply Function
### Derived from a Supply of Labor
### Dependent on the Real Wage Rate

An example of a simple supply schedule of labor dependent on the real wage (the workers have no money illusion) is as follows:

$$L_s = l_{w/p}\left(\frac{W}{P}\right)$$

The amount of labor supplied, $L_s$, is a linear function of the real wage, $W/P$.

$$(9\text{-}29)$$

The demand for labor derived earlier by setting the marginal product of labor equal to the real wage is

$$L_d = c^{1/b} K \left(\frac{W}{P}\right)^{-1/b}$$

The amount of labor demanded is a nonlinear function of the reciprocal of the real wage.

$$(9\text{-}24)$$

We assume that a real wage, $W/P$, will prevail such that $L_s = L_d$. To specify this equilibrium of employment, $L_e$, we solve Eqs. (9-29) and (9-24) simultaneously for $L$ and obtain

$$L_e = (cK^b l_{w/p})^{\,1/(1+b)} \qquad (9\text{-}30)$$

Given the capital stock, $K$, the equilibrium level of employment is uniquely determined by the parameters of the production function and the supply schedule of labor. The equilibrium level of real output, $Q_e$, is also uniquely determined. Substituting $L_e$ as defined by Eq. (9-30) into the aggregate production function,

$$Q_e = K^b L_e^c \qquad b + c = 1.00 \tag{9-14}$$

gives us the following expression for the equilibrium level of output:

$$Q_e = K^{2b/(1+b)}(cl_{w/p})^{(1-b)/(1+b)} \tag{9-31}$$

Equation (9-31) is a "classical" aggregate supply function. The equilibrium level of output is totally insensitive to the price level, $P$, and thereby is totally insensitive to the level of aggregate demand. Graphically, such an aggregate supply curve appears in Figure 9–4 as the vertical line above $Q_e$.

In the classical supply function, the inflation coefficient $a$ approaches infinity ($a \to \infty$). The economy is perpetually at full employment, the level indicated $F.E.$ on Figure 9–1. As indicated in Figure 9–4, an increase in aggregate demand (total expenditures) from $Y_1$ to $Y_2$ will not increase the output of real goods and services but will simply raise the price level from $P_1$ to $P_2$. As previously indicated for an inflation coefficient approaching infinity, the elasticity of output with respect to aggregate demand, $\eta_{Q,Y}$, is zero and the elasticity of the price level with respect to aggregate demand, $\eta_{P,Y}$, is unity. We shall discuss this general type of model in some detail in Chapter 10.

## 2. The Aggregate Supply Function Derived from a Supply of Labor Dependent on the Money-Wage Rate

An example of a simple supply schedule of labor dependent on the money wage (presence of money illusion) is as follows:

$$L_s = l_w W \qquad \qquad \text{The supply of labor is a linear function of the money wage rate.}$$

$$\tag{9-32}$$

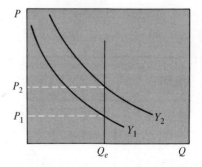

Figure 9–4

We assume that a money wage rate, $W$, will prevail such that the amount of labor supplied equals the amount demanded ($L_s = L_d$). To find the equilibrium level of employment, we solve Eq. (9-32) and the demand equation, Eq. (9-24), simultaneously for $L$ and obtain

$$L_e = (cK^b l_w P)^{1/(1+b)} \tag{9-33}$$

Notice that in this case we need not only the various parameters $b$, $c$, and $l_w$, and the capital stock, $K$, but the price level, $P$, as well, to determine the equilibrium level of employment.

We can derive an aggregate supply curve by substituting the expression for the equilibrium level of employment given in Eq. (9-33) into the aggregate production function, Eq. (9-14), to obtain an expression for the equilibrium level of output:

$$Q_e = K^{2b/(1+b)}(cPl_w)^{(1-b)/(1+b)} \tag{9-34}$$

Note that Eq. (9-34) differs from Eq. (9-31) only by the existence of $P$ in the parentheses on the right-hand side of Eq. (9-34). Solving Eq. (9-34) for the equilibrium level of prices gives

$$P_e = (l_w c K^{2b/c})^{-1} Q^{(1+b)/c} \tag{9-35}$$

Recalling the form of the aggregate supply function,

$$P = AQ^{a-1} \tag{9-2}$$

we can put Eq. (9-34) in this form by assuming

$$A = (l_w c K^{2b/c})^{-1} \qquad a - 1 = \frac{1+b}{1-b} \quad \text{or} \quad a = \frac{2}{c} \tag{9-36}$$

Since we have assumed that the parameter $c$ must be between zero and one, this model implies that the inflation coefficient, $a$, must be greater than two. This formulation also implies that the elasticity of output with respect to aggregate demand, $\eta_{Q \cdot Y}$, must be less than one-half and, conversely, that the elasticity of price with respect to aggregate demand, $\eta_{P \cdot Y}$, must be greater than one-half. These results are summarized algebraically in Table 9–1, along with the results of the other two models.

This model, in contrast to the previous "classical" model, could be termed "Keynesian" since the level of output is sensitive to the level of aggregate demand. An increase in aggregate demand would be reflected both in an increase in output and employment and in an increase in prices.

## Table 9-1

### Summary of Derived Aggregate Supply Relationships

| | CLASSICAL: LABOR SUPPLY AS A FUNCTION OF REAL WAGE RATE | LABOR SUPPLY AS A FUNCTION OF MONEY-WAGE RATE | WAGES FIXED AT LEVEL THAT GENERATES UNEMPLOYMENT |
|---|---|---|---|
| Supply of Labor | $L_s = l_{w/p}\left(\dfrac{W}{P}\right)$ | $L_s = l_w W$ | $L_s > L_d;\ at\ W_0 = $ constant |
| Demand for Labor: | $L_d = c^{1/b}K\left(\dfrac{W}{P}\right)^{-1/b}$ | $L_d = c^{1/b}K\left(\dfrac{W}{P}\right)^{-1/b}$ | $L_d = c^{1/b}K\left(\dfrac{W_0}{P}\right)^{-1/b}$ |
| Equilibrium Level of Employment: | $L_e = (K^b c l_{w/p})^{1/(1+b)}$ | $L_e = (cK^b l_w P)^{1/(1+b)}$ | $L_e = c^{1/b}K\left(\dfrac{W_0}{P}\right)^{-1/b}$ |
| Equilibrium Level of Output:* | $Q_e = K^{2b/(1+b)}(cl_{w/p})^{c/(1+b)}$ | $Q_e = K^{2b/(1+b)}(cl_w P)^{c/(1+b)}$ | $Q_e = Kc^{c/b}\left(\dfrac{W_0}{P}\right)^{-c/b}$ |
| Aggregate Supply Relationship: | $P$ and $Q$ independent | $P = l_w^{-1}c^{-1}K^{-2b/c}Q^{(1+b)/c}$ | $P = Q^{b/c}W_0(cK^{b/c})^{-1}$ |
| Parameter Values of Form $P = AQ^{a-1}$ and $Y = AQ^a$ | $a \to \infty$ | $a = \dfrac{2}{c};\ A = (l_w cK^{2b/c})^{-1}$ | $a = \dfrac{1}{c};\ A = W_0(cK^{b/c})^{-1}$ |
| Implications for $a$, $\eta_{Q,r}$, and $\eta_{P,r}$ | $a \to \infty$<br>$\eta_{Q,r} = 0$<br>$\eta_{P,r} = 1.00$ | $a > 2.00$<br>$\eta_{Q,r} < 0.50$<br>$\eta_{P,r} > 0.50$ | $a > 1.00$<br>$\eta_{Q,r} < 1.00$<br>$\eta_{P,r} > 0$ |

(Aggregate Supply Relationship, Classical column: graph of $P$ versus $Q$ showing a vertical line $Y_s$ at $Q_e$.)

* $Q = K^b L^c$; $b + c = 1.00$ ($0 < b < 1.00$)

### 3. The Aggregate Supply Function Derived from a Fixed Wage Rate Generating Unemployment

As noted earlier, we can construct another "Keynesian" model by assuming that for some reason the money wage is rigid at a level, $W_0$, at which the amount of labor supplied, $L_s$, is greater than the amount demanded, $L_d$. Under such circumstances the amount of labor demanded will be the amount employed: $L_e = L_d$. The demand equation, Eq. (9-24), provides the amount of labor to be substituted into the aggregate production function, Eq. (9-14), to give us the aggregate supply function as follows:

$$L_e = K(cW_0^{-1}P)^{1/b} \tag{9-24}$$

$$Q_e = K^b L_e^c = K^b L_e^{1-b} \tag{9-14}$$

$$Q_e = K(cW_0^{-1}P)^{(1-b)/b} \tag{9-37}$$

Solving Eq. (9-37) for $P$ gives

$$P_e = W_0(cK^{b/c})^{-1}Q^{b/c} \tag{9-38}$$

To put this in the standard aggregate supply form, $P = AQ^{a-1}$, we set

$$A = W_0(cK^{b/c})^{-1} \qquad a = \frac{1}{c}$$

Given that $c$ must be between zero and one, the inflation coefficient must be greater than one. This implies that the elasticity of output with respect to aggregate demand, $\eta_{Q,Y}$, must be less than one and the elasticity of price with respect to aggregate demand must be greater than zero. (See last row of Table 9–1.)

### 4. The Three Aggregate Supply Relationships Compared

An algebraic comparison of the three models is given in Table 9–1 with the implications for the inflation coefficient $a$ (and thereby for $\eta_{Q,Y}$ and $\eta_{P,Y}$) given in the last row.

Clearly the inflation coefficient is largest in the classical model as any change in aggregate demand will be totally reflected in a price change. The inflation coefficient is smaller in the money-wage model but not so small as it is in the unemployment model. It is obvious that the inflation coefficient in the money-wage model will always be exactly twice as large as the inflation coefficient in the unemployment model, regardless of the values of $b$ and $c$.

These aggregate supply models have assumed the level of total expenditures and the capital stock to be given. We shall combine the aggregate supply and demand forces in Chapter 10 and consider changes in the capital stock under the heading of economic growth in Chapter 11.

## EXERCISES

**1.** **a.** Given the production function $Q = K^b L^{(1-b)}$ and assuming that businessmen act in such a way as to maximize aggregate profits, derive a demand curve for labor.

**b.** Given also the aggregate supply function $Q_s = P^{1/2}$, what can you say about the possible results of a given percentage change in total expenditures, $Y$, on the equilibrium level of output, prices, and employment?

**2.** **a.** Given the production function $Q = 10L^{1/2}$, derive a demand curve for labor.

**b.** Given the two supply curves of labor below, derive equations for the equilibrium level of employment and output in each model:

| MODEL I | MODEL II |
|---------|----------|
| $L_s = 10W$ | $L_s = 10\left(\dfrac{W}{P}\right)$ |

**c.** Calculate the following three elasticities for each of the models:

  i   output, $Q$, with respect to total expenditures, $Y$;

  ii   employment, $L$, with respect to total expenditures;

  iii   price level, $P$, with respect to total expenditures.

**3.** **a.** Given the aggregate production function $Q = K^{1/4} L^{3/4}$ derive a demand curve for labor as a function of the real wage, $W/P$.

**b.** If $K = 32$ and the supply curve of labor is $L_s = (1\frac{1}{3})(W/P)$, what is the equilibrium level of employment?

**c.** i   What is the elasticity of employment with respect to total expenditures?

  ii   What is the elasticity of employment with respect to changes in the capital stock?

## RECOMMENDED REFERENCES

Allen, R. G. D., *Mathematical Analysis for Economists*. New York: St. Martin's Press, 1938, Chapter XII.

McKenna, Joseph P., *Aggregate Economic Analysis*, 3rd ed. New York: Holt, Rinehart and Winston, Inc., 1969, Chapters 12 and 13.

# 10 The Equilibrium Level of Output, Prices, and Employment

This chapter combines elements from all the previous chapters in order to complete a model that provides equilibrium levels of the aggregate supply variables—output, prices, wages, and employment. In making these determinations, this chapter will continue to employ the three models developed in Chapter 9. These three models differ primarily in the assumptions concerning the supply of labor. In the "real wage" model (to be designated as Model I), the supply of labor is a function of the real wage $W/P$. In the "money-wage" model (Model II), the labor supply depends on the money wage, $W$; while in the unemployment model (Model III), the supply of labor is assumed to be completely elastic at a fixed money-wage rate, $W_0$. In this last model, whatever quantity of labor is demanded will be forthcoming at the existing wage rate, and that rate cannot fall either to increase the quantity demanded or to decrease the quantity supplied.

Section I of this chapter reviews the underlying aggregate supply and demand concepts. Section II combines aggregate demand with aggregate supply for each of the three labor supply models and then examines the impact on the endogenous variables (determined by the system) resulting from changes in selected exogenous variables (determined outside the system) and changes in selected parameters. Section III is addressed to the effect of monetary and fiscal policy on the equilibrium levels of output, prices, and employment. An appendix to this chapter presents a new formulation of aggregate demand that generates an entirely different set of equilibrium values.

It should be noted that in all of these models the capital stock is assumed fixed, thereby making all of them "short run" in character. In Chapter 11, we remove this restriction in order to discuss economic growth.

## I REVIEW OF AGGREGATE SUPPLY AND AGGREGATE DEMAND

### 1. Aggregate Demand

Chapters 2 through 7 have developed the basic aggregate demand model employed in this text. This model can be quickly summarized in the following sets of equations:

$$Y = C + I + G \tag{1-6}$$

$$C = c_0 + c_y(Y - T) \tag{2-15}$$

$$T = t_y Y - t_0 \tag{2-17}$$

$$I = i_0 - i_r r \tag{4-10}$$

$$S + T = I + G \tag{5-11}$$

These five equations define equilibrium in the commodity market. By proper substitutions, these equations can be reduced to a single equation containing the two variables, $Y$ and $r$, called the $IS$ curve.

$$Y = \frac{c_0 + i_0 + c_y t_0 - i_r r + G}{1 - c_y + c_y t_y} \tag{5-12}$$

Equilibrium in the money market is based upon the following three relationships:

$$M_t = m_y Y \tag{6-18}$$

$$M_s = m_0 - m_r r \tag{6-19}$$

$$M = M_t + M_s \tag{6-21}$$

A solution of these three equations in terms of $Y$ and $r$ yields the $LM$ curve:

$$Y = \frac{M - m_0 + m_r r}{m_y} \tag{6-23}$$

Simultaneous solution of the $IS$ and $LM$ curves yields the equilibrium levels of national income and the rate of interest and thus also the equilibrium levels of consumption, investment, saving, taxes, and the demands for cash balances:

$$Y = \frac{m_r(c_0 + i_0 + c_y t_0 + G) + i_r(M - m_0)}{D} \tag{7-1}$$

$$r = \frac{m_y(c_0 + i_0 + c_y t_0 + G) - (1 - c_y + c_y t_y)(M - m_0)}{D} \tag{7-2}$$

$$C = c_0 + c_y t_0 + \frac{c_y(1 - t_y)[m_r(c_0 + i_0 + c_y t_0 + G) + i_r(M - m_0)]}{D}$$

$$\tag{10-1}$$

$$I = i_0 - \frac{i_r[m_y(c_0 + i_0 + c_y t_0 + G) - (1 - c_y + c_y t_y)(M - m_0)]}{D}$$

$$\text{(10-2)}$$

$$S = -c_0 + (1 - c_y)t_0$$
$$+ \frac{(1 - c_y)(1 - t_y)[m_r(c_0 + i_0 + c_y t_0 + G) + i_r(M - m_0)]}{D}$$

$$\text{(10-3)}$$

$$T = \frac{t_y[m_r(c_0 + i_0 + c_y t_0 + G) - (1 - c_y + c_y t_y)(M - m_0)]}{D} - t_0 \quad \text{(10-4)}$$

$$M_s = m_0 - \frac{m_r[m_y(c_0 + i_0 + c_y t_0 + G) - (1 - c_y + c_y t_y)(M - m_0)]}{D}$$

$$\text{(10-5)}$$

$$M_t = \frac{m_y[m_r(c_0 + i_0 + c_y t_0 + G) + i_r(M - m_0)]}{D} \quad \text{(10-6)}$$

where

$$D = m_r(1 - c_y + c_y t_y) + m_y i_r$$

Note that in the previous six equations, all the equilibrium values are determined by government expenditures, the money supply, the tax rate, and the parameters in the behavioral equations. In this particular formulation, the aggregate supply variables have absolutely no influence upon the aggregate demand variables.

## 2. Aggregate Supply

Chapter 9 has already developed most of the aggregate supply relationships. For purposes of convenience, we shall assume that the aggregate production function is linearly homogeneous of the Cobb-Douglas type:

$$Q = K^b L^c \quad \text{(9-14)}$$

Furthermore, we shall continue the assumption that the demand for labor is derived by equating the real wage rate, $W/P$, to the aggregate marginal product of labor. Thus,

$$L_d = c^{1/b} K \left(\frac{W}{P}\right)^{-1/b} \quad \text{(9-24)}$$

The production function and the demand for labor given by Eqs. (9-14) and (9-24) are relationships that we shall assume to be generally valid throughout the remainder of the chapter. However, we shall not assume that there is any single generally valid labor supply equation. Thus, in order to proceed further, we must again turn to the three models of Chapter 9.

## MODEL I

The assumption of Model I is that the supply of labor depends on the real wage rate. The linear equation employed to express this relationship was

$$L_s = l_{w/p}\left(\frac{W}{P}\right) \tag{9-29}$$

The equilibrium level of labor is determined by the simultaneous solution of Eqs. (9-24) and (9-29).

$$L_e = (cK^b l_{w/p})^{1/(1+b)} \tag{9-30}$$

In the short run, the stock of capital is fixed, so the equilibrium level of employment is a function merely of various constants in the aggregate supply equations. The level of aggregate demand has no influence upon employment.

The real wage is also determined by simultaneous solution of Eqs. (9-29) and (9-30).

$$\frac{W}{P} = (cK^b l_{w/p}^{-b})^{1/(1+b)} \tag{10-7}$$

Similar to employment, aggregate demand variables do not have any impact on the real wage rate.

The equilibrium level of output is found by substituting the equilibrium level of employment given by Eq. (9-30) into (9-14), the production function:

$$Q = K^{2b/(1+b)}(cl_{w/p})^{c/(1+b)} \tag{9-31}$$

Once again, with a fixed capital stock, the level of output is also determined solely by aggregate supply factors, with aggregate demand having no influence at all.

The only variables left undetermined at this point are the price level and the money-wage rate. Equation (10-7) gives the ratio of these two, but an infinite number of combinations of the two are consistent with that ratio. To determine a unique price level, and therefore a unique wage level, we must turn to a reconsideration of aggregate demand. Equation (9-1) gave an

that underpins these relationships has been developed in previous chapters and sections, this section shall be concerned only with the signs of the partial derivatives rather than with their values. In the accompanying tables to this section, an entry of $+$ indicates that the partial derivative is positive, whereas a $-$ or a 0 indicates that it is negative or zero, respectively.

## 1. Aggregate Demand

Table 10–1 presents the signs of the partial derivatives of the aggregate demand endogenous variables with respect to relevant exogenous variables

### Table 10–2

Aggregate Supply
Signs of Partial Derivatives

Model I

ENDOGENOUS VARIABLES

| BLOCK I | | | | | |
|---|---|---|---|---|---|
| *Aggregate Demand* *Behavioral Parameters* | $Q$ | $L$ | $W$ | $P$ | $W/P$ |
| $c_0$ | 0 | 0 | $+$ | $+$ | 0 |
| $c_y$ | 0 | 0 | $+$ | $+$ | 0 |
| $i_0$ | 0 | 0 | $+$ | $+$ | 0 |
| $i_r$ | 0 | 0 | $-$ | $-$ | 0 |
| $m_0$ | 0 | 0 | $-$ | $-$ | 0 |
| $m_y$ | 0 | 0 | $-$ | $-$ | 0 |
| $m_r$ | 0 | 0 | $+$ | $+$ | 0 |
| **BLOCK II** | | | | | |
| *Policy Variables* | | | | | |
| $t_0$ | 0 | 0 | $+$ | $+$ | 0 |
| $t_y$ | 0 | 0 | $-$ | $-$ | 0 |
| $G$ | 0 | 0 | $+$ | $+$ | 0 |
| $M$ | 0 | 0 | $+$ | $+$ | 0 |
| **BLOCK III** | | | | | |
| *Aggregate Supply* *Behavioral Parameters* | | | | | |
| $b$ | $\pm$ | $\pm$ | $\pm$ | $\mp$ | $\pm$ |
| $c = 1 - b$ | $\mp$ | $\mp$ | $\mp$ | $\pm$ | $\mp$ |
| $l_{w/p}$ | $+$ | $+$ | $-$ | $-$ | $-$ |
| $K$ | $+$ | $+$ | $-$ | $-$ | $-$ |

The entry in each column is the sign of the partial derivative of the column variable with respect to the row variable.

and constants in the system. The signs for Block I are those for derivatives taken with respect to behavioral parameters in the aggregate demand equations. Block II contains policy variables which may be set exogenously by the governmental authorities, while Block III contains aggregate supply parameters and the stock of capital.

The reader should examine each of the signs to see if he can explain to himself the reason for each. If he has any difficulty, he should reread the chapter and section dealing with that particular variable. Note that the signs of the derivatives with respect to the aggregate supply constants are all zero. In the formulation of aggregate demand in this book, we have steadfastly assumed that the absolute level of income determines consumption expenditures and the demand for money balances. Thus, aggregate demand is totally independent of the real level of output. Had the authors made the alternate assumption that the *real* level of consumption and money balances is set by the *real* level of income, aggregate demand would have been dependent on aggregate supply, and the partial derivatives in Block III would have had positive and negative signs.[1]

## 2. Aggregate Supply

Tables 10–2, 10–3, and 10–4 present the signs of the partial derivatives for the aggregate supply endogenous variables for each of the employment

**Table 10–3**

Aggregate Supply
Signs of Partial Derivatives

Model II

| | ENDOGENOUS VARIABLES | | | | |
|---|---|---|---|---|---|
| **BLOCK I** | | | | | |
| *Aggregate Demand Behavioral Parameters* | $Q$ | $L$ | $W$ | $P$ | $W/P$ |
| $c_0$ | + | + | + | + | − |
| $c_y$ | + | + | + | + | − |
| $i_0$ | + | + | + | + | − |
| $i_r$ | − | − | − | − | + |
| $m_0$ | − | − | − | − | + |
| $m_y$ | − | − | − | − | + |
| $m_r$ | + | + | + | + | − |
| **BLOCK II** | | | | | |
| *Policy Variables* | | | | | |
| $t_0$ | + | + | + | + | − |
| $t_i$ | − | − | − | − | + |
| $G$ | + | + | + | + | − |
| $M$ | + | + | + | + | − |

---

[1] See the appendix to this chapter for an example of such an aggregate demand model.

## Table 10–3 (Continued)

ENDOGENOUS VARIABLES

| BLOCK III<br>*Aggregate Supply*<br>*Behavioral Parameters* | $Q$ | $L$ | $W$ | $P$ | $W/P$ |
|---|---|---|---|---|---|
| $b$ | ± | − | − | ∓ | ± |
| $c = 1 - b$ | ∓ | + | + | ± | ∓ |
| $l_w$ | + | + | − | − | − |
| $K$ | + | 0 | 0 | − | + |

The entry in each column is the sign of the partial derivative of the column variable with respect to the row variable.

## Table 10–4

Aggregate Supply

Signs of Partial Derivatives

Model III

ENDOGENOUS VARIABLES

| BLOCK I<br>*Aggregate Demand*<br>*Behavioral Parameters* | $Q$ | $L$ | $W_0$ | $P$ | $W_0/P$ |
|---|---|---|---|---|---|
| $c_0$ | + | + | 0 | + | − |
| $c_y$ | + | + | 0 | + | − |
| $i_0$ | + | + | 0 | + | − |
| $i_r$ | − | − | 0 | − | + |
| $m_0$ | − | − | 0 | − | + |
| $m_y$ | − | − | 0 | − | + |
| $m_r$ | + | + | 0 | + | − |

| BLOCK II<br>*Policy Variables* | | | | | |
|---|---|---|---|---|---|
| $t_0$ | + | + | 0 | + | − |
| $t_y$ | − | − | 0 | − | + |
| $G$ | + | + | 0 | + | − |
| $M$ | + | + | 0 | + | − |

| BLOCK III<br>*Aggregate Supply*<br>*Behavioral Parameters* | | | | | |
|---|---|---|---|---|---|
| $b$ | ± | − | 0 | ∓ | ± |
| $c = 1 - b$ | ∓ | + | 0 | ± | ∓ |
| $W_0$ | − | − | + | + | + |
| $K$ | + | 0 | 0 | − | + |

The entry in each column is the sign of the partial derivative of the column variable with respect to the row variable.

models given above. Again, the student should verify for himself the reason for the sign for each of the derivatives. With the exception of the derivatives with respect to the coefficient, $b$, in the production function, the theory should be reasonably straightforward. The difficulty in the particular case cited stems from the fact that a change in the capital coefficient, $b$, also changes the labor coefficient, $1 - b$. Thus, an increase in the value of $b$, if it increases the marginal productivity of capital, also decreases the marginal productivity of labor. If the change in the value of $b$ decreases the marginal productivity of capital, it increases the marginal productivity of labor. Moreover, it is not apparent immediately what the exact impact of a change in $b$ will be on the marginal productivities. If the student returns to Chapter 9 to examine the marginal productivity of labor, he will see that the formula is

$$MP_L = (1 - b)\left(\frac{K}{L}\right)^b \tag{9-18}$$

Whether the change in the capital coefficient increases or decreases the marginal productivity of labor depends on the size of the capital-labor ratio and the initial value of $b$. If the capital-labor ratio is small and the initial value of $b$ is close to unity, an increase in $b$ will decrease the marginal productivity of labor greatly. The equilibrium level of labor will decline more than enough to offset the increased productivity of capital, and total output will decrease. If the capital-labor ratio is large and the initial value of $b$ is small, an increase in the value of $b$ will increase the marginal productivity of labor, expand the equilibrium level of employment, and lead to the result that the utilization of a larger amount of more efficient labor is more than enough to offset the use of the same amount of capital that has become less efficient. Thus, in this latter case, output increases. The only cases where the signs of the partial derivatives with respect to $b$ are straightforward are in Models II and III for endogenous variables $L$ and $W$. As shown above, however, these variables are insensitive to the stock of capital, so it seems only natural that they should not be affected by the efficiency of the stock of capital.

Of particular interest in comparing the three aggregate demand models are the elasticities of the endogenous variables with respect to other variables and constants. Recall that a coefficient of elasticity is nothing more than a percentage change in one variable that results from a change of 1% in some other variable. The formula for the partial elasticity of a variable $x$ with respect to a variable $y$ is

$$\eta_{x,y} = \frac{\partial x}{\partial y} \frac{y}{x}$$

Table 10–5 presents an array of relevant elasticity coefficients for each of the models under examination. In general, notice that as we move from

**Table 10–5**

Aggregate Supply and Aggregate Demand
Coefficients of Elasticity

| | COEFFICIENTS | | |
|---|---|---|---|
| VARIABLES | *Model I* | *Model II* | *Model III* |
| $\eta_{Y,Q}$ | 0 | 0 | 0 |
| $\eta_{Y,P}$ | 0 | 0 | 0 |
| $\eta_{Q,Y}$ | 0 | $\dfrac{1-b}{2}$ | $1-b$ |
| $\eta_{Q,P}$ | 0 | $\dfrac{1-b}{1+b}$ | $\dfrac{1-b}{b}$ |
| $\eta_{Q,K}$ | $\dfrac{2b}{1+b}$ | $b$ | $b$ |
| $\eta_{P,Y}$ | 1.0 | $\dfrac{1+b}{2}$ | $b$ |
| $\eta_{P,Q}$ | $-1.0$ | $\dfrac{1+b}{1-b}$ | $\dfrac{b}{1-b}$ |
| $\eta_{L,K}$ | $\dfrac{b}{1+b}$ | 0 | 0 |
| $\eta_{L,Y}$ | 0 | $\dfrac{1}{2}$ | 1.0 |
| $\eta_{W/P,K}$ | $\dfrac{b}{1+b}$ | $b$ | $b$ |
| $\eta_{W,Y}$ | 1.0 | $\dfrac{1}{2}$ | 0 |
| $\eta_{W,P}$ | $-1.0$ | $\dfrac{1}{1+b}$ | 0 |

Model I to Model III, output and employment generally become more sensitive to other variables in the system, while prices and wages generally become less sensitive. For example, in considering the impact of a change in aggregate demand upon the volume of output, notice that in Model I there is no effect whatsoever, while the effect for Model III is exactly twice as large as for Model II. The same result holds for the elasticity of employment with respect to aggregate demand. On the other hand, wages in Model III are completely insensitive to changes in national income, but the change in Model I is twice as great as it is in Model II.

## 3. A Graphic Presentation

Figure 10–1 presents two of the more interesting relationships above graphically. For Model I, Graph (a) shows that the level of output is independent of the price level at a value $Q_e$. The price level is determined by the

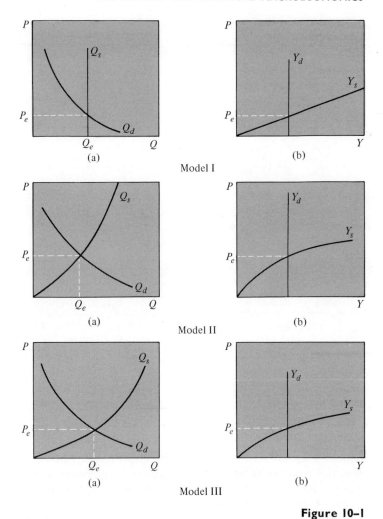

**Figure 10-1**

A Graphic Comparison of the Three Models

intersection with the aggregate demand schedule ($Y = PQ$), giving all possible combinations of $Q$ and $P$ that will equal the fixed level of total expenditures. Graph (b) is an alternative description of the equilibrium. The graph shows aggregate demand fixed at a level of $Y_e$. The upward-sloping straight line is the relationship between $P$ and $Y$ that must hold if the levels of aggregate demand and the fixed total output are to be consistent. Equilibrium price is determined by the intersection of the two curves.

Graphs (a) and (b) for Models II and III are similar to the corresponding graphs in Model I. Note that in Graph (a) for both of these models, however, $Q$ and $P$ are not independent in the aggregate supply sector, so the relationship between them is described by an upward-sloping curved line. Equilibrium is again attained at the intersection of the two curves. Graph (b) for Models II and III is similar to the corresponding graph for Model I, except that prices in the latter two models are not quite so sensitive to changes in aggregate demand. Thus, the upward-sloping lines increase at a decreasing rate.

### III THE IMPACT OF MONETARY AND FISCAL POLICY ON OUTPUT, PRICES, AND EMPLOYMENT

The effect of monetary and fiscal policy on aggregate demand has already been discussed in previous chapters. However, this material is quite relevant to the present section because the role that policy plays in affecting aggregate supply is an indirect one through its influence on aggregate demand. That is, changes in tax rates, government expenditures, or the money supply have no immediate impact on prices and employment. Only by changing the level of aggregate demand will it be possible to affect aggregate supply variables, and only then if the aggregate supply variable under consideration is not independent of aggregate demand.

The signs of the partial derivatives of the aggregate supply variables with respect to the policy variables have already been given in Tables 10–2, 10–3, and 10–4 for each of the three labor supply models. The important difference in the three models is that output, employment, and the real wage are unaffected by policy variables for Model I, whereas the money-wage rate is not affected by policy in Model III. Note that all three models are consistent insofar as the sign of a partial derivative is never reversed in moving from one model to another.

Table 10–6 represents the elasticities of the aggregate supply variables for policy changes of each of the three models. That is, each entry in the table shows the percentage change in the aggregate supply variable resulting from a change of 1% in the policy variable. Only the three most important policy variables—government expenditures, the marginal tax rate, and the money supply—are presented in the table. Note that for output, employment, and the real wage the absolute size of the elasticity coefficient increases as we move from Model I to Model III, with the coefficient in Model III being twice as large in absolute value as the coefficient for Model II. For money wages, the reverse is true, with the elasticity being zero in Model III and twice as large in Model I as Model II. Thus, government policy would have the greatest effect on employment, output, and real wages if Model III were

**Table 10–6**

Aggregate Supply Elasticities for Policy
Changes

| MODEL AND POLICY VARIABLE | AGGREGATE SUPPLY VARIABLE | | | | |
|---|---|---|---|---|---|
| | $Q$ | $L$ | $W/P$ | $P$ | $W$ |
| *Model I* | | | | | |
| $G$ | 0 | 0 | 0 | $\dfrac{m_r G}{DY}$ | $\dfrac{m_r G}{DY}$ |
| $t_y$ | 0 | 0 | 0 | $-\dfrac{m_r c_y t_y}{D}$ | $-\dfrac{m_r c_y t_y}{D}$ |
| $M$ | 0 | 0 | 0 | $\dfrac{i_r M}{DY}$ | $\dfrac{i_r M}{DY}$ |
| *Model II* | | | | | |
| $G$ | $\dfrac{1-b}{2}\dfrac{m_r G}{DY}$ | $\dfrac{1}{2}\dfrac{m_r G}{DY}$ | $\dfrac{-b}{2}\dfrac{m_r G}{DY}$ | $\dfrac{1+b}{2}\dfrac{m_r G}{DY}$ | $\dfrac{1}{2}\dfrac{m_r G}{DY}$ |
| $t_y$ | $-\dfrac{1-b}{2}\dfrac{m_r c_y t_y}{D}$ | $-\dfrac{1}{2}\dfrac{m_r c_y t_y}{D}$ | $\dfrac{b}{2}\dfrac{m_r c_y t_y}{D}$ | $-\dfrac{1+b}{2}\dfrac{m_r c_y t_y}{D}$ | $-\dfrac{1}{2}\dfrac{m_r c_y t_y}{D}$ |
| $M$ | $\dfrac{1-b}{2}\dfrac{i_r M}{DY}$ | $\dfrac{1}{2}\dfrac{i_r M}{DY}$ | $\dfrac{-b}{2}\dfrac{i_r M}{DY}$ | $\dfrac{1+b}{2}\dfrac{i_r M}{DY}$ | $\dfrac{1}{2}\dfrac{i_r M}{DY}$ |
| *Model III* | | | | | |
| $G$ | $(1-b)\dfrac{m_r G}{DY}$ | $\dfrac{m_r G}{DY}$ | $-\dfrac{bm_r G}{DY}$ | $\dfrac{b\,m_r G}{DY}$ | 0 |
| $t_y$ | $-(1-b)\dfrac{m_r c_y t_y}{D}$ | $-\dfrac{m_r c_y t_y}{D}$ | $b\dfrac{m_r c_y t_y}{D}$ | $-b\dfrac{m_r c_y t_y}{D}$ | 0 |
| $M$ | $(1-b)\dfrac{i_r M}{DY}$ | $\dfrac{i_r M}{DY}$ | $-b\dfrac{i_r M}{DY}$ | $b\dfrac{i_r M}{DY}$ | 0 |

The entry in each column is the elasticity of the column variable with respect to the row variable.
$$D = m_r(1 - c_y + c_y t_y) + i_r m_y$$

most descriptive of the economy and the greatest effect on prices and money
wages if Model I were the most realistic. Only if Model II were the true
representation of the economy would government policy be able to have any
impact on all five of the aggregate supply variables. Which of these models
might be the most descriptive is the subject of a later section.

# IV INFLATION AND GOVERNMENT POLICY

Chapter 9 developed the concept of aggregate supply, showing the
alternative combinations of output and price levels that are possible with a
given production function and a given capital stock under different assumptions about labor market behavior. Earlier sections of this chapter combined

aggregate supply with aggregate demand to indicate the static equilibrium levels of output and the price level. This section will expand on the concepts presented earlier and consider some of the problems associated with *rising* prices, or inflation.

Of course, not all the different aspects of inflation can be adequately examined in the static model used in Chapters 7 and 9, because inflation is not just *high* prices (a static phenomenon) but is *rising* prices (a dynamic matter). Accordingly, this chapter will not treat such matters as *how fast* prices rise but merely compare different static positions to see if in fact they *will* rise.

## 1. Demand-Pull Inflation

Demand-pull inflation is said to occur when the aggregate demand schedule increases, the aggregate supply schedule remaining relatively constant. Thus, the increased dollar bids for commodities raises the equilibrium prices of commodities. We may examine this concept more closely by considering the equilibrium price equations for Models I, II, and III above, Eqs. (10-8), (10-11), and (10-18), respectively. In these equations, the level of aggregate demand is indicated by the volume of total expenditures, $Y$. If the level of aggregate demand increases, then

$$\frac{\partial P_e}{\partial Y} = K^{-2b/(1+b)}(cl_{w/p})^{-(1-b)/(1+b)} > 0 \tag{10-22}$$

$$\frac{\partial P_e}{\partial Y} = \tfrac{1}{2}(1+b)K^{-b}[(1-b)l_w Y]^{-(1-b)/2} > 0 \tag{10-23}$$

$$\frac{\partial P_e}{\partial Y} = bY^{b-1}K^{-b}[(1-b)^{-1}W_0]^{1-b} > 0 \tag{10-24}$$

We might also look at the impact that the increase has on the level of real output, $Q$.

$$\frac{\partial Q}{\partial Y} = 0 \tag{10-25}$$

$$\frac{\partial Q}{\partial Y} = \tfrac{1}{2}K^b(1-b)^{(3-b)/2}l_w^{(1-b)/2}Y^{-(1+b)/2} > 0 \tag{10-26}$$

$$\frac{\partial Q}{\partial Y} = (1-b)^{2-b}K^b W_0^{b-1}Y^{-b} > 0 \tag{10-27}$$

With the exception of output in Model I, an increase in aggregate demand increases the equilibrium levels for both the price index and the volume of total output. Only the period of disequilibrium will be an inflationary period, for once the new equilibrium level is reached, price increases will not continue unless there is a further increase in aggregate demand. How severe the interim inflationary period will be depends on how much greater the new equilibrium is and on how rapidly price adjustments are made within the economy.

If governmental authorities attempt to restrain or eliminate inflation, either monetary policy or fiscal policy may be employed to force aggregate demand back toward its previous levels. In the models considered here, however, it is unlikely that government would attempt to restore the previous level of aggregate demand, as that would not only prevent further price increases, it would cause prices to fall back to their previous levels. Equations (7-16), (7-13), and (7-11) have already shown that aggregate demand can be reduced by reducing the money supply, decreasing the level of government expenditures, or increasing the tax rate. Since the partial derivatives of price or output with respect to any of these policy variables are merely the partial derivative of price or output with respect to aggregate demand times the partial derivative of aggregate demand with respect to the policy variable, it can be quickly shown that, with the exception again of Model I, the price level and the volume of output move in the same direction as changes in the money supply and in government spending and in the opposite direction from changes in the tax rate. Alternatively, the reader may reexamine Table 10–6 and inspect the coefficients of elasticity for the price and output variables with respect to the policy variables.

Whether monetary policy or fiscal policy is used to combat inflation or whether a mix of the two is used should depend on other objectives being pursued by society. For example, decreasing the money supply will cause interest rates to rise, forcing contractions in those industries that are sensitive to the interest rate, especially the construction trades. Moreover, municipalities and state governments may delay the construction or completion of various public investments such as schools, highways, and sanitation facilities because of unfavorable bond markets. If government expenditures are decreased, the interest rate will fall somewhat, and the public sector will decrease in size relative to the private sector. Increases in taxes will again cause interest rates to fall, but the basic impact will fall upon the producers of consumer goods.

## 2. Cost-Push Inflation

The cost-push model of inflation assumes that pressures for rising prices develop in the labor markets rather than in the product markets. Any of the three labor markets models employed above can be used to demonstrate cost-push inflation, but the analysis is probably most clear if we use only Model III. In that case, partial differentiation of Eq. (10-18) yields

$$\frac{\partial P}{\partial W_0} = Y^b K^{-b}[(1 - b)^{-1}W_0]^{-b} > 0 \qquad (10\text{-}28)$$

Thus, an increase in the going wage rate causes the equilibrium price level to rise. The impact on the level of output can be observed from differentiation of Eq. (10-19):

$$\frac{\partial Q_e}{\partial W_0} = -K^b(1 - b)^{2-b}Y^{1-b}W_0^{b-2} < 0 \qquad (10\text{-}29)$$

In this case, inflation is accompanied by a *decrease* in real output.

With cost-push inflation, government policy makers face a real dilemma. As already discussed, decreases in the money supply, decreases in government expenditures, and increases in taxes can retard the increase in prices, but these same policies will further reduce the level of output. Accordingly, government policy aimed at solving the problem of inflation can only succeed at the cost of decreased output and employment, while increased production can be attained only through greater inflation. This result has caused some economists to question whether the government has enough policy instruments to attain all the national economic objectives simultaneously. It has been suggested that government should develop new policy weapons that operate on aggregate supply to enhance the policy instruments that already exist for manipulation of aggregate demand. In the early 1960's, the government tried to enforce wage-price guidelines partially to meet this objective. Basically, the guidelines urged businessmen and labor unions to agree on wage increases that roughly paralleled productivity increases in the economy. In areas where productivity increased by more than the national average, prices were to be decreased. Although these guidelines met with some initial success, they were largely abandoned during the mid 1960's in the face of intense pressure for large wage increases. No substitute for the guidelines has yet been adopted.

## 3. The Phillips Curve

The previous section on cost-push inflation raises some interesting questions as to what variables affect the going wage rate, $W_0$. Although several economic variables such as productivity increases, corporate profits, and market expectations all have their separate impacts, one factor that is of considerable interest here is the level of unemployment.[2] Empirically, this

---

[2] For example, see M. Liebenberg, A. Hirsch, and J. Popkin, "A Quarterly Econometric Model of the U.S.," *Survey of Current Business*, May 1966, p. 32.

variable has been found to be quite important in determining the percentage increase in wages in any given period. Theoretically, this could be explained by labor reluctance to seek higher wages when employment security is already threatened and by management's inability to grant large wage increases when profits are reduced. The relationship between wage increases and the level of unemployment might therefore be written as

$$\frac{dW_0}{W_0} = w_0 - w_U U$$

The percentage rate of increase in wages is a function of the level of unemployment, $U$.

(10-30)

Assuming that aggregate demand and the capital stock remain constant, the differential of Eq. (10-18) becomes

$$dP = Y^b K^{-b} (1 - b)^b W_0^{-b} \, dW_0 \tag{10-31}$$

Division of both sides by $P$ yields

$$\frac{dP}{P} = (1 - b) \frac{dW_0}{W_0} = (1 - b)(w_0 - w_U U) \tag{10-32}$$

The previous equation poses another dilemma to modern policy makers. Called the Phillips curve,[3] this relationship demonstrates again the possible incompatibility between price stability and full employment. The equation illustrates that the percentage change in prices will be zero only if unemployment is equal to $w_0/w_U$ and that unemployment will be zero only if prices rise at an annual rate of $(1 - b)w_0$.

# V THE RELEVANCE OF THE MODELS

The three very specific aggregate supply models inadequately reflect the almost infinite complexities of a modern industrial economy, as valid generalities cannot be proved with only three specific examples. However, the models do reflect certain generally accepted postulates concerning contemporary macroeconomic theory.

Model I demonstrates that there can be no unemployment if wages and prices are flexible and if employers and employees behave rationally. Here,

[3] After A. W. Phillips, "The Relation Between Unemployment and the Rate of Change of Money Wage Rate in the United Kingdom, 1861–1957," *Economica*, November 1958, pp. 283–99.

"rationally" means that workers supply their labor in positive correlation with the purchasing power of wages paid them and employers hire labor for the value of what they produce. In such a system the output of the economy is set by "real" factors of production—the production function and the supply of labor. Total money expenditures are relevant only to setting the price level, and changes in aggregate demand brought about by changes in the money supply or changes in government spending and taxing influence neither output nor employment. Under such conditions, if the government increases its claim on the output of the economy, prices and wages will be forced upward and the share of real output going to the private sector will have to be reduced.

Model II drops the assumption of rationality on the part of the workers and assumes in its place that workers are subject to a money illusion by which they offer labor in direct relationship to the money wage rather than the real wage. The point made by this model is that if some members of the economy act as if they are subject to a money illusion, the level of aggregate demand will influence not only the price level but also the level of output and employment. Since the model continues to assume that wages and prices are flexible, unemployment still cannot exist. In this model, however, an increase in government claims on the economy will lead to both an increase in prices and an increase in output and employment. The private sector's share of the output would not necessarily have to decrease in the face of such government claims.

Model III drops the assumption of flexible wages, assuming instead that the money wage is institutionally set at some particular level. The interesting result from this assumption is that unemployment is allowed to exist. Thus, any increase in government claims on the economy will tap a pool of unemployed labor and increase total output with only slight increases in prices. This model might be employed to illustrate the effect of short-run adjustments in an economy where wages and prices were perfectly flexible only over a very long period of time. In other words, Model III could serve as an example of either Model I or Model II during extended periods of disequilibrium if the transition from one equilibrium period to another is sufficiently slow in those models.

In conclusion, in periods of full employment, Model I is probably not a bad approximation, while Model III is adequate to describe an economy in a depression. However, these static models will always be inadequate to the job of observing the dynamic behavior of macroeconomic systems. That much further study of dynamic models is needed is indicated by our brief look at the dynamic phenomenon of inflation and its possible relationship to unemployment via the Phillips curve. It is possible that the structure of the economy is such that we cannot achieve price stability and "full employment" simultaneously. Serious consideration of these matters requires dynamic models beyond the scope of this book and a sophisticated look at the data describing the time path of the economy, the interpretation of which is the field of aggregate econometrics.

## APPENDIX TO CHAPTER 10:
## THE COMPARATIVE STATICS OF
## MACROECONOMIC MODELS WITH
## AND WITHOUT MONEY ILLUSION

In this appendix we shall first establish that a formulation of aggregate demand as presented thus far in the text implies that our economic groups (consumers, investors, and speculators in the money market) are subject to a money illusion. We shall then rewrite the behavioral equations in such a way as to remove the money illusion and evaluate the comparative statics of the two systems. We shall find that the *IS* and *LM* curves are not independent in the absence of money illusion and that unemployment can result from a true "deficiency of aggregate demand" in such a system.

The essential points to be made in this appendix can be illustrated most clearly if a simple system considering only consumers and investors (ignoring government expenditures, taxes, and the foreign sector) is used. Virtually identical results can be obtained using the more complicated models presented in the text. The symbols retain the same definitions as in the text but the numbering of the equations is unique to the appendix.

A behavioral equation implies money illusion if the "real" (price-deflated) values change when all prices, incomes, and wages are changed by a constant proportion. Let us first examine a set of equations that can be used to derive the *IS* curve of a simple macroeconomic model similar to that used in the text:

$$Y = C + I \tag{10A-1}$$

$$C = c_0 + c_y Y \tag{10A-2}$$

$$I = i_0 - i_r r \tag{10A-3}$$

$$S = I \tag{10A-4}$$

Additional definitions:

$$Y = PQ$$

$$S = Y - C$$

Equations (10A-1) and (10A-4) are an identity and an equilibrium condition, respectively, and tell us nothing about money illusion on the part of consumers or investors. We can write them in money terms as presented above or rewrite them in real terms by dividing each equation by the price level. Rewriting Eq. (10A–1) in real terms gives

$$\frac{Y}{P} = \frac{C}{P} + \frac{I}{P} \qquad \frac{PQ}{P} = \frac{C}{P} + \frac{I}{P} \qquad Q = \frac{C}{P} + \frac{I}{P} \qquad \text{(10A-5)}$$

Rewriting Eq. (10A–4) in real terms gives

$$\frac{S}{P} = \frac{I}{P} \qquad \text{(10A-6)}$$

Turning now to the consumption function, Eq. (10A–2), let us determine what would happen to real consumption ($C/P$) if there were a proportionate change in prices, $P$, and income, $Y$, with no change in real output, $Q$. Dividing Eq. (10A–2) by the price level to obtain a real consumption function yields

$$\frac{C}{P} = \frac{c_0}{P} + \frac{c_y Y}{P} \qquad \frac{C}{P} = \frac{c_0}{P} + \frac{c_y PQ}{P}$$

$$\frac{C}{P} = \frac{c_0}{P} + c_y Q \qquad \text{(10A-7)}$$

What happens to real consumption, $C/P$, if prices and money incomes change, holding $Q$ constant?

$$\frac{\partial (C/P)}{\partial P} = -\frac{c_0}{P^2} < 0 \qquad$$ Real consumption will vary inversely with the price level—consumers are subject to money illusion.

Specifically it is the autonomous consumption, $c_0$, that is fixed in money terms that gives rise to the money illusion. The induced portion of the consumption, $c_y Y$, will vary directly with the price level, leaving induced real consumption unchanged.

To remove the money illusion, we may rewrite Eq. (10A–2) as follows:

$$C = c_0 P + c_y Y \quad \text{or} \quad \frac{C}{P} = c_0 + c_y Q \qquad \text{(10A-8)}$$

To test for money illusion, we take the partial with respect to the price level:

$$\frac{\partial (C/P)}{\partial P} = 0 \qquad$$ A change in prices will leave real consumption unchanged—consumers plan their expenditures in real terms and are not subject to money illusion.

The investment function, Eq. (10A–3), also implies money illusion. Dividing Eq. (10A–3) by the price level to find an expression for real investment, we obtain

$$\frac{I}{P} = \frac{i_0}{P} - \frac{i_r r}{P} \qquad (10A\text{-}9)$$

Evaluating the results of a price change, we find that

$$\frac{\partial(I/P)}{\partial P} = -\frac{(i_0 - i_r r)}{P^2} < 0 \qquad$$ Real investment will vary inversely with the price level—investors are subject to money illusion.

$$(10A\text{-}10)$$

It is obvious that Eq. (10A–10) is negative if $(i_0 - i_r r)$ is positive. This expression is total investment as given by Eq. (10A–3) and hence assumed to be positive. The investment function, Eq. (10A–3), may be rewritten without money illusion as follows:

$$I = P(i_0 - i_r r)$$

or

$$\frac{I}{P} = i_0 - i_r r \qquad (10A\text{-}11)$$

We can now compare the model implying money illusion with the one without money illusion:

| MONEY ILLUSION | | NO MONEY ILLUSION | |
|---|---|---|---|
| (10A-1) | $Y = C + I$ | (10A-5) | $Q = \dfrac{C}{P} + \dfrac{I}{P}$ |
| (10A-2) | $C = c_0 + c_y Y$ | (10A-8) | $\dfrac{C}{P} = c_0 + c_y Q$ |
| (10A-3) | $I = i_0 - i_r r$ | (10A-11) | $\dfrac{I}{P} = i_0 - i_r r$ |
| (10A-4) | $S = I$ | (10A-6) | $\dfrac{S}{P} = \dfrac{I}{P}$ |

In the two models, Eq. (10A–1) implies Eq. (10A–5), and Eq. (10A–4) implies Eq. (10A–6). They are the same equations. However, the behavioral equations have a substantive difference. Equation (10A–8) conceives of consumers behaving in an entirely different way than does Eq. (10A–2). The hypothesis regarding the behavior of investors that is expressed by Eq. (10A–11) is entirely different from that of Eq. (10A–3).

These two formulations do, of course, result in differing *IS* curves whether one thinks of the *IS* curve being plotted in a *Y,r* plane or a *Q,r* plane. The four formulae for the *IS* curves with and without money illusion and with *Y* a function of *r* and *Q* a function of *r* are as follows:

FORMULAE FOR *IS* CURVES

| *Investors and Consumers Subject to Money Illusion* | *Investors and Consumers Not Subject to Money Illusion* |
|---|---|
| (A) $\quad Y = \dfrac{i_0 + c_0 - i_r r}{1 - c_y}$ | (C) $\quad Y = \dfrac{P(i_0 + c_0 - i_r r)}{1 - c_y}$ |
| (B) $\quad Q = \dfrac{i_0 + c_0 - i_r r}{P(1 - c_y)}$ | (D) $\quad Q = \dfrac{i_0 + c_0 - i_r r}{1 - c_y}$ |

Note that in the money illusion case an *IS* curve that is independent of the price level (and thereby independent of shifts in the *LM* curve and aggregate supply conditions) is obtained only if income is stated in money terms, *Y*. If, as shown by Eq. (B), the *IS* curve is written as an equilibrium level of the demand for real goods, *Q*, the position of the curve in the *Q,r* plane is a function of the endogenous variable *P* and can be expected to shift with every change in the equilibrium price level.

Conversely, in the case of no money illusion, Eqs. (C) and (D), the *IS* curve is independent of the price level only when the relationship is expressed between real income, *Q*, and the interest rate. The equilibrium level of money expenditures will change (an *IS* curve in a *Y,r* plane will shift) with every change in the price level in the absence of money illusion.

The presentation in the text has used the formulation of Eq. (A). Many other macroeconomic textbooks use the formulation of Eq. (D). Before we can compare the two approaches, we must go on to the *LM* curve.

In the text the *LM* curve is derived from the following equations:

$$M_t = m_y Y \tag{10A-12}$$

$$M_s = m_0 - m_r r \tag{10A-13}$$

$$M = M_t + M_s \tag{10A-14}$$

The last equation is the equilibrium condition and says nothing about money illusion. Equation (10A–14) may be rewritten in real terms as

$$\frac{M}{P} = \frac{M_t}{P} + \frac{M_s}{P}$$

The real value of the money supply must equal the sum of the demand for transactions and speculative balances in real terms.

$$\tag{10A-15}$$

Examining Eq. (10A–12), the demand for transaction balances, for money illusion, we find that

$$M_t = m_y Y$$

$$\frac{M_t}{P} = \frac{m_y PQ}{P}$$

$$\frac{M_t}{P} = m_y Q \qquad\qquad\qquad\qquad (10A\text{-}16)$$

$$\frac{\partial(M_t/P)}{\partial P} = 0 \qquad$$ The real value of transactions balances is insensitive to the price level—there is no money illusion.

Examining Eq. (10A–13), the demand for speculative balances, for money illusion, we find that

$$\frac{M_s}{P} = \frac{m_0}{P} - \frac{m_r r}{P}$$

$$\frac{\partial(M_s/P)}{\partial P} = -\frac{m_0 - m_r r}{P^2} < 0 \qquad$$ The demand for speculative balances in real terms varies inversely with the price level—there is money illusion.

The sign of the partial derivative is unambigous if the sign of $m_0 - m_r r$ is known. This expression is the total demand for speculative balances given by Eq. (10A–13), so the partial derivative is unambiguously negative.

This formulation of the speculative demand for money assumes that at a given interest rate speculators will demand a certain *dollar amount* of speculative balances, regardless of the price level. To reformulate this demand for speculative balances in real terms without money illusion, we may describe the speculators' behavior as follows:

$$M_s = P(m_0 - m_r r)$$

$$\frac{M_s}{P} = m_0 - m_r r \qquad$$ The real balances demanded for speculative purposes are a function of the market rate of interest.

$$\qquad\qquad\qquad\qquad\qquad\qquad (10A\text{-}17)$$

$$\frac{\partial(M_s/P)}{\partial P} = 0 \qquad$$ Real speculative balances are insensitive to changes in the price level—there is no money illusion.

We now have the following two sets of equations underlying an $LM$ curve:

| MONEY ILLUSION | NO MONEY ILLUSION |
|---|---|
| (10A-12)   $M_t = m_y$ | (10A-16)   $\dfrac{M_t}{P} = m_y Q$ |
| (10A-13)   $M_s = m_0 - m_r r$ | (10A-17)   $\dfrac{M_s}{P} = m_0 - m_r r$ |
| (10A-14)   $M = M_t + M_s$ | (10A-15)   $\dfrac{M}{P} = \dfrac{M_t}{P} + \dfrac{M_s}{P}$ |

Formulae for $LM$ curves for both cases can be derived from the equations above and expressed either in the form of $Y$ as a function of $r$ or $Q$ as a function of $r$. The four equations are given below. In the equations where money illusion is present, Eqs. (A) and (B), the $LM$ curve is independent of the price level if it is expressed in terms of current money expenditures, $Y$, as shown in Eq. (A). When the $LM$ curve is expressed in the $Q,r$ plane as in Eq. (B), it must shift everytime there is a change in the price level. In the money illusion case an interest rate level and a money supply will fix the level of total expenditures, $Y$, necessary to have the money market in equilibrium. The value of these expenditures in real terms, $Q$, depends on the price level. This is the formulation used in the book.

FORMULAE FOR LM CURVES

| Speculative Demand for Money Subject to Money Illusion | Speculative Demand for Money Not Subject to Money Illusion |
|---|---|
| (A)   $Y = \dfrac{M - m_0 + m_r r}{m_y}$ | (C)   $Y = \dfrac{M - Pm_0 + Pm_r r}{m_y}$ |
| (B)   $Q = \dfrac{M - m_0 + m_r r}{Pm_y}$ | (D)   $Q = \dfrac{M}{Pm_y} - \dfrac{(m_0 - m_r r)}{m_y}$ |

In the case of no money illusion, Eqs. (C) and (D), there is no way to express the $LM$ curve so that it is independent of the price level. Expressing it in money terms, Eq. (C), the money value of the speculative demand for cash balances, $-Pm_0 + Pm_r r$, will vary with every change in the price level. Expressing it in real terms, Eq. (D), the real value of the money supply, $M/P$, will change with every change in the price level. In other words, in the absence of money illusion, the $LM$ curve contains not just two endogenous variables ($Y$ and $r$ or $Q$ and $r$) but three: the third being the price level, $P$!

In a macroeconomic model formulated completely in "real terms" (no money illusion), it is not sensible to engage in comparative statics of the form in which a shift in the $IS$ curve is assumed to give a new equilibrium position for the entire system by moving along the *LM* curve, although this is frequently done in contemporary textbooks. A shift in the *IS* curve must change aggregate demand, which presumably changes the equilibrium level of output and prices, and the changes in prices must cause a shift in the *LM* curve.

Similarly, any money illusion operating in the savings and investment markets, such as fixed dollar government expenditures, will cause the price level variable to appear in an *IS* curve expressed in real terms. The price level will appear in the expression for real government expenditures, $G/P$, indicating that as prices change the real value of the government purchases of goods and services will vary inversely with the price level. In such a formulation, an *IS* curve in real terms will also contain *three* endogenous variables: $Q$, $r$, and $P$.

The question of which formulation is most applicable to the U.S. economy today, as well as the circumstances under which it would make little difference which is used, lies beyond the scope of this book. However, the student is advised to examine carefully the assumptions regarding money illusion implied by behavioral equations in contemporary economic literature, especially those utilizing the popular "*IS, LM*" analysis.

Let us now derive an aggregate demand curve for each of the models by solving the *IS* and *LM* curves simultaneously. We can express the equilibrium level of aggregate demand either as total expenditures, $Y$, or real goods and services, $Q$, as shown below:

### AGGREGATE DEMAND FORMULAE

| Money Illusion Model | No Money Illusion Model |
|---|---|

(A) $\quad Y_d = \dfrac{m_r(i_0 + c_0) + i_r(M - m_0)}{m_r(1 - c_y) + i_r m_y}$

(C) $\quad Y_d = \dfrac{P\{m_r(i_0 + c_0) + i_r[(M/P) - m_0]\}}{i_r m_y + m_r(1 - c_y)}$

(B) $\quad Q_d = \dfrac{m_r(i_0 + c_0) + i_r(M - m_0)}{P[m_r(1 - c_y) + i_r m_y)]}$

(D) $\quad Q_d = \dfrac{m_r(i_0 + c_0) + i_r[(M/P) - m_0]}{i_r m_y + m_r(1 - c_y)}$

In the case of the money illusion model, Eqs. (A) and (B), the level of total expenditures is set by the exogenous parameters of the behavioral equations and the level of the money supply. This, of course, leaves the aggregate level of total expenditures, $Y_d$, constant, regardless of the aggregate supply conditions. This makes the analysis of the system relatively simple. The ease of illustration with such a model is the main reason for its use in this book.

It is to be noted that in a price-quantity plane the aggregate demand curve is a rectangular hyperbola as given by Eq. (B). The aggregate demand curve in this money illusion model is asymptotic to both axes: as $P \to 0$, $Q \to \infty$; as $Q \to 0$, $P \to \infty$.

In the case of no money illusion, total money expenditures as indicated by Eq. (C) are sensitive to the price level since our consumers, investors, and speculators all think in real terms and behave accordingly. If prices rise, total expenditures will go up; total expenditures decrease for a price decline. However, the change in total expenditures will *not* be exactly proportionate to the price change because *the money supply is fixed in money terms*. Rising prices will require more transactions balances, lower speculative balances, and higher interest rates that will discourage investment. In Eq. (D) it can be seen that the demand for goods and services in real terms, $Q_d$, would be set by only the parameters of the behavioral equations were it not for the term $M/P$ in the numerator.

Under the usual assumptions the aggregate demand curve in the no money illusion case, Eq. (D), is negatively sloped in a $P,Q$ plane. It is not, however, asymptotic to both axes It is asymptotic to the quantity axis and to a fixed quantity of output greater than zero: As $P \to 0$, $Q \to \infty$ and as $P \to \infty$,

$$Q \to \frac{m_r(i_0 + c_0) - i_r m_0}{i_r m_y + m_r(1 - c_y)}$$

There are three basic approaches that are frequently used to make the quantity demanded insensitive to the price level in the no money illusion model. They are as follows:

1. Assume $M/P$ constant.

The money supply is fixed in real terms. $M/P$ is now the exogenous variable instead of $M$. If prices rise, $M$ is increased proportionately, and if prices fall, $M$ is reduced proportionately by the monetary authorities.

2. Assume $m_r \to \infty$ and thereby

$$Q_d \to \frac{i_0 + c_0}{1 - c_y}$$

This is the Keynesian "liquidity trap" in which the liquidity preference becomes infinite at the existing rate of interest. (In our particular linear model it would be at a zero rate of interest.)

3. Assume $i_r = 0$ and thereby

$$Q_d = \frac{i_0 + c_0}{1 - c_y}$$

This accomplishes the same result as the liquidity trap but instead of the interest rate not declining and encouraging investment, it is merely assumed that investment is totally insensitive to the interest rate.

If there is a classical supply curve (Model I, the real wage model) of the type previously discussed, $Q_s$ is constant. If $Q_s > Q_d$, prices may fall; but if one of the three conditions expressed above prevails, the system will never reach equilibrium. The labor market will be in disequilibrium and unemployment will exist.

In case 1, $M/P$ is constant. As prices fall, the money supply is reduced so that interest rates do not fall and investment is not encouraged. Aggregate demand for goods and services remains fixed in real terms in spite of falling prices.

In case 2, $m_r \to \infty$. We are in the Keynesian "liquidity trap" and although falling prices are releasing transactions balances, the demand for speculative balances is totally elastic at a rate higher than the rate required to raise $Q_d$ to $Q_s$ and generate full employment. Many presentations of this approach argue that the level of interest rates required for full employment is negative, which is reasonably assumed to be impossible.

In case 3, $i_r = 0$. Falling interest rates simply have no effect on investment that is assumed to be fixed (at $i_0$) at a level too low to generate enough aggregate demand for $Q_d = Q_s$ and full employment.

These cases are really not "unemployment equilibrium" since equilibrium is never reached, but they do dramatize how the speed of adjustment toward equilibrium depends on these parameters. Indeed, in certain time periods of our history these models may have been reasonable approximations of reality. We must hasten to point out, however, that at present a large sector of the economy is subject to money illusion in the form of fixed dollar government expenditures. This causes such expenditures to have an added "automatic stabilizer" effect.

## EXERCISES

1. Given

   a. aggregate supply: $P = Q^3$
   b. aggregate demand elasticities: $\eta_{Y,M} = \frac{1}{2}$ and $\eta_{Y,G} = 2$

   Quantify the effectiveness of monetary and fiscal policy for the purpose of influencing output in this economy.

2. Contrast algebraically and discuss the equilibrium level of prices (and thereby output and employment) in the following two cases:

Case 1:

   $Y_d = 100$, aggregate demand curve with total money illusion.
   $Q_s = 10$, classical full employment model supply curve.

Case 2:

   $Q_d = 10$, aggregate demand curve with no money illusion and a liquidity trap.
   $Q_s = (P + 110)^{1/2}$, positively sloped Keynesian supply curve.

## RECOMMENDED REFERENCES

Bronfenbrenner, M. and F. Holzman, "Survey of Inflation Theory," *American Economic Review*, September 1963, pp. 593–661.

McKenna, J. P., *Aggregate Economic Analysis*, 3rd ed., New York: Holt, Rinehart & Winston, Inc., 1969, Chapters 14, 15, and 16.

Phillips, A. W., "The Relation Between Unemployment and the Rate of Change of Money Wage Rate in the United Kingdom, 1861–1957," *Economica*, November 1958, pp. 283–99.

Samuelson, P. and R. Solow, "Analytical Aspects of Anti-Inflation Policy," *American Economic Review*, May 1960, pp. 177–94.

Schultze, C., "Recent Inflation in the United States," in *Study of Employment, Growth, and Price Levels*. Washington, D.C.: U.S. Govt. Printing Office, 1959.

# 11 The Process

# of Economic Growth

The previous chapters have been primarily concerned with the explanation of short-run macroeconomic phenomena. The time dimension in these chapters was so short that the capital stock of the economy could not be augmented, and any increase in output had to be gained entirely through increased inputs of labor. The present chapter will address itself to the longer-run aspects that arise when not only the amount of capital but also the level of technology are allowed to change.

Although very many growth models have been developed, this chapter, in keeping with the general theme of the text, will be concerned only with those that have gained widespread popularity. Section I presents what has come to be known as the "Harrod-Domar" model, while Section II is concerned with "neoclassical growth models" emphasizing aggregate production functions.

## I THE HARROD-DOMAR GROWTH MODEL

This model of growth was formulated independently but in similar fashion by the English economist Sir Roy F. Harrod and the American

Evsey Domar.[1] Although some economists present these as different theories that have outstanding similarities, this book will treat this area with only one basic model.

This particular model is concerned with the dual nature of investment, or the change in the capital stock over some period of time. It was pointed out in Chapter 4 that if net investment is positive, the increased capital equipment will expand the potential output of the economy. On the other hand, investment is also a component of *GNP*, and increased investment adds to aggregate demand not only directly but also indirectly through the multiplier effect on consumption. The problem of the Harrod-Domar model is to find an equilibrium growth pattern such that the increase in potential output is consistent with the increased aggregate demand.

## I. The Output–Capital Ratio

A key variable in the Harrod-Domar model is the output-to-capital ratio, which represents the average physical product that is potentially available per unit of capital. In other words, it is the maximum amount of

[1] For a comparison of the two formulations and some extensions, see R. F. Harrod, "Domar and Dynamic Economics," *The Economic Journal*, September 1959, pp. 451–64.

output attainable per unit of capital, although it does not necessarily represent the amount of output that would actually be produced. The developers of the model assume that this ratio is constant for all values of $K$, so that

$$d\left(\frac{Q}{K}\right) = 0 = \left(\frac{1}{K}\right) dQ - \left(\frac{Q}{K^2}\right) dK$$

or

$$\frac{Q}{K} = \frac{dQ}{dK} \tag{11-1}$$

Thus, $Q/K$ is both the *average* and the *marginal* potential output-to-capital ratio. Alternatively, Eq. (11-1) can be rewritten

$$dQ = \left(\frac{Q}{K}\right) dK \tag{11-2}$$

If we assume for the moment that the price level remains constant, however, then the change in the capital stock will be equal to the volume of net investment ($dK = I$). In that case, Eq. (11-2) becomes

$$dQ = \left(\frac{Q}{K}\right) I \tag{11-3}$$

In other words, the change in potential output is a simple proportional function of the level of investment.

## 2. Aggregate Demand

The output-capital ratio of the previous section is essentially concerned with aggregate supply. This section examines the impact of investment on aggregate demand, in much the same manner as Chapter 3.

If increases in the capital stock are to be fully utilized, the entire output that the capital is capable of producing must actually be produced. Accordingly, aggregate demand must increase to absorb the potential increase in physical output. The definition of aggregate demand given by Eq. (9-1) is

$$Y = PQ \tag{9-1}$$

Again, assume that prices remain constant, at least initially. For purposes of convenience, assume that the price index at the original equilibrium is 1.00. Then

$$Y = Q$$

and

$$dY = dQ \tag{11-4}$$

If we further assume a no-government economy, then

$$Y = C + I = Q \tag{11-5}$$

We simplify Eq. (2-4) and assume the following long-run proportional consumption function:

$$C = c_y Y = c_y Q \tag{11-6}$$

From Eqs. (11-5) and (11-6) we obtain

$$Y = \left(\frac{1}{1 - c_y}\right) I = Q \tag{11-7}$$

and

$$dY = \left(\frac{1}{1 - c_y}\right) dI = dQ \tag{11-8}$$

The aggregate demand equation therefore states that the change in output is a simple proportional function of the change in investment, the constant of proportionality being nothing more than the investment multiplier of Chapter 3.

## 3. The Warranted Rate of Growth

Equations (11-3) and (11-8) can be used to construct a warranted rate of growth for investment such that the increased potential output resulting from the investment will exactly be justified by increased aggregate demand resulting from the same investment. Equating the two expressions for $dQ$ in these two equations yields

$$\frac{dI}{I} = (1 - c_y)\left(\frac{Q}{K}\right) \tag{11-9}$$

Since

$$(1 - c_y) = s_y$$

then

$$\frac{dI}{I} = s_y\left(\frac{Q}{K}\right) \tag{11-10}$$

In other words, the percentage rate of growth of investment must be equal to the product of the marginal output-capital ratio and the marginal propensity to save. Moreover, if the warranted rate of growth for investment is maintained, all other relevant variables in the system—output, income, the stock of capital, and savings—will also grow at the same rate. That income grows at the same rate as investment may be seen merely by dividing Eq. (11-8) by (11-7). The assumption of price stability assures that output and income grow at the same rate, and the stability of the output-capital ratio dictates that the rate of growth of output will be matched by the rate of growth of the capital stock. Finally, with a proportional long-run saving function,

$$S = s_y Y$$

$$dS = s_y dY$$

and, by division,

$$\frac{dS}{S} = \frac{dY}{Y} = s_y \left(\frac{Q}{K}\right)$$

Again, the important conclusion of this model is that if the capital stock is to be fully utilized, with neither deficient nor excess demand for output, the volume of net investment must grow by a constant percentage rate equal to the product of the marginal output-capital ratio and the marginal propensity to save. Of course, note that a constant percentage rate means that larger and larger absolute increases in investment must be forthcoming if the equilibrium between income and output is to be maintained.

## 4. The Razor's Edge—An Investment Paradox

As long as investment grows at the warranted rate given by Eq. (11-10), the increase in potential physical output will be exactly matched by an increase in aggregate demand, and prices will remain stable. However, Harrod and others who have examined this particular model are quick to point out that this unique rate of growth is the *only* rate at which the economy can maintain stability. These writers argue that any deviation from the warranted rate will automatically force the economy into unrestrainable inflationary or deflationary spirals, according to whether the actual rate of investment is, respectively, above or below the warranted rate.

For example, assume that the economy is initially in equilibrium but that the rate of growth of investment for that period is greater than the warranted rate. Thus

$$\left(\frac{Q}{K}\right) s_y < \frac{dI}{I} \tag{11-11}$$

or

$$\left(\frac{Q}{K}\right) I < \left(\frac{1}{s_y}\right) dI \tag{11-12}$$

Since the left-hand side of Eq. (11-12) is the potential change in output from Eq. (11-3), while the right-hand side is the change in aggregate demand from Eq. (11-8), it is clear that the change in aggregate demand will be greater than the change in potential output. Thus, prices will be forced up and businessmen, seeing that demand had exceeded their expectations, may even increase their level of investment according to one of the accelerator relationships given by Chapter 4. In that case, the disparity given by Eq. (11-11) will be widened even further, and the inflationary tendency will be accentuated.

Analogously, had investment originally increased by less than the warranted rate, the change in aggregate demand would have been less than the change in potential output. A downward pressure would be placed on the price level, and excess capacity would likely result. In that case, businessmen probably would decrease the rate of investment even more in hopes of absorbing the excess capacity. However, the consequence of such an action would be a further deceleration of the rate of growth of aggregate demand, and excess capacity would likely increase. Thus, a rate of growth of investment that is below the warranted rate would touch off a reinforcing deflationary spiral.

The paradox that arises from this situation is that the warranted rate of growth constitutes a thin "razor's edge" of economic stability, with slight deviations in either direction leading to a spiraling departure from equilibrium. The "paradox" of such a model is that overinvestment (above the warranted rate) causes capital scarcity (due to failure of capacity to grow as rapidly as excess demand), while underinvestment (below the warranted rate) leads to excess capacity (because growth in aggregate demand cannot keep pace with increased capacity).

The previous discussion can perhaps be further clarified by introducing prices into the model. Before doing so, however, let us briefly recall the meaning of some of the variables in question. $Q$ represents the level of output as measured in terms of the $GNP$ of some base period. Thus, $Q$ is $GNP$ in constant dollars, or $Y$ deflated by the price index, $P$. The output-capital ratio should therefore provide a relationship between output in terms of base period prices to the capital stock in terms of base period prices. This last point is quite important, because under this definition the change in the capital stock is no longer equal to the volume of current investment, $I$, but instead equal to the value of investment after adjustment for price changes, the "real" investment, $I/P$. In that case,

$$dQ = \left(\frac{Q}{K}\right)\left(\frac{I}{P}\right) \tag{11-13}$$

or

$$P\,dQ = I\left(\frac{Q}{K}\right) \tag{11-14}$$

If prices are allowed to vary, then from Eq. (9-1)

$$dY = P\, dQ + Q\, dP \qquad\qquad (11\text{-}15)$$

Recalling Eq. (11-8),

$$dY = \left(\frac{1}{s_y}\right) dI \qquad\qquad (11\text{-}8)$$

so, combining Eqs. (11-15) and (11-8),

$$P\, dQ + Q\, dP = \left(\frac{1}{s_y}\right) dI \qquad\qquad (11\text{-}16)$$

Next, assume that capital is always used to capacity, so that differences between potential output and aggregate demand will be eliminated entirely by price adjustments. Dividing Eq. (11-16) by (11-14) then yields

$$\frac{dI}{I} = s_y\left(\frac{Q}{K}\right)\left[1 + \left(\frac{Q}{P}\right)\left(\frac{dP}{dQ}\right)\right] \qquad\qquad (11\text{-}17)$$

As defined in Chapter 9, the elasticity of price with respect to total output, $\eta_{P,Q}$ is equal to the percentage change in price divided by the percentage change in output, or

$$\eta_{P,Q} = \left(\frac{Q}{P}\right)\left(\frac{dP}{dQ}\right) \qquad\qquad (11\text{-}18)$$

So

$$\frac{dI}{I} = s_y\left(\frac{Q}{K}\right)(1 + \eta_{P,Q}) \qquad\qquad (11\text{-}19)$$

which may be rewritten as

$$\eta_{P,Q} = \left[\frac{(dI/I)}{s_y(Q/K)}\right] - 1 \qquad\qquad (11\text{-}20)$$

The previous equation states that if potential output is equal to actual output, *the price elasticity depends on the ratio of the actual rate of growth of investment to the warranted rate of growth.* If investment grows at a rate greater than the warranted rate, this ratio is greater than unity, price elasticity is then positive, and therefore increases in output will be accompanied by increases in the price level. If investment grows by less than the warranted rate, the ratio is less than unity, price elasticity is negative, and therefore increases in output result in decreased prices. Moreover, the greater the divergence between the actual and the warranted rates, the greater the impact on the price level. In effect, the dynamic equilibrium of aggregate demand and supply growing at the same rate requires $\eta_{P,Q} = 0$.

Note also the similarity between Eqs. (11-20) and (9-13). In Chapter 9, the concept of an inflation coefficient was generated to illustrate how general production conditions in the economy resulted in differing price levels. The present analysis extends that concept. If we define the inflation coefficient, $a$, to be equal to the ratio of actual and warranted rates of growth,

$$a = \frac{dI/I}{s_y(Q/K)} \qquad (11\text{-}21)$$

then

$$\eta_{P,Q} = a - 1 \qquad (11\text{-}22)$$

which is exactly the result obtained in Eq. (9-13), and all comments in that section are relevant to the discussion at hand. The dynamic equilibrium of this model requires that $a = 1$. As previously noted, this results in perfectly stable prices.

The results obtained here are only relevant when the potential output of the economy is actually produced. In periods of deflation, it is more likely that excess capacity would be allowed to develop and that the equating of aggregate demand to aggregate supply would be accomplished by both price adjustments and output reductions. In that case, the price elasticity would be smaller in absolute value than what is given by Eq. (11-20) when it is negative. When $\eta_{P,Q}$ is positive, however, Eq. (11-20) would hold since we do not allow for utilization of capital in excess of 100%.

## 5. The Labor Force and the Natural Rate of Growth

The previous sections are concerned with the relationships necessary to ensure that growth of the economy is balanced in the sense that aggregate demand and aggregate supply increase at the same rate. However, the argument up to now has completely ignored the role of the labor force and the effects of the warranted rate of growth on per capita income.

In order to consider these new ideas, we need some indication of the rates of growth of the labor force and the population, which we shall assume to be the same for purposes of convenience. The determinants of these rates will include a large number of factors that are social, psychological, institutional, and economic in character. We shall assume that the economic determinants are small compared to the total effects of all the others, however, so that the rate of growth of the population is substantially independent of the rate of growth of income and may be either above or below the warranted rate as defined above. Also, we must now drop the assumption that the output-capital ratio is constant and note that it could depend on the abundance or scarcity of capital relative to the labor force. The marginal productivity of capital (and thereby the marginal output-capital ratio) will be higher when labor is relatively abundant and lower when capital is relatively abundant.

Consider, now, the consequences if population is growing more slowly than national income, output, and capital—all of which are growing at the warranted rate. In that case, no disequilibrium forces are at work that directly affect the level of output, and per capita income is therefore increasing. However, subtle indirect forces are operating to equate the growth rates of income and population. With the stock of capital growing faster than the labor force, the quantity of capital per worker will be steadily increasing. This increasing capital-labor ratio will exert strong downward pressures on the output-capital ratio via the "law" of diminishing returns. As capital becomes more and more abundant relative to labor, it seems likely that a point will be reached where each additional unit of capital that is added will produce proportionately smaller volumes of output. In other words, the output-capital ratio will be reduced. Since the warranted rate of growth depends directly on the output-capital ratio, that rate of growth will also decrease, with the decline continuing until it is finally equal to the rate of growth of the population, which we may call the "natural" rate.

Analogously, had the rate of growth of population been greater than the warranted rate, labor would have become abundant relative to capital, and additional increments of capital would yield increased amounts of output. Accordingly, the warranted rate of growth would increase directly with the output-capital ratio. Only when the warranted and natural rates were equated would the output-capital ratio again become a constant.

Taking the world as described in the previous paragraphs as a model, increasing income per capita is impossible in the long run (when the warranted and natural growth rates are equal), as income per capita can only increase when the natural rate is less than the warranted rate. This result, however, although true for this particular model, is not particularly foreboding because technological change has been omitted from consideration. Long-run forces tend to equate the natural and warranted rates of growth only in the absence of technological change. Periodic improvements in technology have tended to increase both the productivity of capital and the productivity of labor. Thus, the output-capital ratio is increased so that the warranted rate is maintained above the natural rate. This conclusion, that increasing per capita income is impossible in the absence of technological change, will be considered again in Section II.

## II   "NEOCLASSICAL" MODELS OF ECONOMIC GROWTH

The previous section was concerned with the rate at which investment must grow if the productive capacity created by the investment was to be

matched exactly by the increased aggregate demand generated by the investment. The principal conclusion was that investment had to grow at a rate
equal to the product of the constant output-capital ratio and the marginal
propensity to save. Moreover, if this rate for investment was maintained,
output, income, capital, and saving would all grow at exactly the same rate.
Finally, the growth of the labor force would cause the output-capital ratio to
adjust itself to the point where the warranted rate of growth was equal to the
rate of increase in the labor force. Thus, the resulting system is one of
"steady-state" growth, in which all variables increase at the same rate, and
relative magnitudes remain unaffected. Ignoring technology, increasing per
capita output is impossible in such a system.

A different form of growth analysis from the Harrod-Domar model is
concerned with a general productive relationship that is believed to exist
among the factors of production, with little or no attention given to the role
played by aggregate demand. The basis for this latter type of analysis is the
assumption that changes in the marginal propensity to save are automatically
offset in the long run by changes in the output-capital ratio. This section will
be concerned with an examination of some of the principal elements of
neoclassical growth theory.

## 1. The Aggregate Production Function

As mentioned above, the key to neoclassical growth theory is the
production function, which expresses total output of the economy as a
function of the principal factors of production—the quantity of labor, the
stock of capital, and the level of technology. Unlike the Harrod-Domar
model, which assumed that *potential* output was a function of the amount of
capital *available*, the neoclassical model assumes that *actual* output depends
on the amounts of the factors that are *utilized*. While measurement problems
are obviously quite difficult here, we shall simply assume the problem away.
With respect to technology, we shall assume that technology increases over
time according to some known monotonic function. Thus, the aggregate
production function can be written as

$$Q = F[K, L, A(t)] \qquad (11\text{-}23)$$

In this equation, $A(t)$ is a function of time giving the growth pattern of
technology. Since diminishing returns are thought to be applicable to the
macro level as well as to the micro, output will increase at diminishing rates

as any single factor is increased, other factors held constant. Accordingly,

$$\frac{\partial Q}{\partial L} > 0 \qquad\qquad (11\text{-}24)$$

$$\frac{\partial^2 Q}{\partial L^2} < 0 \qquad\qquad (11\text{-}25)$$

$$\frac{\partial Q}{\partial K} > 0 \qquad\qquad (11\text{-}26)$$

$$\frac{\partial^2 Q}{\partial K^2} < 0 \qquad\qquad (11\text{-}27)$$

$$\frac{\partial Q}{\partial A(t)} > 0 \qquad\qquad (11\text{-}28)$$

$$\frac{dA(t)}{dt} > 0 \qquad\qquad (11\text{-}29)$$

Equations (11-24) through (11-27) merely define diminishing returns for both capital and labor. Equation (11-28) states that technological change always increases production, while Eq. (11-29) indicates that the rate of development of technology must be positive.

## 2. Substitution of the Factors

Assume for the moment that at some point in time the level of technology is fixed so that any change in quantity must be achieved by manipulating either capital or labor, or both. In that case, any given level of output, $Q_0$, can be produced only by different combinations of labor and capital, and the production function may be written as

$$Q_0 = F(K, L) \qquad\qquad (11\text{-}30)$$

The total differential of Eq. (11-30), holding output equal to $Q_0$, is

$$dQ_0 = \left(\frac{\partial Q}{\partial K}\right) dK + \left(\frac{\partial Q}{\partial L}\right) dL = 0$$

or

$$-\frac{dL}{dK} = \frac{\partial Q/\partial K}{\partial Q/\partial L} \qquad\qquad (11\text{-}31)$$

The left-hand side of Eq. (11-31) is called the marginal rate of substitution of labor for capital and will hereafter be referred to as *MRS*. The rate of substitution measures nothing more than the rate at which one factor must be substituted for another if total output is to be held constant. As is clear from Eq. (11-31), the *MRS* is equal to the ratio of the marginal products.

Economists have historically been interested in the degree to which factors tend to be substitutes for each other. One technique for measuring the degree of substitutability is to calculate the percentage change in the ratio of the two factors, given some percentage change in the marginal rate of substitution. The larger the change in the factor ratio relative to the change in the *MRS*, the greater is the substitutability of the factors. Mathematically the *elasticity of substitution* of labor for capital is defined as

$$\sigma = \frac{(K/L)\ d(L/K)}{dMRS/MRS} \tag{11-32}$$

In the case of perfectly complementary factors, the labor-capital ratio must be held constant, as an increase in one factor yields no increase in output unless the other factor is also increased. Thus, the term $d(L/K)$ in Eq. (11-32) is zero, so the elasticity of substitution is equal to zero. If the factors are perfect substitutes, then the marginal rate of substitution is always constant. Therefore, $dMRS$ in Eq. (11-32) is equal to zero, and the elasticity of substitution is equal to infinity.

### 3. The Role of Technology

Exactly how technology enters into the production function is open to question. However, economists generally distinguish between two broad classifications by which it might enter. The first of these is *embodied* technological progress, which assumes that improvements in production or the state of the arts are accomplished by new types of machines and more productive forms of labor. On the other hand, *disembodied* progress assumes that labor and capital are basically homogeneous but that technological progress makes possible new and different combinations of these factors that cause output to increase. Although growth models have been developed for both types of assumption, this chapter will be concerned only with disembodied technological progress.

Even limiting the analysis to disembodied technological progress does not make the analysis entirely straightforward, for various further assumptions may be made concerning the technique by which technological progress affects the combination of the factors of production. One assumption that has been made is that technological change does not affect capital but that it does make labor more efficient. Thus, this approach argues that the production function could be written as a combination of capital and labor efficiency units, where a labor efficiency unit might be defined as

$$L^* = A(t)L \tag{11-33}$$

where $A(t)$ and $L$ are the level of technology and the size of the labor force as defined above. In that case,

$$\frac{dL^*}{L^*} = \frac{dA(t)}{A(t)} + \frac{dL}{L} \tag{11-34}$$

In other words, the rate of growth of the labor efficiency unit is equal to the sum of the rate of growth of technology and the rate of growth of the labor force. Accordingly, labor efficiency increases with technology, and the combination of the more efficient labor with capital that does not change in quality allows output to increase. Technology of this type is said to be *Harrod neutral* technological growth. Since it increases the amount of output that can be obtained with any given level of labor units, it is also said to be *labor-augmenting technological growth.*

By analogy, exactly the same type of model could be developed for *capital-augmenting technological growth*. In that case, the number of capital efficiency units would increase as technology expanded, even if the amount of physical capital remained the same. Thus, letting $K^*$ represent capital efficiency units,

$$K^* = A(t)K \tag{11-35}$$

and

$$\frac{dK^*}{K^*} = \frac{dA(t)}{A(t)} + \frac{dK}{K} \tag{11-36}$$

Technology of this type is said to be *Solow neutral*. Finally, technology may be said to enter the production function in such a way as to increase the efficiency of both labor and capital but leave the optimal combination of the two unaffected, so that the marginal rate of substitution remains the same. In that case, the production function would be

$$Q = A(t)F(K, L) \tag{11-37}$$

and

$$MRS = -\frac{dL}{dK} = \frac{A(t)(\partial Q/\partial K)}{A(t)(\partial Q/\partial L)} = \frac{\partial Q/\partial K}{\partial Q/\partial L}$$

This type of technology is defined as *Hicks neutral*.

## 4. Technological Change and Output Per Capita

Much of the material above can now be combined to illustrate the crucial role played by technology in increasing economic welfare, as measured by output per capita. In making this examination, we shall assume "Hicks neutral" technological change and a production function that is linearly homogeneous in the factors of production. Thus,

$$Q = A(t)F(K, L) \tag{11-38}$$

and

$$\lambda Q = A(t)F(\lambda K, \lambda L)$$

Then, letting $\lambda = 1/L$,

$$\frac{Q}{L} = A(t)F\left(\frac{K}{L}, 1\right)$$

or, defining $F(K/L, 1)$ as $f(K/L)$,

$$\frac{Q}{L} = A(t)f\left(\frac{K}{L}\right) \tag{11-39}$$

So,

$$\frac{\partial Q}{\partial L} = A(t)f\left(\frac{K}{L}\right) - \left(\frac{K}{L}\right)A(t)f'\left(\frac{K}{L}\right) \tag{11-40}$$

and

$$\frac{\partial Q}{\partial K} = A(t)f'\left(\frac{K}{L}\right) \tag{11-41}$$

Substituting Eq. (11-41) into (11-40) yields

$$\frac{\partial Q}{\partial L} = \left(\frac{Q}{L}\right) - \left(\frac{K}{L}\right)\left(\frac{\partial Q}{\partial K}\right) \tag{11-42}$$

In order to examine the rate of change of output per capita, the total differential of output per capita with respect to all variables must first be calculated. From Eq. (11-39),

$$d\left(\frac{Q}{L}\right) = A'(t)f\left(\frac{K}{L}\right) dt + \frac{A(t)}{L}f'\left(\frac{K}{L}\right) dK - A(t)f'\left(\frac{K}{L}\right)\left(\frac{K}{L^2}\right) dL \tag{11-43}$$

Dividing Eq. (11-43) by $(Q/L)\, dt$,

$$\frac{d(Q/L)/(Q/L)}{dt} = \frac{A'(t)}{A(t)} + \frac{(K/L)f'(K/L)}{f(K/L)}\left[\frac{(dK/K)}{dt} - \frac{(dL/L)}{dt}\right] \tag{11-44}$$

The last bracketed term on the right-hand side of Eq. (11-44) is merely the percentage rate of growth of capital minus the percentage rate of growth of labor. In other words, this term is equal to the percentage rate of growth of capital per worker. As a very long-run matter, it is impossible for the rate of growth of output per worker to be different from the rate of growth of capital per worker. A rate of growth of output per worker that was lower than the rate for capital per worker would imply that capital was growing faster than output. Since the capital equipment produced is merely one part of total output, however, a long-run rate of growth for capital equipment above the rate of growth for output would imply that ultimately the former would have to be larger than the latter, which is impossible by definition. By analogy, it seems equally unlikely that the rate of growth of capital per worker should be permanently less than the rate of growth of output per worker. The only reasonable assumption seems to be that the long-term rates of growth for capital and output are equal. Therefore, from Eq. (11-44),

$$\frac{d(Q/L)/(Q/L)}{dt} = \left(\frac{K}{L}\right)\left[\frac{f'(K/L)\,d(Q/L)}{f(K/L)(Q/L)\,dt}\right] + \frac{A'(t)}{A(t)} \tag{11-45}$$

Next, consider the elasticities of output with respect to the factors of production:

$$\eta_{Q,L} = \left(\frac{L}{Q}\right)\left(\frac{\partial Q}{\partial L}\right) = \left(\frac{L}{Q}\right)\left[\left(\frac{Q}{L}\right) - \left(\frac{K}{L}\right)\left(\frac{\partial Q}{\partial K}\right)\right]$$

$$= 1 - \left[\frac{(K/L)}{(Q/L)}\right]\left(\frac{\partial Q}{\partial K}\right)$$

$$= 1 - \left[\frac{(K/L)}{(Q/L)}\right]A(t)f'\left(\frac{K}{L}\right) \tag{11-46}$$

but

$$\frac{Q}{L} = A(t)f\left(\frac{K}{L}\right)$$

so, by substitution into Eq. (11-46),

$$\eta_{Q,L} = 1 - \left(\frac{K}{L}\right)\left[\frac{f'(K/L)}{f(K/L)}\right] \tag{11-47}$$

and

$$\eta_{Q,K} = \left(\frac{K}{Q}\right)\left(\frac{\partial Q}{\partial K}\right) = \left[\frac{K/L}{Q/L}\right]\left(\frac{\partial Q}{\partial K}\right)$$

$$= \left[\frac{K/L}{Q/L}\right]\left[A(t)f'\left(\frac{K}{L}\right)\right]$$

$$= \left(\frac{K}{L}\right)\left[\frac{f'(K/L)}{f(K/L)}\right]$$

$$= 1 - \eta_{Q,L} \qquad (11\text{-}48)$$

Substitution of Eq. (11-48) into (11-45) yields

$$\frac{d(Q/L)/(Q/L)}{dt} = \frac{d(Q/L)}{(Q/L)\,dt}\eta_{Q,K} + \frac{A'(t)}{A(t)} \qquad (11\text{-}49)$$

so

$$\frac{d(Q/L)/(Q/L)}{dt} = \frac{A'(t)}{A(t)(1 - \eta_{Q,K})} \qquad (11\text{-}50)$$

or

$$\frac{d(Q/L)/(Q/L)}{dt} = \frac{A'(t)}{A(t)\eta_{Q\,L}} \qquad (11\text{-}51)$$

According to Eq. (11-51), the long-run rate of growth of output per capita is equal to the rate of growth of technology divided by the elasticity of output with respect to the labor input. If technology is held constant, per capita income cannot increase, which is the same conclusion as that presented at the end of Chapter 11, Section I.

The result given here, however, although mathematically correct, is merely a very simple consequence of combining a linearly homogeneous production function with the requirement that the capital stock increase at the same rate as total output. The following illustration should clarify this point. Suppose we stipulate that both capital and output will increase by annual rates of 10% and that technology is to be held constant. What, then, can be said about the rate of growth of the labor input? First, it should be clear that if the rate of growth of labor is also 10%, we have the simple case in which expansion of all factors in a linearly homogeneous production function increases output by the same percent. Secondly, consider what happens if labor increases at a rate of 15%. This is done by first taking an increase of 10%, then adding enough extra labor to make the total increase equal to 15%. As seen above, the original 10% increase, coupled with the 10% increase in capital, will lead to a 10% increase in output. Assuming that marginal factor products are always positive, the next increment of labor will add even more to output (although under diminishing returns), so total output must increase by more than 10% over its original level. However, this result must be dropped from consideration by the requirement that the percentage rate of growth of output must be exactly equal to 10%. Finally, consider the outcome of labor increasing by less than 10%, say 8%. In this case, we can look upon the increase in capital as being composed of an initial

8% increase and then being augmented by enough extra growth to allow the total increase to be 10%. The first 8% increase in both factors will cause output to expand by 8% also. Moreover, the next increase in the capital stock will cause output to increase even more but less than proportionate to the increase in the capital stock. Thus, the total increase in output must be less than 10%, which also does not fit the assumptions of the problem being studied.

The end result of the previous paragraph is that with a linearly homogeneous production function, equal rates of growth for any two of the variables requires that the third grow at the same rate. The only solution to the problem is one of steady-state growth, in which capital, labor, and output all grow at the same percentage rates. When the rate of growth of output must equal the rate of growth of capital, not only can per capita output not increase without technological advance, it also cannot decrease without technological decline. Moreover, if consumption is a constant fraction of output, consumption per capita also must remain constant. The proper area of investigation, then, is to see if there is one particular level of steady-state growth such that economic welfare, measured in terms of consumption per capita, is higher at all points in time than under any other level of steady-state growth. This question will be addressed in the following section.

### 5. Economic Growth and the Marginal Propensity to Save

Up to now, the present chapter has tended to diminish the importance of the marginal propensity to save in determining the growth rate of the economy. Although the Harrod-Domar model indicated that an increase in the *MPS* would raise the warranted rate of growth, neoclassical growth theory in turn argues that the resulting increase in the capital stock caused by the increase in saving would reduce the output-capital ratio through diminishing returns to capital. Thus, the smaller output-capital ratio exactly offsets the larger marginal propensity to save. While rejecting much of Harrod-Domar analysis, however, neoclassical theory still provides a key role for the savings coefficient in determining optimum consumption patterns.

Recall for a moment the findings of the previous section. With a linearly homogeneous production function and in the absence of technological change, the capital stock, the labor force, and the level of total output will all grow at the same percentage rate after the passage of a sufficient length of time. Since relative magnitudes do not change under this model, the capital-labor ratio, the capital-output ratio, and the output per capita ratio all remain constant. The problem then is to find that output per capita and its accompanying capital-labor and capital-output ratios that maximize well-being in the economy. Assuming away problems of the optimum distribution of income, the highest level of well-being will be associated with the highest consumption per capita ratio.

The standard approach to this problem is as follows. Remember that the change in the capital stock per time period is equal to the level of investment, which, with a constant marginal propensity to save, is a constant fraction of total output.

$$\frac{dK}{dt} = I = s_y Q$$

Division by the capital stock, $K$, yields

$$\left(\frac{1}{K}\right)\left(\frac{dK}{dt}\right) = s_y\left(\frac{Q}{K}\right) \tag{11-52}$$

However, the left-hand side of Eq. (11-52) is the constant growth rate of the capital stock, or $g$ symbolically. Thus,

$$s_y\left(\frac{Q}{K}\right) = g$$

or

$$s_y = \left(\frac{K}{Q}\right)g$$

and so

$$s_y = \frac{g(K/L)}{(Q/L)}$$

and

$$s_y = \frac{g(K/L)}{f(K/L)} \tag{11-53}$$

Next, note that consumption per capita is equal to output per capita minus saving per capita:

$$\frac{C}{L} = \frac{Q}{L} - \frac{S}{L}$$

$$= \frac{Q}{L} - s_y\left(\frac{Q}{L}\right)$$

$$= f\left(\frac{K}{L}\right) - s_y f\left(\frac{K}{L}\right)$$

$$= f\left(\frac{K}{L}\right) - g\left(\frac{K}{L}\right) \tag{11-54}$$

In order to maximize consumption per capita, the first derivative of Eq. (11-54) must be set equal to zero. Since $K/L$ is the only variable in the equation,

$$\frac{d(C/L)}{d(K/L)} = f'\left(\frac{K}{L}\right) - g = 0$$

or

$$g = f'\left(\frac{K}{L}\right) \tag{11-55}$$

Thus, maximum consumption per capita requires that the rate of growth be equal to the marginal product of capital. The saving ratio required to bring about this rate of growth can be determined by substituting the value of $g$ from Eq. (11-55) into (11-53):

$$s_y = \frac{(K/L)f'(K/L)}{f(K/L)} \tag{11-56}$$

or, from Eq. (11-48),

$$s_y = \eta_{Q,K} \tag{11-57}$$

Equation (11-57) indicates that if consumption per capita is to be maximized, the saving ratio must be set equal to the elasticity of total output with respect to capital. Moreover,

$$1 - s_y = c_y = 1 - \eta_{Q,K} = \eta_{Q,L} \tag{11-58}$$

The optimal propensity to consume is equal to the elasticity of total output with respect to the labor input. Or, a different way of stating this is that to maximize output per capita a competitive society should consume its labor income and invest its returns to capital.[2]

This last statement may perhaps be clarified by considering Euler's theorem, which states that for linearly homogeneous functions the sum of the products for all partial derivatives and their respective variables should equal the dependent variable. Thus, for linearly homogeneous production functions,

$$Q = \left(\frac{\partial Q}{\partial L}\right)L + \left(\frac{\partial Q}{\partial K}\right)K \tag{11-59}$$

If Eq. (11-59) is met, then

$$s_y = \left(\frac{\partial Q}{\partial K}\right)\left(\frac{K}{Q}\right)$$

[2] For the original formulation of this result, see E. S. Phelps, "The Golden Rule of Accumulation: A Fable for Growthmen," *American Economic Review*, September 1961, pp. 638–43.

or

$$s_y\left(\frac{Q}{K}\right) = \frac{\partial Q}{\partial K} \qquad (11\text{-}60)$$

or

$$\frac{I}{K} = \frac{\partial Q}{\partial K} \qquad (11\text{-}61)$$

Moreover, from Eq. (11-58),

$$\frac{C}{L} = \frac{\partial Q}{\partial L} \qquad (11\text{-}62)$$

Finally, substitution of Eqs. (11-61) and (11-62) into (11-59) yields

$$Q = \left(\frac{C}{L}\right)L + \left(\frac{I}{K}\right)K = C + I \qquad (11\text{-}63)$$

Equation (11-59) states that total product is exactly accounted for when each factor is paid its marginal product, a commonly developed result for a competitive economy at the microeconomic level. On a normative basis, this is often said to be desirable since each factor takes from society only what it is capable of producing. Equations (11-61) through (11-63) state that the returns to labor and capital, respectively, equal consumption and investment, the only components of GNP in a no-government model. Any other mix of consumption to investment will necessarily result in a lower per capita consumption along the corresponding steady-state growth path. A saving ratio greater than the capital elasticity would have enlarged the capital stock and increased total output but the smaller MPC would mean that less of this output would go for consumption. On the other hand, a larger MPC (per capita consumption greater than the marginal output of labor) would devote a larger share of total output to consumption but the MPS would dictate a smaller capital stock than otherwise would have been accumulated, so that even with the higher MPC, per capita consumption would be reduced. Thus, the saving ratio given by Eq. (11-57) is the optimum under the assumptions of this model. At any point in time, this saving ratio will define the capital-labor ratio that maximizes consumption per capita. Of course, the results of this section do not necessarily remain valid when production functions are not linearly homogeneous or when the marginal propensity to consume is allowed to change over time.

## III SUMMARY

Contemporary growth theory contains two different forms of growth models: those pattened on the older Harrod-Domar analysis and the newer "neoclassical growth models" built around aggregate production functions.

The Harrod-Domar models emphasize the constancy of the ratio of potential output to the capital stock and show that equilibrating aggregate demand to aggregate supply produces a "warranted" rate of growth that is equal to the product of the output-capital ratio and the marginal propensity to save. When investment grows at this warranted rate, a "steady-state" pattern of economic growth emerges, with output, saving, consumption, and the capital stock all growing at the same warranted rate. Growth of investment either above or below the warranted rate produces either unrestrainable inflation or incurable depression, respectively. In the Harrod-Domar model the rate of growth of the labor force, "the natural rate," influences the output-capital ratio through the forces of diminishing returns and ultimately causes the natural rate and the warranted rate to be equal. Accordingly, only technological advance can increase per capita output.

Neoclassical growth analysis is based upon the assumption that the relationships among output, technology, and the factors of production can be adequately explained by continuous aggregate production functions, generally specified to be homogeneous of degree one. Analysis of these functions again illustrates the theorem that output per capita cannot increase without technological advance. Even within the framework of a constant technology, however, it is possible to achieve maximum consumption attainable per person by selecting the proper marginal propensity to save. This analysis indicates that the *MPS* should be set equal to the elasticity of output with respect to capital so that consumption is equal to "labor's share" of income, while investment is always equal to the returns to capital.

## EXERCISE

1. A model of economic growth is as follows:

   *Aggregate supply: $Q_{s,t} = vK_t$*

   *Aggregate demand: $Q_{d,t} = I_t + C_t$ and $C_t = bQ_t$*

   *Definition: $I_t = \Delta K_t = K_t - K_{t-1}$*

Derive the necessary condition in terms of the percentage rate of growth in investment, $I_t$, for this economy to have neither inflationary nor deflationary problems with its growth.

## RECOMMENDED REFERENCES

Ackley, Gardner, *Macroeconomic Theory*. New York: The Macmillan Co., 1961, Chapters XVIII and XIX.

Allen, R. G. D., *Macroeconomic Theory*. New York: St. Martin's Press, 1967, Chapters 10 through 14.

Arrow, K., H. Chenery, B. Minhas, and R. Solow, "Capital-Labor Substitution and Economic Efficiency," *The Review of Economics and Statistics*, August 1961, pp. 225–50.

Dernburg, Thomas F. and Judith D. Dernburg, *Macroeconomic Analysis*. Reading, Mass.: Addison-Wesley Pub. Co., 1969, Chapters 10 and 11.

Domar, Evsey, "Capital Expansion, Rate of Growth, and Employment," *Econometrica*, April 1946, pp. 137–47.

————, "Expansion and Employment," *American Economic Review*, March 1947, pp. 34–55.

————, *Essays in the Theory of Economic Growth*. Fair Lawn, N.J.: Oxford University Press, 1957.

Griliches, Z. and Y. Grunfeld, "Is Aggregation Necessarily Bad?" *The Review of Economics and Statistics*, February 1960, pp. 1–13.

Harrod, R. F., "An Essay in Dynamic Theory," *Economic Journal*, March 1939, pp. 14–33.

————, *Towards a Dynamic Economics*. London: Macmillan and Co., 1949.

Nelson, R. R., "Aggregate Production Functions and Medium Range Growth Projections," *American Economic Review*, September 1964, pp. 575–606.

Peston, M. H., "A View of the Aggregation Problem," *Review of Economic Studies*, July 1960, pp. 58–64.

Phelps, E. S., "The Golden Rule of Accumulation: A Fable for Growthmen," *American Economic Review*, September 1961, pp. 638–43.

Solow, R. M., "Technical Change and the Aggregate Production Function," *Review of Economics and Statistics*, August 1957, pp. 312–20.

# 12 International Economics

International economic relationships are in many ways quite similar to those within a particular national economic system. Due to the absence of a sovereign world government, however, there are many special problems. Most of these problems of international economics arise from the fact that while the nations are politically independent, they are continuously forced to recognize that they are economically interdependent. One country can indeed ignore requests for cooperation in international trade from another country, but it cannot ignore the fact that it is dependent on the other country both for the supply of its imports and the demand for its exports and perhaps also dependent on various capital market arrangements in the foreign country.

In the presence of different monetary systems and the absence of a sovereign world government to arbitrate between the politically independent domestic governments, it is perhaps surprising that international economic relationships operate as well as they do. It is the purpose of this chapter to give the reader the basic ideas of just what these relationships are and to explore the requirements for equilibrium in an "open" economy. Most problems of international economics are reflected in the payments made between countries. The record of such transactions is called the "balance of payments" and this is the subject to which we now turn.

# I THE BALANCE OF PAYMENTS

## I. The Balance of Payments Accounts

The balance of payments of a particular country is a bookkeeping record of the payments by that country to other countries (called "debits") and receipts from other countries (called "credits") that took place during a particular time period. The term "balance" can be misleading since in bookkeeping terms the balance of payments is more nearly analogous to a profit and loss statement than a balance sheet; it is a statement of flows over a period of time rather than a statement of stocks or balances at a point in time.

For most industrialized countries such accounts are broken down into many detailed subaccounts. For illustrative purposes here, let us consider only four major income and expense accounts:

BALANCE OF PAYMENTS ACCOUNTS

| Credits<br>(Receipts or Income) | Debits<br>(Payments or Expenditure) |
|---|---|
| 1. Exports of goods and services ($X$) | 1. Imports of goods and services ($I_m$) |
| 2. Sale of financial assets ($F_s$) | 2. Purchase of financial assets ($F_p$) |
| 3. Sale of gold or other international reserves ($R_s$) | 3. Purchase of gold or other international reserves ($R_p$) |
| 4. Unilateral receipts ($U_r$) | 4. Unilateral payments ($U_p$) |

Item 1 is self-explanatory. Item 2 is somewhat more complex. It consists not only of such obvious transactions as the sale of stocks or bonds by the citizens or government of one country to the citizens or government of another country (long-term financial assets) but the incurring of a short-term debt such as an accounts receivable (a short-term financial asset). If for example the country about which we are speaking imports some goods but has not yet paid for them during the period for which the accounts are applicable, there would be a debit to account 1 and a credit of an equal amount to account 2 as the accrual of the debt to foreigners is classed as the sale of a financial asset.

This is perhaps the point at which it should be noted that, strictly speaking, the balance of payments *always* balances. The accounts are defined in such a way that if there were no errors or omissions, debits would exactly equal credits for each and every country. In fact, however, there are errors and omissions and the reported figures include an account so labeled. We shall defer for the moment what is meant by the statement that a country has a "surplus" or "deficit" in its balance of payments, in which case the term "balance of payments" must necessarily be redefined.

The definition of item 3, the sale or purchase of gold or other international reserves, depends to some extent on the existing international monetary agreements in force at the time. If gold is the only acceptable international currency, then that is all that is included. As we shall discuss in some detail below, there are other forms of international currency. In any case, this account refers to an outflow (sale) or an inflow (purchase) of whatever is classed as international monetary reserves under the institutional arrangements existing at the time. In the simple case of a country that imports substantially more goods and services than it exports and has no other receipts to pay the difference, the net debit balance on trade would have to be offset by an equal credit balance as it paid off in gold or other internationally acceptable reserves.

Item 4, unilateral receipts or payments, covers all transactions for which there is no automatically offsetting transaction. For example, a foreign aid grant from one country to another would be a unilateral payment (debit) for the grantor and a unilateral receipt (credit) for the grantee. Similarly, private remittances in the form of gifts for family support or whatever from citizens of one country to citizens of another country are classed as unilateral payments and receipts.

We can define a new set of accounts that net each of these accounts on the receipts side as follows:

$$X_n = X - I_m \qquad \text{Net exports equals exports minus imports.}$$

$$(12\text{-}1)$$

$$F_n = F_s - F_p$$

Net sales of financial assets equal sales of financial assets minus purchase of financial assets.

(12-2)

$$R_n = R_s - R_p$$

Net *decrease* in the *stock* of international reserves equals the sale (outflow) of reserves minus the purchase (inflow) of reserves.

(12-3)

$$U_n = U_r - U_p$$

Net receipts from unilateral transfers equal unilateral receipts minus unilateral payments.

(12-4)

With such a set of accounts it follows by definition that

$$X_n + F_n + R_n + U_n = 0 \tag{12-5}$$

Equation (12-5) merely restates the proposition that the balance of payments accounts will always balance. If net exports $(X_n)$ falls from one period to the next, net receipts from the sale of financial assets must increase $(F_n)$, a decrease in international reserves must occur $(R_n)$, or income from unilateral transfers must go up $(U_n)$.

## 2. Balance of Trade

The balance of trade is distinguished from the balance of payments in that it refers only to that portion of the balance of payments included in the import and export of goods and services accounts. As formulated here, the balance of trade is indicated by whether $X_n$ is by itself greater than, less than, or equal to zero. If it is greater than zero (exports are greater than imports), a country is said to have a trade "surplus" or sometimes a "favorable" balance of trade. Conversely, if imports exceed exports and thereby $X_n$ is less than zero, a country is said to have a trade "deficit" or an "unfavorable" balance of trade. The quotation marks around "favorable" and "unfavorable" are doubly meaningful as it is impossible to say without further information whether a trade surplus or deficit is the more advantageous to a particular country over a particular time period. The desirability of one over the other in particular circumstances will be discussed in greater detail below.

## 3. Surplus or Deficit in the Balance of Payments

As indicated above, the balance of payments always balances in the sense that each and every transaction gives rise to equal debits and credits and Eq. (12-5) must hold for any particular time period. However, the term "balance of payments" is used in a different sense than as a label for all the accounts showing payments and receipts by one country to others. The basic idea of this other definition is whether or not a country is gaining or losing gold and other international reserves. We have defined $R_n$ as a net *decrease* in the stock of international reserves. As a result, if $R_n$ is a positive number, the country is said to have a deficit or "unfavorable" balance of payments; if $R_n$ is negative, the country is said to have a surplus or "favorable" balance of payments. Equation (12-5) can be rewritten as follows:

$$-R_n = X_n + F_n + U_n \tag{12-6}$$

Since we have defined $R_n$ to be the magnitude of the decrease in the stock of international reserves, we could add the following definitional equation:

$$\Delta R = -R_n \tag{12-7}$$

where $\Delta R$ is the amount by which a country's international reserves grow (if $\Delta R$ is greater than zero) or decline (if $\Delta R$ is less than zero). Substituting Eq. (12-7) into (12-6) gives

$$\Delta R = X_n + F_n + U_n \tag{12-8}$$

With this formulation, a balance of payments surplus is one with a $\Delta R$ greater than zero or an increase in international reserves, while a balance of payments deficit is one with a negative $\Delta R$ and a decrease in the country's international reserves over the time period.

Defining the balance of payments surplus or deficit in terms of the change in the stock of international reserves is something of a gross over-simplification. In the first place there is no world central bank to define legally what constitutes international reserves. At the present time gold stocks certainly qualify, and to a greater or lesser degree most countries include foreign currencies that are freely convertible into gold. Also, some countries include short-term claims (financial assets) that are redeemable in currencies freely convertible into gold. If these assets are added to the gold stock to get the international reserves, the country usually also subtracts short-term claims on its stock of gold and foreign currencies. As a result there are numerous definitions of a country's stock of international reserves and thereby numerous definitions as to the amount of the surplus or deficit in the balance of payments. Under some definitions, part of the transactions are removed from account 2, "Purchase and sale of financial assets," and put in account 3, "Purchase and sale of gold or other international reserves." The short-term assets or liabilities are the ones that may be considered as additions to or subtractions from the stock of international reserves. The long-term financial instruments are not counted, but the definition of "long term" and "short term" is not entirely unambiguous, although one year is the customary point of demarcation. As a result of these ambiguities, measures of the balance of payments surplus or deficit are not always comparable between countries, and many countries will calculate and publish figures for more than one definition of the balance of payments surplus or deficit.

From Eq. (12-8) it is apparent that the balance of trade, $X_n$, may be positive while the overall balance of payments, $\Delta R$, may be negative and vice versa, depending on what goes on with respect to the purchase and sale of financial assets, $F_n$, and the magnitude and direction of the unilateral transfers, $U_n$. For example, it is possible for a country to have a large surplus in its balance of trade accounts (exports much more than it imports) and still have a zero or negative balance of payments flow if foreigners borrow a great deal of money in this country's capital markets (this country "imports" a large amount of financial assets) and this country has large foreign aid commitments (large negative unilateral transfers). This was the position of the United States for a number of years.

The foregoing has described the bookkeeping system of international accounts, but to know thoroughly what might go into any of these accounts one must have in mind a particular mechanism through which the countries settle their accounts with one another. This is the subject to which we must now direct our attention.

## II INTERNATIONAL PAYMENTS MECHANISMS

Historically there have been a wide variety of international payments mechanisms and such arrangements have almost always been in a state of change due to disruptions of war and other manifestations of international politics. We shall look at four different arrangements, that seem to make some sense as an analytical division. None of the four has ever existed in a pure state, and at all times some elements of each of these four mechanisms have been in operation.

### 1. A Full Gold Standard

The international payments mechanism is virtually an "automatic" system if each and every country has in operation a domestic gold standard as described in Chapter 8 and does not depart from it. As noted in that chapter, under such a monetary system the government stands ready to buy and sell the domestic currency (or accept demand deposits in exchange) for gold at a set price. The size of the domestic money supply is then set by the supply of gold mined domestically plus or minus gold imports or exports.

A primary function of any international payments mechanism is to set the value of one currency in terms of other (foreign) currencies. If two countries are both on a gold standard, the relative value of one in terms of the other is set by the common denominator of gold.

For example, to those demanding dollars for gold, there is a completely elastic supply at a gold price, $\$F_1$, set by the U.S. government:

$$\frac{\$}{G} = \$F_1 \tag{12-9}$$

If the gold were located overseas, say in London, the cost of shipping, insurance, etc., $T$, would have to be deducted. The net cost of dollars in terms of gold for a British trader would then be

$$\frac{\$}{G} = \$(F_1 - T) \tag{12-10}$$

For those demanding a foreign currency, say British pounds sterling, there would be a completely elastic supply at a gold price, $£F_2$, set by the British government:

$$\frac{£}{G} = £F_2 \tag{12-11}$$

or if the gold were located in New York, the transactions cost, $T$, would have to be deducted. The net cost of pounds in terms of gold for a U.S. trader would then be

$$\frac{£}{G} = £(F_2 - T) \tag{12-12}$$

In the absence of transaction costs it follows that the price of pounds in terms of dollars would be the ratio of the prices of each in terms of gold set by the two governments:

$$\frac{\$}{£} = \frac{\$}{G} \div \frac{£}{G} = \frac{F_1}{F_2} \tag{12-13}$$

from Eqs. (12-9) and (12-11).

For example, if the U.S. government stands ready to buy and sell gold at a price of \$35 per ounce ($F_1$) and the British government stands ready to buy and sell gold at a price of £17.50 per ounce ($F_2$), then it follows that the exchange rate cannot depart too far from $2 per pound ($F_1/F_2$). Actually, the exchange rate can depart only by an amount equal to the cost of moving gold from one country to another. The upper and lower bounds of the exchange rate under a gold standard are called *gold points*. Let us see exactly why the gold points are effective.

First, consider the meaning of the two governments' guarantees of their currency in terms of gold to a British trader seeking dollars with which to buy American goods. It assures him that the minimum number of dollars he need ever accept for his pound is the amount to be obtained by selling pounds to his government at the fixed rate $F_2$ for gold, shipping the gold to the United States, and selling it to the U.S. government, where he would net the fixed rate less the cost of shipment, $F_1 - T$. Therefore, the *minimum* rate of dollars in terms of pounds is

$$\frac{\$}{£} = \frac{\$}{G} \div \frac{£}{G} = \frac{F_1 - T}{F_2} \qquad (12\text{-}14)$$

by substituting Eq. (12-10) for the first term and Eq. (12-11) for the second term.

Now consider the meaning of the fixed price of gold in terms of the two currencies to the U.S. trader seeking to obtain pounds with which to buy British goods. The maximum amount of dollars he would pay for £1 is that obtainable from exchanging dollars for gold at the rate guaranteed by the U.S. government, $F_1$, shipping the gold to Great Britain, and selling it for pounds to net the guaranteed rate less transactions cost, $F_2 - T$. Therefore the *maximum* rate for pounds in terms of dollars is

$$\frac{\$}{£} = \frac{\$}{G} \div \frac{£}{G} = \frac{F_1}{F_2 - T} \qquad (12\text{-}15)$$

by substituting Eq. (12-9) for the first term and Eq. (12-12) for the second term.

In day-to-day operations of the foreign exchange market, various supply and demand forces, to be discussed in detail later, will set the price of pounds in terms of dollars somewhere between these two limits. If the demand and supply situation is such as to push the price outside the gold points, gold will move from one country to another. Specifically, in our example, if

$$\frac{F_1 - T}{F_2} < \frac{\$}{£} < \frac{F_1}{F_2 - T}$$

there will be no gold flow. If

$$\frac{\$}{£} \leq \frac{F_1 - T}{F_2}$$

gold will move from Great Britain to the United States. If

$$\frac{\$}{£} \geq \frac{F_1}{(F_2 - T)}$$

gold will move from the United States to Great Britain.

To illustrate numerically, let us assume that

$$F_1 = \$35 \qquad F_2 = £17.50$$

and that $T = \$0.35$ in dollars and £0.175 in pounds, which is to say that the United States is on a gold standard under which the government stands ready to buy and sell gold at \$35 per ounce; the British are on a gold standard at £17.50 per ounce of gold; and the cost of transporting an ounce of gold from the United States to Great Britain or from Great Britain to the United States is \$0.35 or £0.175. Under such an arrangement the following statements would be true: If the exchange rate of dollars for pounds, $\$/£$, were between \$1.98 $[(35 - 0.35)/17.50]$ and \$2.02 $[35/(17.50 - 0.175)]$, there would be no gold flow. If the exchange rate were equal to or less than \$1.98, gold would move from Great Britain to the United States. If the exchange rate is equal to or greater than \$2.02, gold would move from the United States to Great Britain.

It should be obvious that as long as both governments had a sufficient supply of gold, the exchange rate could never move very far outside the limit set by the gold points because traders on both sides of the Atlantic would prefer to ship gold rather than pay or receive a less favorable price than that obtainable by so doing.

What if the supply and demand forces caused one country to begin to lose all its gold stock? Could it run out of gold and cause a drastic change in the exchange rate? The answer is no. Let us see why. Recall the effect of changes in the government's gold stock on the domestic money supply under the gold standard. Each dollar's worth of gold exported would reduce the domestic money supply by \$1. A massive gold outflow from one country would result in an equally massive contraction in its money supply. A massive gold inflow into the other country would result in an equally massive increase in its money supply. Eventually (and perhaps painfully), if this situation were allowed to take its course, the country losing gold would undoubtedly fall into recession or depression, and the country receiving the gold would experience a substantial degree of inflation. Through these deflationary and inflationary effects, we shall now illustrate that "balance of payments problems" under a gold standard are self-correcting and no country would ever exhaust its gold supply, i.e., have its money supply reduced to zero.

In this case the change in international reserves, $\Delta R$, would be the change in the nation's gold stock. Repeating Eq. (12-8),

$$\Delta R = X_n + F_n + U_n \qquad (12\text{-}8)$$

We should note that each element in this equation is a component of the net demand for a nation's currency on the foreign exchange market. If $\Delta R$ is less than zero and the country is losing gold, then there is a net supply (a negative demand) for this nation's currency. This net supply is, in effect, turned in to the government in exchange for the exported gold. It is shown below that under some fairly realistic assumptions a gold outflow and the corresponding reduction in the money supply will cause the net exports component of demand for this country's currency, $X_n$, to rise as well as the net sale of financial assets, $F_n$. There is not much the economist can say in general about unilateral transfers, $U_n$.

We shall restate this mechanism using linear relationships, although any set of relationships with the same first derivatives would give the same results.

$\Delta R = X_n + F_n + U_n < 0$      Net demand for this country's currency is negative and it is thereby losing gold reserves.

$$(12\text{-}8)$$

$dR = dM$      The change in the gold reserves results in an equal change in the money supply.

$$(8\text{-}11)$$

$P = kM$      The price level, $P$, is positively related to the money supply, $M$.[1]

$$(12\text{-}16)$$

$X_n = x_0 - x_p\left(\dfrac{P}{P_w}\right)$      Net exports are negatively related to the ratio of this country's price level, $P$, to price levels in the rest of the world, $P_w$.

$$(12\text{-}17)$$

---

[1] Model I of Chapter 10 yields such an equation. For Models II and III, the price–money relationship is nonlinear.

Substituting Eq. (12-16) into (12-17) gives

$$X_n = x_0 - x_p\left(\frac{kM}{P_w}\right) \tag{12-18}$$

Differentiating Eq. (12-18) with respect to $M$ gives

$$\frac{dX_n}{dM} = -\left(\frac{x_p k}{P_w}\right) < 0$$

The relationship between net exports and the money supply is negative.

(12-19)

From Eq. (8-11) we know that $dM$ is negative when $dR$ is negative so

$$dX_n > 0$$

That is, a *decrease* in gold reserves will lead to an *increase* in net exports via a reduced money supply and falling prices.

The effect on $F_n$ takes place through a similar mechanism.

$$r = r_0 - r_m M$$

Interest rates in this country are negatively related to the money supply.

(12-20)

$$F_n = f_r\left(\frac{r}{r_w}\right) - f_0$$

Financial investment by foreigners in this country (sale of financial assets by this country) are positively related to the ratio of interest rates in this country to those in the rest of the world.

(12-21)

Substituting Eq. (12-20) into (12-21) gives

$$F_n = \frac{f_r r_0 - f_r r_m M}{r_w} - f_0 \tag{12-22}$$

Differentiating Eq. (12-22) with respect to $M$ gives

$$\frac{dF_n}{dM} = -\frac{f_r r_m}{r_w} < 0$$

The relationship between the net sale of financial assets and the money supply is negative.

(12-23)

From Eqs. (12-8) and (8-11) we know that $dM$ is negative so

$$dF_n > 0$$

That is, a *decrease* in gold reserves will lead to an *increase* in the sale of financial assets via a reduction in the money supply and a rise in the interest rate.

The foregoing mechanism can be reversed to show that the gold-receiving nations should eventually stop showing a balance of payments surplus. An increasing money supply will cause a decline in net exports (via rising prices) and a decline in the sale of financial assets (via falling interest rates).

From the general macroeconomic relationships discussed in the previous chapters of this book, it should be obvious why the international gold standard has never been allowed to work unfettered. For a gold outflow to be stopped by increased exports, the country losing the gold has to have a relative price decline. In many cases prices are not flexible downward, and they are not determined solely by the money supply but by the general level of aggregate demand relative to the productive capacity of the economy. Similarly, interest rates in the deficit country must rise relative to the rest of the world. Interest rates also are not solely determined by the money supply. In general, what is required of the gold-losing country to overcome its balance of payments problem is a significant decline in aggregate demand (and probably employment) along with rising interest rates. This is not palatable medicine for most national policy makers. On the other hand, the gold-receiving country is required to encourage inflation by allowing interest rates to fall. Again, this is not an appealing package to policy makers, and the country accumulating gold reserves by running a surplus does not really feel it has a problem.

Although a pure international gold standard has never really been allowed to function, these same basic elements are contained in all alternative fixed exchange rate systems. Hence, the mechanics of the gold standard system must be understood if more complex fixed exchange rate systems are to be comprehended. To reiterate, under the gold standard, if a country runs a balance of payments deficit, it must pay the difference out of its gold stock and reduce its domestic money supply accordingly. Eventually the reduced money supply of the deficit country and the expanding money supply of the surplus country will cause the surplus and deficit to cease *with no change in the exchange rate* beyond that allowed by the gold points. Under the gold standard, currencies are never devalued; economies are only deflated.

## 2. A Gold Exchange Standard

A gold exchange standard is the term applied to the international payments mechanism in effect in the world today. Just what is the gold exchange standard? Under this arrangement, the countries have a domestic monetary system of any variety they desire, but the central banks (or some other governmental monetary authority) agree with each other that each will redeem their own currency with gold at a fixed price. No central bank need honor the request of a private individual to redeem currency with gold, but it will honor the demand of a foreign central bank.

Specifically, most of the major trading countries of the world are members of the *International Monetary Fund.* Under the agreements binding on members of this organization, each country stands ready to redeem its own currency in dollars on demand by the central bank of other members at an agreed price. The United States has agreed to redeem dollars with gold at a fixed price. Also, each member country agrees to sell its own currency for dollars at this same price. The price may vary only by 1% on either side of this stated price without notification of the *IMF.* A nation may unilaterally change its exchange rate (which is the price at which it will exchange dollars for its own currency and vice versa) by as much as 10% simply by "consulting" with the Fund. A change of greater magnitude requires the "approval" of the Fund. In fact, changes in these rates have been relatively infrequent so that the present arrangements are similar to a pure gold standard in that the rates of exchange between any two countries do not usually fluctuate by more than plus or minus 1%.

The gold exchange standard is a direct outgrowth of the pure gold standard. As noted in the discussion of that system, under the pure gold standard each country must necessarily have a domestic monetary system based upon gold, either 100% or a fractional gold reserve. As a result the maximum domestic money supply is set by a country's gold stock, and its gold stock is set by its domestic production plus or minus what it gains or loses in foreign trade. The gold exchange standard has grown up in an attempt to reduce the connection between a country's balance of payments and its domestic money supply. Also, under the pure gold standard, the world's stock of acceptable international reserves can grow no faster than the stock of gold held for monetary purposes, that is, no faster than gold production minus industrial demand and private hoarding. As we shall see below, the gold exchange standard provides, at least temporarily, the possibility of a growth in international monetary reserves at a rate faster than the growth of the available gold stock.

Allowing nations to have monetary systems not based upon gold means that changes in a country's gold stock need not cause it to change its money supply. Also, if a central bank knows that its holdings of foreign currency are convertible on demand into dollars and thence into gold, it may well hold balances of foreign currency rather than demanding the gold, in which case both the gold and the "strong" currency come to be acceptable in international exchange.

Let us illustrate the operation of the gold exchange standard with a hypothetical example involving the United States and Great Britain. Let us assume that more U.S. dollars are spent (or loaned) to residents of Great Britain than British pounds are spent (or loaned) to U.S. residents. This would mean that a "surplus" of U.S. dollars would pile up in the hands of British citizens. In all probability, the citizens of Great Britain will turn their excess dollars into British banks in exchange for pounds. The banks then turn them into the British central bank in exchange for a deposit at the central bank. If nothing were done to offset this, British bank reserves and the potential money supply would be increased accordingly. Under the gold exchange standard, however, it would be permissible for the British central bank to take some offsetting action (such as selling government securities to the public) if it deemed an increase in bank reserves inappropriate.

At this point the British central bank has the option of holding the dollars, probably in the form of an interest-bearing time deposit with a U.S. bank, or turning them into the U.S. central bank in exchange for gold at the guaranteed rate of exchange. When and by how much the U.S. money supply might be reduced by either of these actions (in the absence of offsetting action by the U.S. central bank) depends on the monetary system of the United States and how the "domestic money supply" is defined. If the dollar balances held by foreigners are not counted as part of the domestic money supply, this figure is of course reduced dollar for dollar as soon as title passes from U.S. to British citizens, but the U.S. bank reserves remain unchanged.

If the British central bank exercises its option to demand gold for its dollars, there will be an equal reduction of U.S. bank reserves. The British central bank will pay the U.S. central bank for the gold with a check drawn on a U.S. commercial bank and the reserve account of that commercial bank will be reduced accordingly. If the United States were on a 100% reserve system, only the dollars held by the British need go out of existence. If the United States were on some fractional reserve system, the potential maximum U.S. money supply would be reduced by some multiple of the gold flow. As noted above, however, under the gold exchange standard it is up to the U.S. central bank to decide whether it wants to allow the contraction of bank reserves to take place. It could take some offsetting action such as lowering reserve requirements or buying securities in the U.S. market.

Since dollar deposits earn interest and gold holdings do not, it is highly likely that the British central bank will want to hold the dollars as long as it thinks the rate at which it can exchange them for gold will not change. In fact, if at some later date the British have a deficit in their balance of payments with a third country, they may settle this deficit by paying the dollars. Under a gold exchange standard the major currencies of the world come to be used as international reserves virtually on par with gold. Such currencies are known as international "reserve currencies." In the world today the primary reserve currencies are the British pound and the U.S. dollar. These currencies are literally "as good as gold" to the central bank of a third country *as long as the exchange rates remain unchanged.* And, as noted in the discussion of the gold standard, exchange rates will remain unchanged as long as each central bank holds the redemption rate of its currency vis-à-vis gold or the dollar constant.

Under the gold exchange standard as it has in fact operated, there have been frequent changes in the gold conversion price of minor currencies. This has not upset the functioning of the system. However, there have been occasional changes in the gold conversion price of a reserve currency. Such changes strike at the very foundation of the gold exchange standard, for if the reserve currencies are not as "good as gold," they cannot be used as international reserves, and this is supposed to be one of the major improvements of the gold exchange standard over the gold standard.

Under a certain set of assumptions, the gold exchange standard is inherently defective in that periodic changes in the gold conversion price of the reserve currencies are inevitable, and these changes will eventually cause the system to be abandoned. This is the so-called "Triffin paradox." In its simplest form it is merely a statement that in order for reserve currency countries to provide an increase in international reserves over time they must necessarily run a continuing deficit in their balance of payments. These deficits will increase the claims of foreign central banks on their monetary gold stock. With no increase in their gold stock, the ratio of claims to gold stock will rise to such a point that holders of the reserve currency will cease to consider it as good as gold (fearing that it cannot be redeemed for gold when desired). The holders of the reserve currency will all begin to demand gold for their reserve currency. If there is not enough gold to redeem it all, the rate at which it is redeemed will have to be lowered (less gold per unit of currency); and even if there is sufficient gold, the gold exchange system is gone as the world is then back on a system that restricts international reserves to the world gold stock.

This simplified version of the problem ignores the possibility of the reserve currency countries increasing their gold stock in an attempt to maintain the "gold cover" (the ratio of their gold stock to foreign holdings of their currency) at an acceptable level. It can be shown that if the purpose of the gold exchange standard is to allow international monetary reserves to increase at a faster percentage rate than the increase in the world's gold stock, a decline in the gold cover is inevitable. First let us define the total international reserves and the gold cover algebraically, assuming that the reserve currency countries could somehow obtain the total gold stock of the world to back their currencies (the *best* we could hope for).

$$R = G + \int_0^t D_r \, dt$$

The total monetary reserves of the world, $R$, are composed of the world's gold stock, $G$, plus the summation of the balance of payments deficits run by reserve currency countries up to the present time, $\int_0^t D_r \, dt$.

(12-24)

$$C = \frac{G}{\int_0^t D_r \, dt}$$

The gold cover, $C$, is equal to the ratio of the world's gold stock to the summation of the balance of payments deficits run by the reserve currency countries up to the present time.

(12-25)

In this case $D_r$ is the balance of payments deficit run by the reserve currency countries and is assumed to be a function of time.

The question to be answered here is: "If the percentage rate of growth in total international reserves $[(1/R)(dR/dt)]$ is greater than the percentage rate of growth in the gold stock $[(1/G)(dG/dt)]$, must the gold cover ratio necessarily decrease?" The question may be answered very simply from manipulation of the previous equations. For ease of notation, let

$$\dot{R} = \frac{dR}{dt} \qquad \dot{C} = \frac{dC}{dt} \qquad \dot{G} = \frac{dG}{dt} \qquad H = \int_0^t D_r \, dt$$

If the rate of growth of reserves is greater than the growth rate of the gold stock, then

$$\frac{\dot{R}}{R} > \frac{\dot{G}}{G} \tag{12-26}$$

Differentiating Eqs. (12-24) and (12-25) with respect to time yields

$$\frac{\dot{R}}{R} = \frac{\dot{G} + D_r}{G + H} \tag{12-27}$$

$$\frac{\dot{C}}{C} = \frac{\dot{G}}{G} - \frac{D_r}{H} \tag{12-28}$$

Substitution of Eq. (12-27) into (12-26) yields

$$\frac{\dot{R}}{R} = \frac{\dot{G} + D_r}{G + H} > \frac{\dot{G}}{G} \tag{12-29}$$

Working with the inequality on the right-hand side of Eq. (12-29),

$$\frac{(\dot{G} + D_r)G}{G(G + H)} > \frac{\dot{G}(G + H)}{G(G + H)}$$

or

$$G\dot{G} + D_rG > \dot{G}G + \dot{G}H$$

or

$$0 > \frac{\dot{G}}{G} - \frac{D_r}{H} = \frac{\dot{C}}{C} \qquad (12\text{-}30)$$

Equation (12-30) clearly indicates that the gold cover must decrease if total reserves are going to increase at a rate faster than the increase in the stock of gold.

The foregoing is simple manipulation of identities. What it implies for foreign exchange arrangements depends on the validity of the critical assumption that the use of reserve currencies will be impeded if the gold cover falls. Also, the gold cover could be allowed to rise or be held constant while reserve currencies were utilized to allow international monetary reserves to grow faster than they would have in the absence of their use. If a gold cover of less than 100% can prove workable, then reserve currencies can be utilized without an ever smaller gold cover. If one requires that the gold cover not be allowed to fall, then the reserve currencies outstanding simply must not grow any faster than the world's stock of gold or, more precisely, than the stock of gold held by the reserve currency countries.

What happens under a gold exchange standard when the exchange rate on a reserve currency is changed? Perhaps nothing, perhaps a great deal. We are in the realm of speculating on psychological reaction. Certainly many of those countries holding the reserve currency that was "devalued" will wish that prior to the devaluation they had converted those reserves into gold or some currency that was not devalued. If the devaluation of the reserve currency causes most of the countries of the world to redefine their currencies in terms of gold (a generalized devaluation), there may be no currency into which the country could have fled. At the same time there may be no great disruption of world trade because all the exchange rates among currencies are maintained at their old level.

In practice, as the gold exchange standard operates in the world today, it is one under which each country tries to pick an "equilibrium" exchange rate and hold within 1% of it. In this context the term "equilibrium" means an exchange rate for a country that, in conjunction with the exchange rates of its trading partners, will not cause it to run an intolerable deficit (this country might use up all its reserves) or an intolerable surplus (this country's trading partners might use up all their reserves). It does appear that under such a system somebody is likely to always have a "balance of payments problem." Both the surplus and the deficit countries have a problem but, although a country can pile up a surplus year after year, the country with the deficit will be forced into doing something as it will eventually run out of reserves. Hence, the gold exchange standard has brought forth, and will likely continue to bring forth, many more devaluations (more currency for a fixed amount of gold) than appreciations or revaluations (less currency for a fixed amount of gold). In this case, the world's international monetary reserves will be increased by a long-term increase in the monetary value of gold, and those speculators betting on this price rise are essentially betting on a continuation of the gold exchange standard.

## 3. A Fiat Reserve Standard

As discussed in Chapter 8, a domestic fiat money system is one without any commodity backing whatsoever, one that is completely cut loose from gold or any other commodity. It is perfectly possible in theory to have an international monetary mechanism of similar nature in which the balance of payments surpluses and deficits between countries are settled not in gold but in some purely fiat reserve unit created by some sort of international monetary authority. Proposals for such a system abound in the literature, but thus far the implementation of such a system has not been possible. It is to be noted that it took some centuries for the domestic economies to break the tie between the domestic money supply and gold and that this has been possible only through the force of the central government. A pessimistic view would be that an international fiat reserve system will have to await the arrival of a world government.

Proposals for an international monetary unit independent of gold have called it everything from a Currency Reserve Unit ("*CRU*") to "paper gold," and most recently "Special Drawing Rights" ("*SDR*'s"). The mechanics of such a system are relatively simple (it is the implementation that is difficult). Some international agency such as the existing International Monetary Fund would be authorized to issue a "credit" on its books to individual countries. All nations party to the agreement would agree that such credits would be acceptable in the settlement of international accounts. The central bank in each country would stand ready to buy and sell the currency of that country in exchange for the *IMF* credits. As in the case of the gold standard, such fixed rates between each currency and the *IMF* credits would effectively fix the rates between currencies. The total international reserves to finance the deficits of some countries (and the corresponding surpluses of others) could then be set by this international organization.

The reader is probably aware of the continuing controversy that surrounds the application of domestic monetary policy in the United States and other countries. There are analogous problems with any proposed international fiat reserve currency—what should "world monetary policy" be? The critical questions are: How much of the fiat international reserves should be created? To which countries should they be made available? On what terms should such reserves be made available? There are no strictly economic answers to such questions, and an economic evaluation of the various proposals on the subject goes beyond the scope of this book.

Given the basic mechanics of any system of fixed exchange rates as outlined in the discussion of the gold exchange standard, some economic implications of a fiat reserve system are apparent. If a country has an exchange rate, that, in conjunction with its domestic economic policies, causes it to run perpetual deficits, the exchange rate can only be maintained with an unending supply of international reserves. The availability of such reserves will enable the country to obtain from its trading partners more real goods and services than it gives to them. The alternative is not to make the reserves available, in which case the deficit country must change its exchange rate or deflate its economy. Presumably in today's world the change in the exchange rate would be preferred.

Both the gold exchange standard and the fiat reserve standard are called "fixed" exchange rate systems. In an ever changing world however, there obviously cannot be any such thing as a truly *fixed* exchange rate system. Realistically, both systems seek to *minimize* the frequency of changes in exchange rates. If agreement could be reached on the implementation of a fiat reserve currency system, it *could* come closer to the ideal of minimizing the frequency of changes in exchange rates than the gold exchange system simply because the freedom to decide when exchange rates should be changed would not be limited by the availability of gold or any other commodity.

### 4. A System of Fluctuating Exchange Rates

The alternative to a "fixed" exchange rate system such as the gold or gold exchange standard is a system of fluctuating exchange rates. The mechanics of such a system are based upon the fact that the moneys of the world are commodities and the supply of, and demand for, these currencies in the foreign exchange market can be allowed to establish the price of each in terms of the others. Of course, a set of prices of each in terms of the others is a set of exchange rates.

To understand how such a system would operate, we must examine the supply and demand factors of a particular currency, say dollars. The demand for dollars in the foreign exchange market results from the need by foreigners to make payments to citizens (or the government) of the United States. The supply of dollars in the foreign exchange market results from the payment of dollars to foreigners by the citizens of the United States. We can therefore describe the supply and demand factors for dollars in terms of the balance of payments accounts previously discussed. Balance of payments credits (receipts) constitute the demand for a nation's currency, and debits (payments) constitute the supply of a nation's currency. Using the accounts presented in the table on page 257, we can put down the supply and demand equations for dollars as follows:

$$D_\$ = X + F_s + R_s + U_r$$

The demand for dollars equals exports plus sale of financial assets plus sale of monetary reserves plus unilateral receipts.

(12-24)

$$S_\$ = I_m + F_p + R_p + U_p$$

The supply of dollars equals imports plus purchases of financial assets plus purchase of international reserves plus unilateral payments to foreigners.

(12-25)

As in any market, the amount bought and the amount sold always are equal for any recorded market period. Hence, we may repeat the equation previously used to state that the balance of payments always balances, which, in the present context, is a statement of the fact that net demand for a nation's currency must be zero.

$$X_n + F_n + R_n + U_n = 0$$

The observed or recorded *net* demand (demand minus supply) for a nation's currency in the foreign exchange market will always be zero.

(12-5)

Just as with any other microeconomic market, supply and demand forces are brought into equality by changes in price, in this case by changes in the exchange rate. If there were a sudden surge in demand for the dollar (resulting, for example, from a sudden strong demand for U.S. exports), the price of the dollar in terms of other currencies, the exchange rate, would rise. Conversely, if there were a sudden increase in the supply of dollars in the foreign exchange market (resulting, for example, from a sudden strong demand by citizens of the United States for imported goods), the exchange rate would tend to fall.

At this point we must point out certain conventions with respect to the discussion of the "exchange rate." In this chapter we have treated it as any other price. The exchange rate would be 0.5 if $2 traded for £1. As a matter of convention, on this side of the Atlantic, we quote rates in terms of dollars per pound or the reciprocal of the price of the dollar in terms of the pound. In this case we would quote the rate as 2.00. When the price or the value of the dollar falls, the quoted exchange rate rises. In Great Britain and on the Continent, rates are also quoted in terms of dollars per unit of domestic currency so that from their point of view the quoted exchange rate is indeed the price of their currency in terms of dollars. In the present discussion the term "exchange rate" will always mean the exchange ratio of foreign currency to domestic currency. Hence, as in the example above, an increase in the demand for a nation's currency will cause a rise in the exchange rate; and an increase in the supply, a fall in the rate.

The role of international reserves (gold and foreign currencies held by the government) in a system of fluctuating exchange rates would depend on the details of a particular system. They need not play any role at all if their level is held constant. In all probability, however, each government would attempt to "stabilize" the market for its currency by at times injecting a net demand or supply of its currency through variations in its stock of international reserves. The utilization by the government of its stock of gold and foreign currencies to influence the exchange rate of its currency can be presented algebraically by differentiating Eqs. (12-24) and (12-25) as follows:

$$\frac{dR_s}{dD_\$} = 1.00$$

or

$$dR_s = dD_\$$$

A sale of monetary reserves generates an equal increase in the demand for that nation's currency.

$$(12\text{-}26)$$

$$\frac{dR_p}{dS_\$} = 1.00$$

or

$$dR_p = dS_\$$$

A purchase of monetary reserves generates an equal increase in the supply of that nation's currency.

$$(12\text{-}27)$$

It should be apparent at this point that a system of fluctuating exchange rates with some government intervention would be similar to our current gold exchange standard except that there would be no commitment by the governments to keep the price of their currencies within a fixed percentage of a previously specified level.

Strictly speaking, with a system of "freely" fluctuating exchange rates (no government intervention), it would be impossible for a country to have a balance of payments problem. If a country sought to take more out of the world economy than it could pay for by exporting and borrowing, the supply of its currency would be excessive and the value of its currency in the foreign exchange market would fall. There would be a concomitant decrease in the price of that country's exports and an increase in the price of imports to them.

Let us take a closer look at why a balance of payments problem should not exist under a system of freely fluctuating exchange rates. Such a problem was defined above in the gold exchange standard as a situation in which the government was in danger of running out of gold or some other acceptable medium of international payment. This need never occur under a system of freely fluctuating exchange rates because the government need never sell any of its gold or other reserves. Under the gold exchange standard it was obliged to sell reserves at a fixed price for its own currency, to guarantee a perfectly elastic demand for its own currency at a set exchange rate. Under a system of fluctuating exchange rates, if supply would exceed demand at the existing price, the rate would simply be allowed to fall.

A fall in the exchange rate should help to alleviate the underlying causes of the falling rate by making imports more expensive to the domestic population and making exports cheaper to foreign purchasers. Let us look at the mechanics of this using dollars, $, and pounds, £. First we must define the following symbols:

$$U_m = \text{one unit of imports (in physical terms).}$$
$$U_x = \text{one unit of exports (in physical terms).}$$
$$E = \text{£}/\text{\$, the exchange rate, the price of dollars in terms of pounds.}$$
$$P_{m\$} = \text{\$}/U_m = \text{price of imports in terms of dollars.}$$
$$P_{m£} = \text{£}/U_m = \text{price of imports in terms of pounds.}$$
$$P_{x\$} = \text{\$}/U_x = \text{price of exports in terms of dollars.}$$
$$P_{x£} = \text{£}/U_x = \text{price of exports in terms of pounds.}$$

We can now express the price level of products moving in international trade as seen from the point of view of the buyer of the product as follows:

$$\frac{\$}{U_m} = \left(\frac{£}{U_m}\right)\left(\frac{\$}{£}\right)$$

or

$$P_{m\$} = (P_{m£})\frac{1}{E}$$

The price of imports in dollars equals the price of imports in pounds times the reciprocal of the exchange rate.

(12-28)

$$\frac{£}{U_x} = \left(\frac{\$}{U_x}\right)\left(\frac{£}{\$}\right)$$

or

$$P_{x\pounds} = (P_{x\$})(E)$$

The price of exports in pounds equals the price of exports in dollars times the exchange rate.

(12-29)

If the United States has a falling exchange rate, what would happen to the prices of its imports and exports as seen from the point of view of the buyer? Differentiating Eqs. (12-28) and (12-29) gives

$$\frac{dP_{m\$}}{dE} = \frac{-(P_{m\pounds})}{E^2} < 0$$

The price of imports in dollars will rise as the exchange rate falls.

(12-30)

$$\frac{dP_{x\pounds}}{dE} = P_{x\$} > 0$$

The price of exports in terms of pounds will fall as the exchange rate falls.

(12-31)

If the demand for imports is sensitive to their dollar price, they should fall as the exchange rate falls. If the demand for exports is sensitive to their price in the foreign currency, pounds, they should rise as the exchange rate falls. If this is in fact the case, according to Eqs. (12-24) and (12-25), the demand for dollars should increase and the supply should decrease. Such a result would cause the exchange rate eventually to stop falling. The question of the necessary and sufficient conditions for a system of freely fluctuating exchange rates to have a stable equilibrium value (one rate toward which the system would tend to move smoothly) is a complex problem of microeconomic dynamics into which we shall not go further. Even the question itself is a problem; how stable is stable enough?

The major liability of a system of fluctuating exchange rates is that if the fluctuations are substantial, they could prove very disruptive to international trade. Transactions in goods and services between countries typically involve long time lags between commitment and payment. If the true cost or revenue to the buyer or seller could not be known with any certainty because of possible future changes in the exchange rate, businessmen might be deterred from engaging in foreign trade. It is argued that forward markets in foreign exchange would allow merchants to "hedge" their risk, that is, transfer it to professional risk takers. This might or might not make fluctuating exchange rates a usable system. The world has never experimented with freely fluctuating exchange rates long enough to find out.

## III MACROECONOMIC EQUILIBRIUM IN AN OPEN ECONOMY

Most of this chapter has discussed the equilibrium level of exchange rates among the currencies of the world as this is a major contemporary problem of international economics.

The preceding discussion was of equilibrium in the supply of and demand for national currencies at the present point in time—the "spot" market for foreign exchange. Full equilibrium would require simultaneous equilibrium not only in the "spot" foreign exchange market but in the entire world's interconnected money and capital markets and in the world trade markets for goods and services.

Equilibrium in the international money and capital market that connects all the domestic money and capital markets of the world is an open issue of the day on which there is much literature; however, it is a relatively specialized area of study and to a large extent lies outside the scope of this book. We shall merely note that not only are the interest rates of the various countries interrelated as mentioned in our previous discussion but the "forward" exchange rates (the price of one currency in terms of another for delivery at some future time period) are interrelated with each other and with the domestic interest rates.

## I. The Foreign Trade Multiplier

The other market that must be in equilibrium is the demand for goods and services in each country when we include the export demand and the import supply of such goods and services. We can include imports and exports in our model by adding the net exports, $X_n$, to aggregate demand as follows: Instead of Eq. (1-6)

$$Y = C + I + G \tag{1-6}$$

we use

$$Y = C + I + G + X_n \tag{12-32}$$

Net exports by definition equal total exports less total imports. This sum may be either positive or negative depending on whether exports exceed imports or vice versa. Assuming the stability of the exchange rate and the relative price levels, we can assume that exports are fixed or at least exogenously determined. Imports, however, typically vary in the same direction as aggregate domestic spending. Let us assume that imports are some constant percentage, $u_y$, of total expenditures in the economy. The parameter, $u_y$, is then by definition both the average and marginal propensity to import, and net exports will be

$$X_n = x_0 - u_y Y \tag{12-33}$$

Repeating the remainder of the aggregate demand model for convenience,[2]

$$C = c_0 + c_y(Y - T) \tag{2-15}$$

$$T = t_y Y - t_0 \tag{2-17}$$

$$I = i_0 - i_r r \tag{4-10}$$

---

[2] Only the equations defining the $IS$ curve are given since we are excluding consideration of money market equilibrium.

we find that the equilibrium level of aggregate demand is

$$Y = \frac{c_0 + i_0 + c_y t_0 - i_r r + G + x_0}{1 - c_y + c_y t_y + u_y} \qquad (12\text{-}34)$$

We now have a "super multiplier" of $1/(1 - c_y + c_y t_y + u_y)$. The addition of the marginal propensity to import, $u_y$, to the denominator of this expression reduces the size of the multiplier. Foreign trade is stabilizing in this respect. However, the export component of aggregate demand can be destabilizing just as fluctuations in domestic investment or government expenditures can be destabilizing.

A large marginal propensity to import means that a country can "export" a portion of the fluctuations in autonomous expenditures; the absolute size of the multiplier is reduced as the size of the marginal propensity to import is increased. For example, with respect to the investment multiplier,

$$\frac{\partial(\partial Y/\partial i_0)}{\partial u_y} = -\frac{1}{(1 - c_y + c_y t_y + u_y)^2} < 0 \qquad (12\text{-}35)$$

On the other hand, a large export component in aggregate demand means that a country is vulnerable to fluctuations in the level of aggregate demand in foreign countries through its export sales since

$$\frac{\partial Y}{\partial x_0} = \frac{1}{1 - c_y + c_y t_y + u_y} > 0 \qquad (12\text{-}36)$$

Unfortunately a large marginal propensity to import (which would be stabilizing) and relatively large fluctuations in exports (which are destabilizing) usually go together.

Without going into the details, it should be obvious that a large marginal propensity to import reduces the effectiveness of fiscal policy. If a country is trying to increase aggregate demand through increased government expenditures, a portion of the impact will be lost as expenditures on foreign goods and services are increased. This is illustrated by the fact that the equilibrium condition for savings and investment is, with this model, not Eq. (5-20)

$$S + T = I + G \qquad (5\text{-}20)$$

as it was before but

$$S + T = I + G + X_n \qquad (1\text{-}13)$$

Exports are analogous to domestic investment and government expenditures (injections to the spending stream), while imports are analogous to savings and taxes (withdrawals from the spending stream).

One frequently sees reference in the literature to the *foreign trade multiplier*. This refers to the change in total expenditures resulting from a change in exports taking account of the fact that imports will also increase. In our case the foreign trade multiplier is Eq. (12-36) given above. In many cases the effect on tax revenues is ignored and the foreign trade multiplier is said to be the reciprocal of one minus the marginal propensity to consume plus the marginal propensity to import, as follows:

$$\frac{\partial Y}{\partial x_0} = \frac{1}{1 - c_y + u_y} \qquad \text{when} \quad t_y = 0 \qquad (12\text{-}37)$$

We have considered here only the direct effects of imports and exports on aggregate demand. There are important indirect effects. As noted earlier, the balance of trade affects the supply and demand for foreign exchange. The level of aggregate demand affects the domestic price level which in turn affects the demand for foreign goods. In short, all three markets we mentioned at the beginning of this section have interdependencies too involved to study in detail, but we can take a brief look at some of the complexities as we consider the efficacy of monetary and fiscal policy in an open economy.

## 2. The Efficacy of Monetary Policy and Fiscal Policy Under Fixed and Fluctuating Exchange Rates

Orthodox economic theory concludes that fiscal policy will be more effective in changing the level of aggregate demand under fixed exchange rates rather than flexible exchange rates, while monetary policy will be more effective under a system of fluctuating exchange rates than under a system of fixed exchange rates. In order to derive these conclusions, the following two assumptions are necessary:

1. The flow of money capital among nations is sensitive to the relative interest rates in those nations.
2. The elasticity of exports and imports with respect to the price paid by the buyer is greater than unity.

For purposes of exposition, let us make these two assumptions in their most extreme forms. We shall assume that the supply of capital to a country is infinitely elastic. In other words, interest rate differentials cannot endure— massive investing in the capital market of the high interest rate country (creating a strong demand for its currency in the foreign exchange market) and massive borrowing in the capital market of the low interest rate country (creating a large supply of its currency) will eventually equalize interest rates. Looking at the comparative statics of such a system, the domestic interest rate cannot be permanently changed by the monetary authorities but rather is set by the world money market. The extreme form of the second assumption means that a rise in the value of a nation's currency vis-à-vis other nations' as a result of a rise in the exchange rate will cause a substantial decline in net exports, $X_n$; a fall in the exchange rate will cause a substantial increase in net exports.

In order to look at the mechanics of monetary and fiscal policy under alternative exchange rate systems, let us use a simplified model specifying only the four following endogenous variables:

$Y$ = equilibrium level of aggregate demand.

$r$ = equilibrium level of interest rates.

$E$ = equilibrium level of the exchange rate.

$X_n$ = equilibrium level of net exports.

The equilibrium levels of these variables will be determined by the following exogenous variables subject to some degree of control by the government:

$G$ = the level of government expenditures and other autonomous components of aggregate demand.

$M$ = the domestic money supply.

$R$ = the rate of accumulation of foreign exchange reserves.[3]

When considering equilibrium in an open economy, we need to specify not only that the domestic market for goods and services (the *IS* curve) and the domestic money market (the *LM* curve) are in equilibrium but also that the foreign exchange market (the *FX* curve) and the export-import market (the *XM* curve) are in equilibrium. Indicating these four markets in generalized functional notation, we have

*IS:*        $Y = f_1(G, r, X_n)$          The equilibrium level of demand for goods and services is a function of government expenditures, the level of interest rates, and the level of net exports.

(12-38)

---

[3] Note the change in the definition of $R$ from its previous usage earlier in the chapter. $R$ as defined here is the equivalent of $\Delta R$ as defined by Eq. (12-7).

LM: $r = f_2(M, Y)$       The equilibrium level of interest rates is a function of the money supply and the level of aggregate demand.

$$(12\text{-}39)$$

FX: $E = f_3(r, X_n, R)$       The equilibrium level of the exchange rate is a function of the level of interest rates, the level of net exports, and the change in the country's stock of foreign exchange reserves.

$$(12\text{-}40)$$

XM: $X_n = f_4(Y, E)$       The equilibrium level of net exports is a function of the level of aggregate demand and the exchange rate.

$$(12\text{-}41)$$

Let us take the total differential of each of these four equations using a slightly different notation from that used previously. We shall indicate the partial derivatives of $Y$ with respect to $G$ taken from Eq. (12-38) as $y_g$, the partial of $Y$ with respect to $r$ as $y_r$, and so on. The total differentials are then

IS: $$dY = y_g\, dG + y_r\, dr + y_x\, dX_n$$

LM: $$dr = r_m\, dM + r_y\, dY$$

FX: $$dE = e_r\, dr + e_x\, dX_n + e_R\, dR$$

XM: $$dX_n = x_y\, dY + x_e\, dE$$

The signs of each of the partial derivatives are as follows:

$$y_g = y_x > 0$$

These partials are equal to the simple multiplier.

$$y_r < 0$$

The slope of the IS curve is assumed to be negative, as given in Chapter 5.

$$r_m < 0$$

The interest rate is inversely related to the money supply.

$$r_y > 0$$

As in Chapter 6, the slope of the LM curve is positive.

$$e_r > 0$$

The exchange rate is influenced by the level of interest rates through the effects of international capital flows discussed above. The relationship is assumed to be positive. Thus, a rise in the interest rate will increase the demand for a nation's currency and thereby put upward pressure on its exchange rate.

$$e_x > 0$$

As previously discussed, exports create a demand for a nation's currency in the foreign exchange markets and imports create a supply. Therefore, a change in net exports will change the equilibrium level of the exchange rate in the same direction.

$$e_R < 0$$

$R$ is defined as the rate of *increase* in foreign exchange reserves, so a rise in $R$ means an increase in the supply of a nation's currency in the foreign exchange market and downward pressure on $E$. Conversely, if a nation liquidates reserves or slows down its rate of accumulation, the exchange rate would tend to rise.

$$x_y < 0$$

Net exports are assumed to have a negative relationship to the level of aggregate demand since, as previously discussed, the level of total exports is not dependent on aggregate demand, and imports vary directly with aggregate demand.

$$x_e < 0$$

Net exports are assumed to be negatively related to the exchange rate since a rise in the exchange rate will increase the cost of exports to the buyers and decrease the cost of imports to domestic citizens. Of course, the opposite holds for a fall in the exchange rate.

Since this model is more complex than necessary, further simplification is useful. Recalling our earlier assumption that one country's interest rate could not long depart from that dictated by the world money markets, we shall assume that from one equilibrium position to the next the interest rate cannot change: $dr = 0$. Rewriting the differential equations with $dr$ equal to zero, we obtain

*IS:*  $$dY = y_g \, dG + y_x \, dX_n \qquad (12\text{-}42)$$

*LM:*  $$0 = r_m \, dM + r_y \, dY \qquad (12\text{-}43)$$

*FX:*  $$dE - e_x \, dX_n + e_R \, dR \qquad (12\text{-}44)$$

*XM:*  $$dX_n = x_y \, dY + x_e \, dE \qquad (12\text{-}45)$$

Turning to the effectiveness of fiscal policy under conditions of fixed exchange rates, we have a system in which $dE$ is zero, $dR$ is not equal to zero, and $dG$ is not equal to zero. Although we are explicitly considering fiscal policy, this does not mean that the money supply cannot or will not be changed. Indeed, if equilibrium is to be restored after a change in government expenditures, the money supply will have to be changed, as indicated below.

The effect of fiscal policy can easily be determined by combining Eqs. (12-42) and (12-45):

$$dY = y_g \, dG + y_x x_y \, dY \qquad (12\text{-}46)$$

which gives

$$\frac{dY}{dG} = \frac{y_g}{1 - y_x x_y} > 0$$

The multiplier in this system is positive but less than the simple multiplier $y_g$. The effect of government expenditures is reduced by the negative effect of increased aggregate demand on net exports. Only if $x_y$ is zero will fiscal policy have the "full" multiplier effect.

We can measure the amount of loss of the impact of fiscal policy via increased imports by using Eq. (12-45) with $dE = 0$ to obtain

$$dX_n = x_y \, dY$$

$$\frac{dX_n}{dY} = x_y$$

Since

$$\frac{dX_n}{dG} = \frac{dY}{dG} \frac{dX_n}{dY}$$

then

$$-1 < \frac{dX_n}{dG} = \frac{y_g x_y}{1 - y_x x_y} < 0$$

The previous equation states that an increase in government expenditures will decrease net exports but by a smaller amount than the original increase in government expenditures. Obviously, if all the increase in government expenditures were for imports, there would be no effect on domestic aggregate demand.

Turning to the necessary change in the money supply, Eq. (12-43) indicates that

$$\frac{dM}{dY} = -\frac{r_y}{r_m} > 0$$

Combining this result with the effects of fiscal policy on aggregate demand, we find that

$$\frac{dM}{dG} = \left(\frac{dY}{dG}\right)\left(\frac{dM}{dY}\right) = -\frac{y_g r_y}{(1 - y_x x_y)r_m} > 0$$

If total demand is, say, expanded by fiscal policy under a system of fixed exchange rates, the increased imports will cause an excess supply of this nation's currency on the foreign exchange markets. This excess must be absorbed by the sale of foreign exchange if the exchange rate is to hold constant. The change in the rate of accumulation of reserves can be shown to be

$$\frac{dR}{dG} = -\frac{e_x y_g x_y}{e_R(1 - y_x x_y)} < 0$$

Thus, an increase in government expenditures will result in a decrease in the rate of accumulation of foreign exchange reserves (or an increase in the rate of liquidation of such reserves).

To designate these interactions as "fiscal policy" instead of "monetary policy" (although a combination of both actually has to be used) is something of an analytical convenience rather than a necessity. This activity is classed as fiscal policy since the effects are those typically associated with fiscal policy—increases in autonomous expenditures and resulting increases in aggregate demand via the multipler.

To consider the implementation of monetary policy as conventionally defined under conditions of fixed exchange rates and perfect capital markets is pointless. One cannot change interest rates, so one cannot affect domestic investment. It is obvious from Eq. (12-46) that if fiscal policy is not used (so that $dG$ is zero), then the equilibrium level of income cannot be changed.

Having determined that under a system of fixed exchange rates fiscal policy (supported by the appropriate monetary policy) will likely be effective and that monetary policy alone is not possible, let us now consider the effectiveness of monetary and fiscal policy under conditions of freely fluctuating exchange rates (so that $dE$ is not zero). Again, we shall make the most extreme assumption for purposes of illustration. We shall assume that the government never buys or sells in the foreign exchange market and hence $dR$ is zero. We shall find that the case of fluctuating rates is just the opposite of the case of fixed rates. Something we shall call "monetary policy" (initiated by a change in the money supply) will be effective if supported by the proper change in autonomous expenditures (so that $dG$ is not zero).

Just as monetary policy alone made no sense in the case of fixed rates, fiscal policy alone is pointless in the case of fluctuating rates. For example, if $dM$ is zero, Eq. (12-43) becomes

$$r_y \, dY = 0$$

or

$$dY = 0$$

so

$$\frac{dY}{dG} = 0$$

Such an attempt at changing aggregate demand via fiscal policy will merely result in an equal and offsetting change in net exports as indicated by Eq. (12-42). If $dY$ is zero, then

$$\frac{dX_n}{dG} = -\frac{y_g}{y_x} = -1$$

If we use monetary policy under a system of fluctuating rates, Eq. (12-43) gives us the monetary multiplier as

$$\frac{dY}{dM} = -\frac{r_m}{r_y} > 0$$

If we required all the markets to be in equilibrium, however, an increase in autonomous expenditures must be part of the policy package (so that $dG$ is not equal to zero). This is necessary for the comparative statics of the model since we cannot change interest rates and thereby change private investment. Without going through the derivation step by step, we may note that the ratio of the change in autonomous expenditures to the change in money supply will have to be as follows:

$$\frac{dG}{dM} = \frac{r_m}{r_y} \left( \frac{x_y}{1 - x_e e_x} - \frac{1}{y_g} \right) > 0$$

This change in autonomous expenditures in the same direction as the change in the money supply will have to be larger than the resulting change in aggregate demand as the change in aggregate demand will cause net exports to change in the opposite direction. The ratio of the change in net exports to the change in the money supply may also be derived from the original basic equations:

$$\frac{dX_n}{dM} = -\frac{x_y r_m}{r_y(1 - e_x x_e)} < 0$$

That the change in government expenditures is greater than the change of net exports can be shown by

$$\frac{dX_n}{dG} = \frac{dX_n}{dM}\frac{dM}{dG} = -\frac{y_g x_y}{1 - x_e e_x - y_g x_y} > -1.0$$

If income, say, rises as the result of an increase in the money supply and government expenditures, the resulting increase in imports will give us a new lower equilibrium level of net exports. It follows that the lower level of net exports means a greater supply of the country's currency for the foreign exchange market and a lower equilibrium level for the exchange rate. This can be illustrated by determining the sign of the ratio of the change in the exchange rate to the change in the money supply, or

$$\frac{dE}{dM} = -\frac{x_y r_m e_x}{r_y(1 - x_e e_x)} < 0$$

A mathematical model of sufficient sophistication to allow us to examine the dynamics of macroeconomic equilibrium in an open economy would involve many more equations and each would be more complicated than we have used here. However, the dynamics of what we have been discussing can be covered fairly well verbally.

Under fixed exchange rates, monetary policy is thought to be relatively ineffective since any attempt to alter the domestic interest rate by changing the money supply will tend to be offset by international capital movements. For example, if the money supply were increased to lower domestic interest rates, there would be a net capital outflow which (unless offset) would decrease bank reserves and tend to reduce the money supply back down to its original level. If the government did not allow the money supply to constrict as a result of the capital outflow, the country would continue to lose reserves indefinitely. In the process, with lower interest rates, some domestic investment might be induced with a resulting increase in aggregate demand. More realistic assumptions than those used on the model above will not show monetary policy to have no effect under a system of fixed exchange rates but merely less effect than such policy would have under flexible exchange rates.

Under a system of flexible exchange rates an attempt to change aggregate demand by changing the rate of interest will cause the exchange rate to vary in such a way as to induce a change in net exports that affects aggregate demand in the desired way. For example, if the money supply is increased and rates fall, the resulting capital outflow will decrease demand for this nation's currency and cause the exchange rate to fall. This fall in the exchange rate will cause imports to look more expensive to domestic citizens and exports to look cheaper to foreigners. The resulting increase in net exports will, via the foreign trade multiplier, result in the desired increase in aggregate demand. This is, of course, in addition to whatever domestic investment might be induced by the lower interest rates that prevail during the period of disequilibrium.

Fiscal policy is more effective under fixed exchange rates because it will induce a change in the money supply via international reserves that supports the change in aggregate demand. For example, if government expenditures were increased, interest rates would initially rise. The resulting capital inflow would increase bank reserves and expand the money supply until interest rates were reduced to their original level. Government expenditures would have been increased and therefore caused aggregate demand to increase without the usual penalty of raising interest rates that depresses domestic investment.

On the other hand, under a system of fluctuating exchange rates, the increase in interest rates initially resulting from an increase in government expenditures will cause a capital inflow that will affect the exchange rate and not the stock of reserves and the domestic money supply. The exchange rate will rise as investors seek to invest in this country and this will cause net exports to fall, partially or totally offsetting the increase in aggregate demand brought about by the original increase in government expenditures.

It is important to note that such models as this merely indicate that monetary policy is likely to be more effective under a system of fluctuating rates and *not* that monetary policy will be "more effective" than fiscal policy—whatever "more effective" might mean in such a context. Similarly, we may say that fiscal policy is likely to be more effective under fixed exchange rates than under fluctuating rates and *not* that fiscal policy will be more effective than monetary policy under fixed rates.

## IV  ADDITIONAL COMPLICATIONS

In this chapter we have discussed how countries of the world actually conduct international economic relations and briefly considered equilibrium in an international macroenonomic system. The material on the balance of payments and related international payments mechanisms is fairly straightforward and can easily be generalized beyond the two-country model within which it was presented here. However, multinational macroeconomic equilibrium involves much more of a substantive nature than has been presented.

One of the additional complications that is more important to international economics than to other material in this book is what are frequently called "second-order effects." For example, a more general expression of the foreign trade multiplier must take account of the marginal propensity to import of all the countries involved since the imports of one country are the exports of another and vice versa. If a foreign country suddenly has a change in tastes that causes our exports to them to increase, the initial effect would be to increase our income and decrease theirs. As a second-order effect, this in turn would cause us to import more from them, increasing their income and reducing ours. As their income rose, there would be a "third-order effect" increasing our exports and income a second time around. Such a process can be continued as a geometric progression which has a fairly simple limit in the two-country model, but in a multi-country model the number of possible outcomes becomes very large, with each possible outcome depending on the specific assumptions about the marginal propensities to import, elasticities of goods with respect to price, the sensitivity of capital movements to interest rates, the type of exchange rate system, and governmental policies in the various countries.

In concluding this chapter we want to point out to the student that when one considers all the relevant markets (domestic goods, goods traded internationally, spot and forward foreign exchange markets, and domestic money markets) in a two-country or multi-country model, the superficially simple question of the necessary and sufficient conditions for the existence of an equilibrium becomes very complex. The complexities multiply, of course, as one moves to the dynamic questions of stability and speed of adjustment.

We have concentrated here on the institutional mechanisms that are reflected in *ex post* data. For the student concerned with the equilibrium values of the economic variables in international trade, *ex ante*, there are many and varied hypotheses in the literature expressed in a host of mathematical models.

## EXERCISES

1. Assuming a monetary policy of keeping interest rates constant,

   a Calculate the investment, government expenditures, and foreign trade (exports) multipliers for the economic system represented by the following equations:

   i. $Y = C + I + X_n + G$

   ii. $C = c_0 + 0.85Y$

   iii. $I = i_0 - i_r r$

   iv. $X_n = x_0 - 0.10Y$

   **b.** Recalculate the multipliers with Equation (iv) as

      iv.   $X_n = x_0 - 0.25\,Y$

**2.** Indicate for each of the following occurrences whether

   **a.** Under a system of fixed exchange rates the foreign exchange reserves of a country would tend to go up $(+)$ or down $(-)$.

   **b.** Under a system of fluctuating exchange rates, the exchange rate (value of the domestic currency in terms of foreign currency) would tend to go up $(+)$ or down $(-)$.

      i.   An increase in government expenditures,

      ii.   an increased preference for foreign goods by domestic consumers;

      iii.   a depression in the domestic economy;

      iv.   an investment boom in the domestic economy;

      v.   a decrease in the money supply;

      vi.   an increase in foreign investment (purchase of foreign corporations' assets) by domestic companies;

      vii.   a tax on foreign bonds sold in the domestic market;

      viii.   an increase in the average propensity to save.

## RECOMMENDED REFERENCES

Baumol, W. J., "Speculation, Profitability and Stability," *Review of Economics and Statistics*, August 1957.

Chipman, J. S., "The Multi-Sector Multiplier," *Econometrica*, October 1950, pp. 355–74.

Clement, M. O., R. L. Pfister, and K. J. Rothwell, *Theoretical Issues in International Economics*, Boston, Mass.: Houghton Mifflin Co., 1967.

Friedman, Milton, "The Case for Flexible Exchange Rates," in *Essays in Positive Economics*. Chicago: University of Chicago Press, 1953.

Johnson, H. G., "Equilibrium under Fixed Exchange Rates," *American Economic Review*, May 1963, pp. 112–19.

Kindleberger, C. P., *International Economics*, 4th ed. Homewood, Ill.: Richard D. Irwin, Inc., 1968.

Mundell, Robert A., *International Economics*. New York: The Macmillan Company, 1968.

Triffin, Robert, *Gold and the Dollar Crisis*. New Haven, Conn.: The Yale University Press, 1960.

### Chapter I

1. $\dfrac{\partial P_e}{\partial b} = \dfrac{1}{a+c} > 0$

$\dfrac{\partial P_e}{\partial c} = \dfrac{-b}{(a+c)^2} < 0$

$\dfrac{\partial Q_e}{\partial b} = \dfrac{a}{a+c} > 0$

$\dfrac{\partial Q_e}{\partial c} = \dfrac{-ab}{(a+c)^2} < 0$

2. a. $Y_1 = a + bY_0$

$Y_2 = a + ab + b^2 Y_0$

$Y_3 = a + ab + ab^2 + b^3 Y_0$

$\qquad = a\left(\dfrac{1-b^3}{1-b}\right) + b^3 Y_0$

**b.** $Y_t = a\left(\dfrac{1 - b^t}{1 - b}\right) + b^t Y_0$    or    $Y_t = \dfrac{a}{1 - b} + b^t\left(Y_0 - \dfrac{a}{1 - b}\right)$

**c.** If $b$ is a positive fraction, $Y_t$ converges monotonically.
If $b$ is a negative fraction, $Y_t$ converges cyclically.
If $b$ is positive and greater than unity, $Y_t$ grows larger and larger monotonically.

**d.** $\dfrac{a}{1 - b}$

## Chapter 2

**1.**   **a.**     $APC = \dfrac{C}{Y} = \dfrac{10}{Y} + 0.6 - 0.01Y$

$\dfrac{\partial(APC)}{\partial Y} = -\dfrac{10}{Y^2} - 0.01 < 0$

**b.**     $MPC = \dfrac{\partial C}{\partial Y} = 0.6 - 0.02Y$

$\dfrac{\partial (MPC)}{\partial Y} = -0.02 < 0$

**2.** The true equation is

$$C = c_0 + c_y Y$$

The estimated equation is

$$\frac{C}{P} = c_0 + c_y^* \left(\frac{Y}{P}\right) \quad \text{or} \quad C = c_0 P + c_y^* Y$$

In the estimated equation, part of the change in $C$ is attributed to changes in $P$. Thus, $c_y^*$ is less than $c_y$.

## Chapter 3

**1.**     $\dfrac{\partial Y}{\partial I} = \dfrac{1}{1 - c_y}$

$\dfrac{\partial (\partial Y / \partial I)}{\partial c_y} = \dfrac{1}{(1 - c_y)^2} > 0$

**2. a.**     $Y_t = c_y Y_{t-1} + I_t$

$\dfrac{\partial Y_t}{\partial I_t} = 1 = c_y^0$

**b.**     $Y_t = c_y(C_{t-1} + I_{t-1}) + I_t$

$Y_t = c_y C_{t-1} + c_y I_{t-1} + I_t$

$\dfrac{\partial Y_t}{\partial I_{t-1}} = c_y$

**c.**     $Y_t = c_y(c_y Y_{t-2}) + c_y I_{t-1} + I_t$

$Y_t = c_y^2 C_{t-2} + c_y^2 I_{t-2} + c_y I_{t-1} + I_t$

$\dfrac{\partial Y_t}{\partial I_{t-2}} = c_y^2$

**d.**     $\dfrac{\partial Y_t}{\partial I_{t-n}} = c_y^n$

3.  a.  $$\frac{\partial Y}{\partial I} = \frac{1}{1 - c_y(1 - t_y + f_y)}$$

    b.  $$\frac{\partial Y}{\partial t_0} = \frac{-c_y}{1 - c_y(1 - t_y + f_y)}$$

        $$\frac{\partial Y}{\partial f_0} = \frac{c_y}{1 - c_y(1 - t_y + f_y)}$$

## Chapter 4

1.  $Y_t = c_0 + c_y Y_{t-1} + i_0 + k_y(Y_{t-1} - Y_{t-2})$

    $Y_t = c_0 + i_0 + (c_y + k_y) Y_{t-1} - k_y Y_{t-2} + G_t$    Reduced form of model

    $Y_t = G_t + 20.00 + 1.70 Y_{t-1} - 0.90 Y_{t-2}$    Empirical estimate

Therefore,

    a.  $k_y = 0.90 =$ accelerator coefficient

    b.  $c_y + k_y = 1.70; c_y = 1.70 - 0.90 = 0.80 =$ the marginal propensity
        to consume

    c.  From Table 4–5, since

$$k_y = 0.90 < 1.00$$

and

$$c_y < 2\sqrt{k_y} - k_y \qquad 0.80 < 1.00$$

then in disequilibrium this model will experience cycles of decreasing magnitude converging toward the new equilibrium.

## Chapter 5

1.  a.  $Y = 1233.33 - 83.33r$

    b.  If $r = 10$,

        $Y = 400$

        $T = 40$

        $C = 308$

        $I = 50$

        $G = 42$

        $S = 52$

**Chapter 6**

1.  a.   $Y = 90 + 30r$
    b.   If $r = 10$,

$$Y = 390$$
$$M_t = 130$$
$$M_s = 50$$

2.  $$\frac{\partial Y}{\partial m_0} = -\frac{1}{m_y}$$

$$\frac{\partial Y}{\partial m_r} = \frac{r}{m_y}$$

$$\frac{\partial Y}{\partial m_y} = -\frac{M + mr_r - m_0}{m_y^2}$$

$$\frac{\partial r}{\partial m_0} = \frac{1}{m_r}$$

$$\frac{\partial r}{\partial m_y} = \frac{Y}{m_r}$$

$$\frac{\partial r}{\partial m_r} = -\frac{m_y Y - M + m_0}{m_r^2}$$

**Chapter 7**

1.  $r = 10.08$
Values of the other variables are roughly the same as those found for Chapters 5 and 6.

**Chapter 8**

1.  a.   $\Delta M = 0$
    b.   $\Delta M = 0$
    c.   $\Delta M = \left(\dfrac{1}{K}\right)(\Delta F) = \left(\dfrac{1}{0.2}\right)(\Delta F) = 5\,(\Delta F)$

2.  a.   $\Delta M = 0$
    b.   $\Delta M = 0$
    c.   $\Delta M = (1.00)\,(\Delta F)$

3.  a.  $\Delta M = \$1$ million

    b.  $\Delta M = \left(\dfrac{1}{K}\right)(\$1 \text{ million})$

4.  $\Delta M = \left(\dfrac{1}{1.00}\right)(\$1 \text{ million}) = \$1$ million in all cases as there would be no "excess" reserves

## Chapter 9

1.  a.  $L_d = (1-b)^{1/b}K\left(\dfrac{W}{P}\right)^{-1/b}$

    b.  Elasticity of output with respect to total expenditures $= \frac{1}{3}$.
        Elasticity of prices with respect to total expenditures $= \frac{2}{3}$.
        Elasticity of employment with respect to total expenditures $= 1/(3-3b)$.

2.  a.  $L_d = 25\left(\dfrac{W}{P}\right)^{-2}$

    b.

    | MODEL I | MODEL II |
    |---|---|
    | $L_e = (2500)^{1/3}(P)^{2/3}$ | $L_e = (2500)^{1/3}$ |
    | $Q_e = (10)(2500)^{1/6}(P)^{1/3}$ | $Q_e = (2500)^{1/6}$ |

    $Q_e$ as a function of $P$ is an aggregate supply curve.

    c.

    | | MODEL I | MODEL II |
    |---|---|---|
    | i. | $\eta_{Q,Y} = \dfrac{1}{4}$ | $\eta_{Q,Y} = 0$ |
    | ii. | $\eta_{L,Y} = \dfrac{1}{2}$ | $\eta_{L,Y} = 0$ |
    | iii. | $\eta_{P,Y} = \dfrac{3}{4}$ | $\eta_{P,Y} = 1.00$ |

3.  a.  $L_d = \left(\dfrac{4}{3}\dfrac{W}{P}\right)^{-4}K$

    b.  $L_e = 2$

    c.  i.  $\eta_{L,Y} = 0$

        ii.  $\eta_{L,K} = \frac{1}{5} = 0.20$

## Chapter 10

1.  $Y = PQ$ and $P = Q^3$; therefore, $Y = Q^4$ and $Q = Y^{1/4}$. Hence $\eta_{Q,Y} = \frac{1}{4}$

    $\eta_{Q,M} = (\eta_{Y,M})(\eta_{Q,Y}) = (\frac{1}{2})(\frac{1}{4}) = \frac{1}{8} = 0.125$ or $12\frac{1}{2}\%$

    $\eta_{Q,G} = (\eta_{Y,G})(\eta_{Q,Y}) = (2)(\frac{1}{4}) = \frac{1}{2} = 0.50$ or $50\%$

2.  Case 1:

$$Y = PQ = 100 \qquad Q_d = \frac{100}{P}$$

$$Q_s = Q_d \qquad 10 = \frac{100}{P} \qquad P = 10$$

The comparative statics would indicate a feasible (positive) price level and presumably full employment could be achieved.

Case 2:

$$Q_s = Q_d \qquad (P + 110)^{1/2} = 10 \qquad P + 110 = 100 \qquad P = -10?$$

The comparative statics indicates that a negative price level is required for equilibrium, which indicates that at any positive price level the amount that suppliers want to supply will be greater than the amount demanded in real terms. Presumably this economy would be in a perpetual state of unemployment (insufficient real aggregate demand) with downward pressure on prices.

## Chapter 11

1.  Change in aggregate supply: $\Delta Q_{s,t} = Q_{s,t} - Q_{s,t-1} = vK_t - vK_{t-1} = vI_t$

    Equilibrium level of aggregate demand:

$$Q_{d,t} = I_t + bQ_t \qquad Q_{d,t} = \frac{I_t}{1 - b}$$

Change in aggregate demand:

$$\Delta Q_{d,t} = \frac{\Delta I_t}{1 - b}$$

For noninflationary growth:

$$\Delta Q_{s,t} = \Delta Q_{d,t} \qquad vI_t = \frac{\Delta I_t}{1 - b}$$

In terms of percentage rate of growth in investment:

$$\frac{\Delta I_t}{I_t} = v(1 - b)$$

Percentage rate of growth in investment = the output-capital ratio times the marginal propensity to save.

## Chapter 12

1. a. $\dfrac{\partial Y}{\partial i_0} = \dfrac{\partial Y}{\partial G} = \dfrac{\partial Y}{\partial x_0} = \left(\dfrac{1}{0.25}\right) = 4.00$

   b. $\dfrac{\partial Y}{\partial i_0} = \dfrac{\partial Y}{\partial G} = \dfrac{\partial Y}{\partial x_0} = \left(\dfrac{1}{0.40}\right) = 2.50$

2.

|      | a. CHANGE IN RESERVES UNDER FIXED RATES | b. CHANGE IN EXCHANGE RATE UNDER FLUCTUATING RATES |
|------|:---:|:---:|
| i.   | − | − |
| ii.  | − | − |
| iii. | + | + |
| iv.  | − | − |
| v.   | + | + |
| vi.  | − | − |
| vii. | + | + |
| viii.| + | + |

# Index